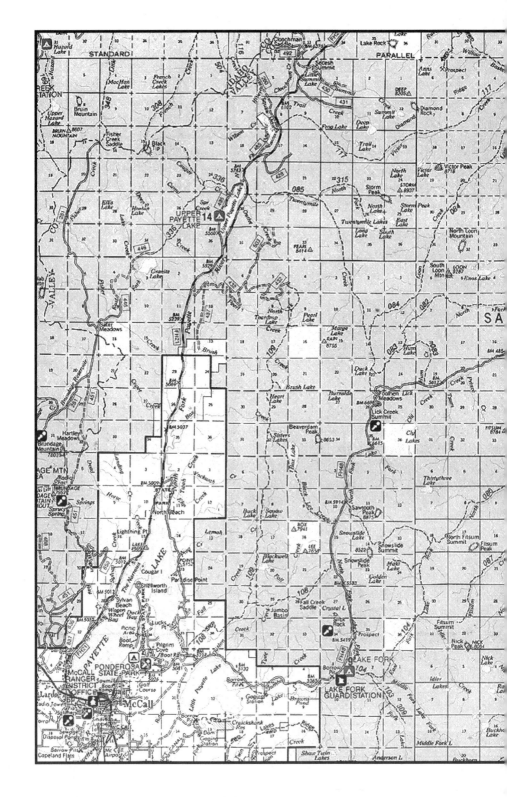

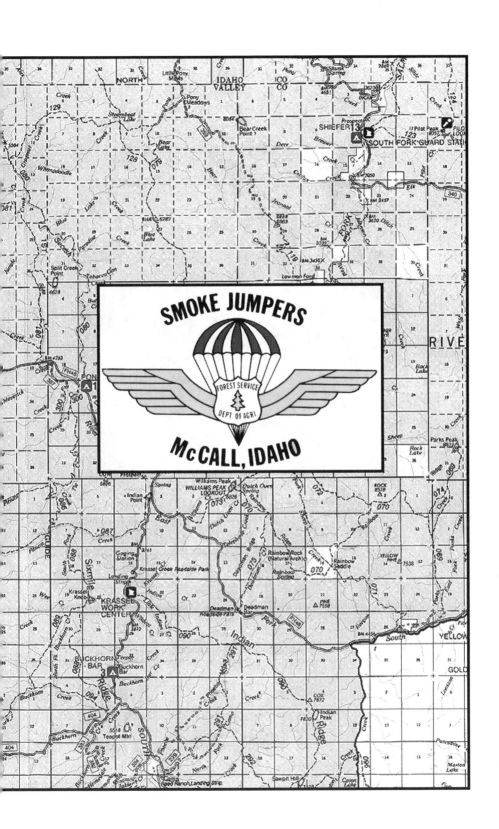

JUMPING SKYWARD

JUMPING SKYWARD

STAN TATE

JUMPING SKYWARD

Edited, Designed and Published by
Cabinet Crest Books
124 Highway 200
Heron, Montana 59844

The Author gratefully acknowledges permission to
reprint excerpts from the following:

Collects from the Book of Common Prayer
Scripture from the New Revised Standard Translation
Sawtooth Tales, from Caxton Publishers, Caldwell, Idaho

Tate, Stanton Davis, 1932 -
     Jumping Skyward

     Library of Congress Catalog Card Number: 95-69735

     Includes bibliographical reference.
     1. Wilderness Areas - popular works 2. Christian Spirituality.
     3. Meditation Techniques 4. Smokejumping, US Forest Service

     ISBN: 1-886591-03-2

ACKNOWLEDGMENTS

UPON COMPLETING A MARRIAGE WORKSHOP IN HOUSTON, TEXAS, a celebrated author recommended I publish my unique experiences as a smokejumping priest. I selected my most breathtaking parachute jumps and spiritual encounters in the Idaho wilderness, and *Jumping Skyward* leaped into print.

Although *Jumping Skyward* is a novel in which names have been disguised to protect anonymity, locations like Whangdoodle Creek are from Idaho maps. Events are based on personal experiences. I am grateful for many colorful and personal visions of spirituality in the forests, including actual dialogues with wild animals, such as the moose, bighorn sheep and bobcat.

I've never attained the ethical and spiritual maturity of the book's hero, Ken Shuler, or in the men who inspired him, Ken Salyer and John Shuler, but I am indebted to Ken, a coach, and John, a juvenile counselor, for their friendship. I was highly honored to have wandered the Idaho woods with them before they moved on. While their stroll in the Idaho wilderness was far too short, as heroes of everyday goodness, they continue soaring like hawks above the rest of us.

Skip Knapp, a courageous pilot, was another friend who emulated bioethics and whose walk beside the still waters was far too short. Lyn Clark, one of Idaho's intrepid female pilots and one of Idaho's finest backcountry pilots, taught me the art of airborne consultation, and I appreciate her skill and friendship.

Foremost is my gratitude in being accepted by some of the wildest - and best - people in the world; the McCall smokejumpers. It is not possible to list all the names, but they will recognize themselves throughout the story.

I have the deepest respect for smokejumpers like 'Tex' Lewis, Bob Rawlins, Walt Rumsey, Jim Thrash, and others who are now on the other side. After officiating at the burial of Jim Thrash, who died in the Storm King fire, I understand why this superb man was one of the most respected guides in America. I honor Jim, Roger Roth, and Don Mackey, smokejumper heros who died in the Colorado fire, and all 28 forest firefighters who died in 1994.

I am indebted to spiritual leaders everywhere, especially the late Rev. Mike Jenkins, who loved the unique forests of Eastern Montana. Sometimes it is heartbreaking for pastors to leave homes, lands, and families, to follow their call. I hope *Jumping Skyward* elevates parishioners' value of the courage it takes to leave comfortable homes in order to move into the unknown.

Bland and Eugene Williams' story in the deathhouse of the New Jersey Maximum Security Prison is true. Their courageous faith could fill a separate book. I envisioned sacred forgiveness in years of friendship with my courageous brothers. After seventeen years of injustice and incarceration, bitterness is unknown in their daily walk.

I would like to thank Princeton Theological Seminary's support of me in the Williams ordeal, especially Dr. Dick Armstrong, Dr. Christy Wilson and the Rev. Walter Wright, Esq. You were there when we needed you.

As national advisor for the Advocates of Indian Youth Empowerment, I gained some of the marvelous spiritual insights from their pow-wows near Wounded Knee, Wind River and the Sun Dance in South Dakota. Thanks to all of you, especially Della Warrior, Art Zimiga, Tonya Garcia, and Dennis Sun Rhodes.

Teachers learn from students. I am no exception. I want to thank the students in my religion classes at Boise State, my ethics classes at the University of Idaho, my Christian meditation groups at Oregon State, and physicians and nurses in my classes in biomedical ethics. I've incorporated wisdom from these disciplines throughout the story.

I applaud my students at Oregon State University, who helped construct the Merton Meditation Chapel and were colleagues in designing new approaches to prayer at Canterbury House. I am especially indebted to Sharon Chen, R.N., Kris Brooks, Ph. D., and Jane Ramp, M.D., who researched new methods of Christian meditation and explored spirituality in the wilderness.

To my own cherished family — my wife Lynn, my delightful children, Teri, Scott and Flip — who understand my anguish in leaving a beautiful family home, I owe unending gratitude. No one will ever take the homesteads within our hearts away from us.

I am indebted to the expertise of Cabinet Crest Books, and to my superb editor, Sandy Compton. I appreciate his personal reverence for the wilderness. A word of thanks to Charlene Vecchi, Nola Steuer, Marjorie Cochrane, and Chris Crutcher, who enhanced the story by their comments and suggestions.

Finally, I thank God for the privilege of parachuting into Idaho's bioscathedral and living with wild members of that blessed biodiversity. My hope is that all people will cherish the wilderness areas throughout the world while loving the One who created them.

Stan Tate
Moscow, Idaho, May, 1, 1995

To my wife,
Lynn Campbell Tate

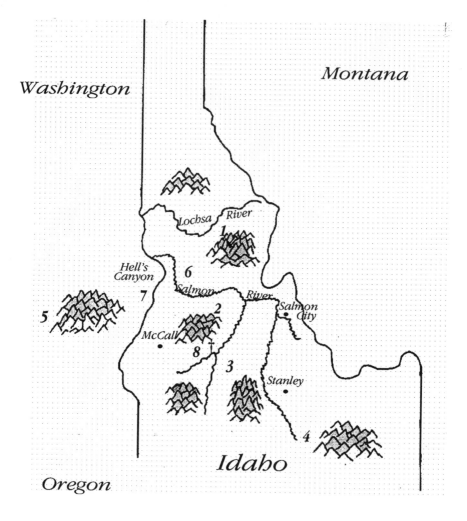

LEGEND

1 — *Selway-Bitterroot Mountains*
2 — *The River of No Return*
3 — *Idaho Primitive Area*
4 — *White Cloud Mountains*
5 — *Wallowa Mountains*
6 — *Gospel Hump Wilderness*
7 — *Seven Devils Mountains*
8 — *Indian Creek Airstrip*

Map by Stan Tate

A TABLE OF CONTENTS

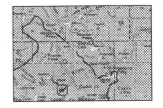
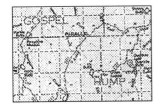

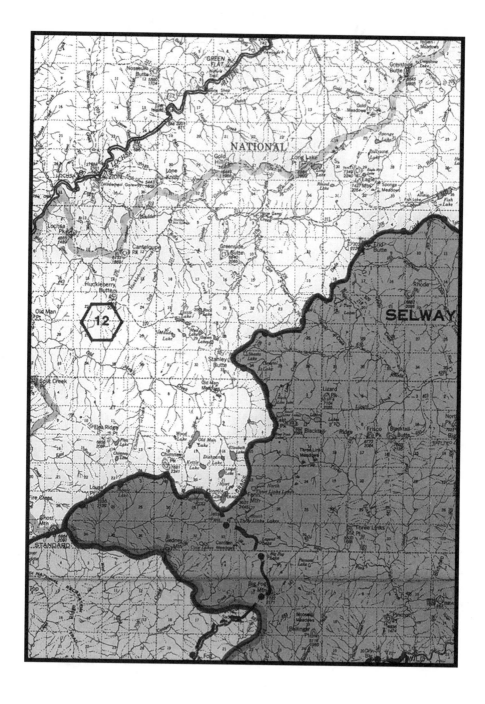

THE SELWAY-BITTERROOT MOUNTAINS

BIOSCATHEDRALS

 IN A FEW MOMENTS, I will leap from the questionable safety of an old airplane into an awesome physical and spiritual abyss. Precariously balanced on the metal step under the round doorway of a Ford Trimotor, I'm poised to plummet into the rugged Selway-Bitterroot Wilderness in Idaho. If the parachute opens properly, I'll experience a new burst of life. I prefer not to consider the alternative.

Other smokejumpers will follow. We're the elite among fire fighters in roadless America. Today, we're parachuting into one of the nation's most remote areas, where the only quick access is by parachute, to extinguish a lightning-caused forest fire.

Concentrating on the wilderness, I visualize mountains peaked 2,000 feet below as flying buttresses supporting granite steeples in nature's bioscathedral. I soar like a hawk high above a natural clerestory, a Selway-Bitterroot sanctuary inhabited by Indian spirits.

We drone high above Kinnikinnick Creek between Gray Bear and Freezeout Peaks, south of the Lochsa River, looking for a safe jump spot. Bob Fogg, a premier backcountry pilot, flys the Tin Goose, as our aircraft is affectionately known. He looks like Bogart and knows the wilderness like the back of his hand.

Spotter Marvin Caldwell shouts, "Mark, stop staring at the scenery. Hold on to the rail before a wind gust yanks you out!"

Marvin is a muscular professor of philosophy at the University of Idaho. He usually enjoys discussing philosophical dilemmas, but the professor is in an unphilosophical mood. As jump master, he will direct us out the little door, and now is time for action, not dialogue.

He has tossed a drift chute over a selected jump zone, testing the wind's velocity and direction. Conditions are favorable, and he checks my riser snaps and shroud lines.

He bellows at me above the noise of the plane, "Put your weight on the step, but hang on to the handrail and don't lose your balance!"

Balancing in the doorway of the jostling three-engine plane above the jagged cliffs rimming the Selway River is a formidable task. Unpredictable winds from yesterday's lightning storm push violently against the reliable old plane, tossing it like a volleyball above an enormous verdant playground. If I lose my balance while the Ford zigzags over these cliffs, it may be the last as well as the first jump I make into this area. I tighten my hand grip on the smooth metal pipe around the oval door and concentrate on the imminent task of entering the bioscathedral safely.

Parachuting is the art of balancing. Success or failure in guiding the nylon canopy into a preselected location depends on proper distribution of weight. Jumpers who can't refine this art often spend the fire season balancing body casts or crutches.

Parachuting follows the spiral flight of birds of prey. Movement through the air creates the canopy's lifting action.

The wind whips across my nervous face through the door of the lumbering plane. I'm ready — if one is ever ready — to parachute into the unknown.

Pilot Fogg holds a steady altitude toward the jump spot. Caldwell hunkers behind me, shouting above the whine of three Pratt and Whitney engines.

"There's about four football fields of drift. I'll carry you past the jump spot 400 yards and then release you. The wind should carry you back to that green bushy ridge just below the fire. You may hit a rock, but at least you won't float over the next ridge."

It's Marvin's way of saying I'm lucky. At 185 pounds, I weigh enough to prevent the wind from blowing me and my 28-foot chute into Canada.

We'll jump two-man "sticks," propelling two fully equipped men out a four-foot opening in a matter of seconds. The second jumper, Ken, the Iowa Hawkeye, crouches behind me in the doorway.

I've known Ken Shuler several years but he's still a mystery. He seldom speaks, but when he does, it reflects awareness of an ethic from another world. He waits calmly, a portrait of peace in the midst of turbulence.

I'm nervous about parachuting, but it will be a relief to leap off this turbulent platform. Men and equipment in the Trimotor are banging around like leather bags strapped to a speeding stage coach.

The plane flies directly into the wind which will theoretically carry me back to the clearing. The jump spot is what every jumper hopes for — an acre of soft soil with a smattering of jack pines surrounded by a few piano-sized boulders. The noisy engines begin idling. I know in a few seconds Caldwell will slap my leg, the signal to jump. The wait seems endless. Bob cuts the engines. Total silence. It is time.

Caldwell slaps my leg, bellowing, "Go!" With eyes fix on the Canadian horizon, I uncoil freely into space, screaming "Geronimo!" as I leap into the crisp Idaho air. Macho jumpers prefer diving straight down. I maintain an upright position as the parachute unwinds neatly from my backpack.

I catch a glimpse of Ken exiting and racing toward the outdoor church, and seconds later my canopy opens with a jolt that almost knocks me unconscious. Then, euphoria.

Instantly my lively being is like a red-tailed hawk soaring above a magnificent wonderland. Huge trees a thousand feet below appear as miniature green shrubs in a Japanese bonsai. Ribbons of blue water scratch inviting paths between untamed mountain peaks. I am at one with a good universe and humbled by her unspoiled beauty.

We soar like angels above the altar in the dome of London's St. Paul Cathedral, but even Christopher Wren's masterpiece pales before God's Bitterroot bioscathedral, whose parishioners include mountain lions and bobcats. The enormous basalt basilica splashes spiritual splendor throughout the natural courtyard

Gothic cathedrals were never constructed from artificial materials. High, arched, stone vaults supported attics called "forests" containing hundreds of wooden timbers. The lofty vault of the bioscathedral is supported by living timbers on granite foundations. There is nothing plastic in the natural composition of God's creation below.

Flying parallel with one another under our orange and white chutes, Ken and I spiral around in the ambiance of celestial beauty. This lofty view of existence may account for the Gospel of St. John sporting an eagle for its emblem.

Soaring a hundred feet below Ken, I shout "I'll beat you to the center of the spot, so don't land on top of me."

"Watch those dead snags to the right," he yells back.

I have forgotten to concentrate on chute handling. I pull hard on the right guide line moving away from the grove of weathered snags looming below like

3

quills on an enormous gray porcupine.

Close to landing, I glide toward a group of small alpine firs. It's nice to land on a small tree. Piling straight into the steep hillside is like tackling a logging truck. Landing directly downhill, I might roll like a basketball until I splash into the river.

In spite of my good intentions, I shoot over the fir trees and make contact with mother Earth among a cluster of blue elder and syringa bushes. It is less than two minutes since I jumped. My chute and lines are tangled in the elder branches, but I've landed safely. Exuberant, I untangle the lines and pause to thank God for being alive.

Unsnapping the heavy, wire face mask from my helmet, I scan the hillside for Ken. He narrowly avoids a prickly snag that could have impaled him with its weathered armor and lands closer to the fire in deep soft soil. He doesn't gloat over being closer to the spot like the rest of us might. He stands up, waves, smiles and begins folding his nylon canopy.

No broken bones today, so I stretch out a five-foot orange streamer on the ground forming the number 7, signaling Caldwell we are safe.

Loosening my harness, I look up to see Tex and Phil exit the Trimotor. The breeze has stiffened since we jumped and I predict the wind will carry Phil to Canada. Weighing a mere 150 pounds, he sails 600 feet above the landing spot toward the next wooded ridge. Tex, who closed both eyes on his first practice jump, is drifting down the ridge toward a grove of tall white pines. We won't see either of them for hours. Since they don't carry flashlights, moonlight will be their guide to the fire.

Hauling my jump gear and chutes on my shoulders, I walk up the mountain ridge toward a clearing below the heavy smoke. A flock of mountain chickadees, black masked and gray cheeked, accompany me. The silence of the ridge is punctuated by the sound of little chirps and the flutter of tiny wings.

It will be a while before the Trimotor drops our equipment. I sit down to rest on a large igneous rock covered with lichens acquired over centuries. It occurs to me that I may be the first human ever to sit here.

English cathedrals had similar stone chairs called "misercords" for clergy to rest on during elaborate liturgies. A litany of love emanates from the tiny chickadees, providing sweet solos of joy. This lumpy rock will serve as my misercord in the midst of a living basilica, patiently fashioned over the centuries.

An ancient philosopher named Thales perceived rocks as living entities. The durable beauty of the Bitterroot batholith, with sheared sections of shiny mylonite, crystallizes as a colorful stone chapel. The Creator uses rocks, instead of paint, to decorate His sanctuary. Their subtle colors endure for centuries as backdrops for the temporary coloration of wildflowers and wild trees. Rocks appear in gorgeous varieties of settings with a thousand shades of gray - all beautifully evoking gratitude.

4

As I peer through a panoramic "rose window" at miles of immaculate radiance, Kinnikinnick beckons me home. Resting in nature's hallowed space pushes the dull slumber out of ordinary awareness. I feel exalted, detecting a fresh vision of world harmony, and my awareness of universal design is complemented by a local resident, a little short-tailed, round-eared pika, who pokes her head out of the rock formation. She whistles "Welcome" to her pastoral homeland.

Sharing the pika's home, awaiting the cargo drop, I get tangled in a paradox. When I consider this indescribable splendor, instead of feeling insignificant, I feel authenticated. The reality of feeling good about myself reverberates with the cosmos ... the mountains, the big sky, the spiraling galaxies; and last, but not least, a bright yellow wildflower growing out of what appears to be solid stone.

The miracle is this: both the flower and I make a difference to God who created this enormous cathedral. Everything living matters to Almighty God.

Spirituality cannot be manufactured but it can be a gift of the wilderness. Jesus suggests building faith on things as durable as stone, rather than on fleeting-sand fads.

Peter said, "Come to Jesus, a living stone, and be like living stones, allowing yourselves to be built into spiritual homes."

There is a delay in getting our supplies dropped, and I begin dreaming about my past. A hushed, gentle breeze pumps fragrant vitality into my memories of smokejumping in the wilderness of Idaho. The sacred atmosphere prompts me to discern the direction my life is taking, like discerning the trails we scribed in the sky today.

I am both a smokejumper and a priest and each career dances with the other to melodies embracing these quiet forests. I hear these mysterious tunes more distinctly here than when I'm bogged down in the frantic pace of the business world.

I am home.

THE FIRST TIME I EVER SAW A SHORT-TAILED, ROUND-EARED PIKA, I was visiting my sister Elizabeth at her forest service lookout. One afternoon, as I watched her feed the plump little pikas, her radio crackled a message. Smokejumpers were on their way to fight a fire below her lookout.

I was in high school that summer as I watched them descending like mammoth butterflies below the lookout tower, but as their bright orange and white chutes unfurled over the blue-green hills, I absolutely knew that I wanted to become a smokejumper more than anything.

I was a graduate student in Princeton Theological Seminary before I received a letter of acceptance from the Forest Service. It had taken two years to get, and I felt as if I'd been accepted for a tryout with the San Francisco '49ers.

Smokejumper camp opened the first week of June. When I drove into camp in my beat-up Studebaker, it had been raining and the ground was soggy from rain and piles of dirty snow were melting on the shady side of the main barracks.

A group of jumpers were slugging it out in a game of rough-style rugby-football near where I parked, playing with Vibram-sole loggers and no helmets. I recognized the man calling signals as quarterback for the University of Idaho Vandals. Several players were World War II combat veterans from the Screaming Eagle airborne unit. The game promised to be far too violent for seminarians.

I introduced myself to a jumper nursing a few bruises on the sidelines.

"Hi, my name's Mark Davis. I'm a new smokejumper."

He shook my hand, pointed out the barracks and told me to put on my loggers and get in the game if I had any guts.

" … and don't call yourself a smokejumper 'til you make your first fire jump. For now, you're just a lowly 'ned'."

The barracks were CCC buildings left from the Depression, rebuilt into attractive cottages, painted Forest Service green. I lifted my duffel out of the car, walked through the door and found a bed with my name on it. Sitting on the next bed was a lanky kid with a southern drawl, appropriately named Tex, I found out. I estimated he wasn't more than 16 years old.

"Pardon me for saying so, but you don't look old enough to be a jumper."

"One of the jumpers broke a leg yesterday," Tex told me. "I was hanging around looking for work and they said I could take his place. I'd told them I'd soon be 18. I didn't say how soon. This morning I bought a pair of loggers and black 'frisco jeans and here I am.

"Some of these fellas from the war seem pretty old, but I guess we'll get used to that."

Fortunately, the football drill was over when Tex and I reported.

Early next morning, we awoke to "Get up and hit the floor running!" Neds who didn't respond immediately found themselves under beds tipped over by the seasoned jumpers. In a matter of minutes we were in the dining hall.

I've seen royal banquets of food at church potlucks, but my first jumper breakfast was beyond imagination; platters of sausage, ham, eggs, fried potatoes, muffins and fruit with steaks and fried chicken left over from the day before.

After breakfast, I waddled to the calisthenics area.

Physical torture began in earnest.

At Seminary, I had been struggling through 25 pushups, but the smokejumper minimum was 50. We put our legs through leather loops on a log and did back bends. Lying flat on our backs, with heavy logger boots, we lifted our legs six inches high and held them until given permission to lower them. We did so many side-straddle hops, my arms wouldn't extend higher than my shoulders.

By the Grace of God, physical fitness had time limits, but ended with 30

6

minutes of fire fighter's volleyball. This is different from Olympic volleyball. We were encouraged to hit the net and try to poke the opposition in the same play. In a good summer we trashed four or five nets. Kicking was outlawed since players wore loggers, but everyone endured a few bruised shinbones.

After volleyball, we gathered on the manicured lawn in front of the smokejumper loft. Squad leaders had met earlier in the week to choose squads of eight men, and we were to be assigned today. I only knew one other man, or one boy, that is: Tex. I hoped we'd be in the same squad.

I was the only man with a crew cut. My brand-new black 'frisco jeans indicated I had just arrived. Beneath my orange sweatshirt hung a Celtic cross on a strong silver chain. I stood a little over six feet tall and was in good physical shape for a seminarian, but not so good among fire fighters.

Wayne Weber, a popular leader, announced our names randomly as we waited on the newly mowed grass.

"Ken Shuler, get your Iowa lard over there behind Paperlegs, right now," Weber blared over his portable loudspeaker.

Squad leader Paperlegs Peterson was a tall, thin, Swede, an airborne veteran with a body and mind cast in steel. The name "Paperlegs" didn't fit him at all, but he had broken both legs in a football game and the name stuck. He was everybody's first choice for trainer, so I felt lucky when Weber called me.

"Mark Davis — get your fragile body over there, too."

Paperlegs and Ken extended handshakes that nearly crushed my academic hands, but it felt good to be accepted.

Don Wakan Stephens, a Native American from Lapwai, Idaho, quietly took his place near me. He walked with a natural gait, and his dark eyes were nearly hidden beneath shoulder-length, black hair. From his powerful grip, I knew he would pass the rigorous physical requirements. We were both rather shy and enjoyed instant rapport.

"Phil Guy, stand up. Oh, my mistake, you are standing. Get over there with the big guys behind Paper."

Weber didn't phase Phil one bit. Small and wiry, he was not intimidated by anyone, though I thought, *This character will never be able to tote a 90-pound pack around the backcountry.*

Phil taught us not to judge a book by its size. His large and genuine smile made up for his size, and after the first major fire, we knew he lived by what he preached. His long, scruffy hair didn't fit the portrait of a Mormon missionary, but he had just returned from a mission in a violent area of Central America. Upon completion of a Master of Social Work degree, he wanted to return to El Salvador.

Weber continued team assignments.

"Just a few left here. Where's John Lewis?"

"Right here, sir, and you can call me Tex. Ever heard of Texas? You'll be hearing a lot more this summer. Where do you want me? Over by Larry Clark?"

7

Weber didn't know whether to laugh at or with the Southern youngster.

"I don't know if we want you or your older brother. Are you the kid who just turned 18 last week?"

"That's me, and I can outwork ..."

"Tex, get over there. Those Northerners will teach you a thing or two about Idaho humility. Now move! And no more Lewis and Clark jokes."

Tex headed toward our group, and Wayne noticed he was wearing cowboy boots.

"Hold it right there. What's on your feet? Didn't you receive instructions to wear White Logger boots?"

"Yes sir, Mr. Weber, sir, " Tex said politely, "But I was born in cowboy boots. When we begin parachuting, I'll change into my loggers."

"You'll change right after doing 20 fast pushups — NOW!"

Tex did 20 and Webb gave him five minutes to go to the barracks and change boots. Tex came back in less than four, out of breath, but not out of spirit

A bit arrogant about being a Texan, Tex feared no man and this was a problem. He was half bobcat, with a drawl, a spitting image of a young Gary Cooper. He stood taller than a lot of the older men even without his black cowboy hat. His dark hair was clipped short and he wore long sideburns like Elvis Presley. When he smiled, he unleashed a perfect set of teeth. He had a pitifully small mustache which he hoped might make him look older, but made him look tacky.

Wayne made another assignment.

"Nick Shaffer, front and center. I hear you jumped Airborne. I jumped Airborne myself, and the training's a lot tougher here than at Fort Benning. "

Wayne told us it was smokejumpers, not the military, who started the physical training rigmarole at the beginning of World War II.

He also told us a friend who helped start the smokejumper's unit in McCall had parachuted onto the top of a Japanese barracks in the Philippines one dark morning. Most of the Japanese were out of the building, and the few who rushed out while he was on the roof didn't notice him and his collapsed chute. He got out of that alive and considered smokejumping a piece of cake.

Wayne was so wrapped up in his wartime memories, he forgot Nick.

"Well, where do I belong sergeant, sir?" Nick asked.

Wayne pointed to Peterson's squad.

Nick was a handsome, standoffish fellow who drove a fancy car. He was a slender five feet, eight inches tall, with small shoulders that supported muscular arms. He worked out regularly and his body showed it. When he spoke, you knew he was from the South. While he and Paperlegs seemed to like each other, he was bored with non-veterans. He grudgingly muttered a Tennessee "howdy" and stood beside us.

Nick avoided close contact with men. Women? That was a different story.

Wayne called Larry David; a tall kid with a scowl on his face who had been pacing back and forth. His black jeans were pressed, which made me wonder, and he saluted rather than simply saying "Here."

"Larry, you have the honor of training with Paperlegs. Please join that squad."

Larry stood erect and marched over to the rest of us as if to the beat of a drum. He was a state debate champion in Georgia and wore a red letter sweater with lots of awards sewed on. We must have looked like a motley crew to such a well-kept perfectionist as Larry. I figured he might be hard to get to know.

The eighth man to join our squad was a bull-riding coal miner from Wyoming, the toughest guy in camp if you could believe his own raucous words.

"Kent Barnes, you're assigned to Paper's squad," Weber told him. "Show Tex that a hard-rock miner has the right boots for the job."

Kent shook hands with no one. He didn't walk, he strutted; growling at the rest of us as if he were sizing up a Brahma bull at the rodeo. He stood about five feet, ten inches tall and weighed maybe 160 pounds, soaking wet. His face showed the signs of wind and sun, and he wore tight Levi's rather than loose 'frisco jeans. I decided not to mess with him. He let us know what would happen to anyone who did, and his glare kept most of us at a safe distance, but not Paperlegs. He tried to get a rise out of the tough one.

"Did you hear we have an annual bash with the local miners at the Jersey Lilly Tavern every summer? Whose side you gonna choose if we get into a brawl, Kent?"

"It doesn't matter to me. I never start fights, but I always finish them."

That's how our squad came together. We would become family. We fought, laughed, and worked together; and came to know our lives depended upon each man being proficient.

DURING TRAINING, we acquired skills we'd need to fight wildfires and fine-tuned our bodies. One of our first physical tests was climbing a thick, hemp rope 18 feet long, using only hands and arms. A brass bell rested on top of the rope tower. Paperlegs climbed quickly to the top, rang the bell and returned hand-over-hand.

"That's how it's done. Let's have the strong-arm wearing the Iowa sweatshirt ring the bell."

Heavy, but immensely strong, Ken carefully scaled the rope and rang the bell, loud and clear. Then, he defiantly held onto the wooden tower with just one hand, swinging back and forth like an ape until Paper called him down.

I made it two-thirds of the way up before sheepishly returning to the ground. I waited for Paper to scold me and demand some pushups, but he didn't.

"Davis made a wise move. If you can't do it safely, don't do it. Safety comes before anything else. Mark this was all right, but you have to make it to pass the physical. Work on it, OK?"

Every year, five percent failed and had to check out. I didn't want to be one of them. I understood that our lives depended on being physically disciplined.

Afternoons were spent studying fire fighting techniques.

We watched "Red Skies Over Montana," starring Richard Widmark. The movie was based on a fire at Mann Gulch in Montana, in which a group of Missoula smokejumpers parachuted onto a steep hillside as a wild fire became a raging fire storm. Flames raced uphill at over 600 feet per minute in cheat grass and fescue. It was estimated that the ground heat reached four hundred degrees, nearly exploding bodies.

Two escaped by reaching a rock ledge merely seconds ahead of death. Wagner Dodge, fire boss, escaped by building a back fire and racing through its wall of fire. Dodge remained face down as the angry flames leaped over his escape fire. Others panicked and tried to outrun the holocaust. Thirteen smokejumpers died.

The Missoula jumpers who died were just our age, but it seemed impossible that we could ever die. I explained the existential concept that until people face the reality of death, they never experience being fully alive and fully human, but only Ken understood.

Ken knew that death opens the door for existence beyond this mortal life; that the life-spiral never stops spinning new explorations beyond planet Earth. He explained how the forest recycles itself continually through fires, and compared it to human death and resurrection. Old deadfall, consumed by flames, creates ashes for the phoenix of renewal. He said there ought to be a balance among natural fires creating new life and destroying old materials for a healthy forest system. I wondered how an Iowa athlete could know so much about forests ... and humanity.

When Paperlegs talked about the deaths at Mann Gulch, he became very serious, and we sensed he really cared about our well being. Paper reminded me of the big, tough man in the red-striped shirt from the old magazine ads for piston rings. The ads featured a man in the first scene bending a railroad tie. In the next scene he was petting a little kitten. It read: "Tough, but oh, so gentle."

EATING FRESH, NUTRITIOUS FOOD, pushing our bodies to their physical limits, breathing pure mountain air and living with men who knew how to laugh and pull together made excellent conditions for sleeping, but the night before our first parachute jump, the "neds" were rudely awakened, thrown out of our bunks at 11:30.

When things quieted down, they told us to prepare for a visit from a local celebrity, and began telling stories of gory accidents; when canopies failed to open or dead branches tore suits to shreds. One of them told of when he "streamered in." His main chute came out so twisted it never opened and the orange and white canopy merely waved like a streamer.

As their stories became more incredible, we became more annoyed, but then, a bearded man in a black suit with a tall "Abraham Lincoln" hat appeared. He had a large Bible under his arm and a tape measure in his hand. His black beard was somewhat unglued and his yellow scruffy sideburns showed, and Phil asked the guest why he wore loggers with a suit. This took "Abe" Peterson by surprise, but thinking "on his feet," he said the boots were those of a "ned" who died on his first practice jump.

"Abe" distributed literature on late model caskets, offered with prepayment plans to new jumpers, carefully measured each of us, as a good mortician would, and agreed to allow us to be buried in our loggers.

Tex asked if he could paint the Texas flag on his casket and we all began to laugh. The veteran jumpers then brought out refreshments, and we managed little sleep before the squad leaders yanked us out of bed.

THERE WAS SOMETHING INTRIGUING ABOUT KEN SHULER. When we arrived at the airport, for our first jump, Ken knew our group would be the second plane load, but no one had told him we'd be second.

As we waited, Ken asked Don about the wrist he had sprained. It hurt plenty, but Don didn't want to miss his first jump.

"Just let me massage it a bit."

In a few minutes, Don's pain was gone. Ken wandered away.

I watched Ken with bewilderment. Earlier in the week, we were boating across Payette Lake when a terrific wind and three-foot waves came up. We were worried we would sink, but Ken laughed and waved at the danger and soon the rest of us laughed the storm away. Ken loved to tell stories that had a bigger impact on us a day later, after we thought about them. Refreshing bits and pieces of wisdom popped out of his mouth at exactly the right times.

Ken also had an extraordinary ability to listen and share his strength, which was demonstrated when Kent nervously sidled up to him.

"Kent, you look worried. Is something bothering you?" Ken asked.

"I've not lived a very good life ... all that fighting and cussing with the miners, you know. What happens if ..."

I think Kent was worried that if he died that day, God might judge him harshly.

"God loves everyone, Kent. You don't have to be tough and scare people. Don't worry about checking it all in this morning. If you can go down a mine shaft, you can go down on a parachute."

Ken then asked Kent to describe the person he really would like to be. Kent talked excitedly for 30 minutes about a gentle man who wanted to train horses. Ken understood the reality gap and said God would help him become whatever he really wanted to be.

"Start living that vision now ... this moment. God's love is unconditionally good. God will be with you in your quest. God is a win-win friend."

Kent stood up and walked toward the plane as if someone had poured new life in him. I wondered what extraordinary well Ken drew his vitality from.

W̲E̲ ̲W̲E̲R̲E̲ ̲O̲U̲T̲F̲I̲T̲T̲E̲D̲ ̲F̲O̲R̲ ̲T̲H̲E̲ ̲F̲I̲R̲S̲T̲ ̲T̲I̲M̲E̲ ̲I̲N̲ ̲J̲U̲M̲P̲ ̲S̲U̲I̲T̲S̲ with two heavy parachutes, and it was hard to walk around. The nylon covering our jump suits protected us from sharp tree limbs. The high collars prevented branches from sticking us under the chin. The webbing above the knees and below the crotch was to prevent us from splitting into two separate but equal parts if we landed crossways on a downed log.

Every jumper had his own plastic helmet and many featured a favorite symbol. Mine sported a Celtic cross from a Presbyterian monastery on the Isle of Iona in Scotland.

A strong screen snapped into place on the helmet to protect our faces. The logger boots were soft-toed with a metal shaft in the sole and heel to prevent a broken foot if we landed on rocks. If an experienced jumper knew he was headed for rocks or downed logs, he would try to hook up in trees. A good tree landing felt like landing on a haystack as long as the canopy settled over the top.

Soft leather gloves prevented burns from the nylon riser cords. Each man had a large hunting knife sewed on the top of his reserve chute pack in case the lines tangled. A large pocket on the right leg held several items: a nylon rope in case we landed in a tall tree; two bright orange cloth strips to signal we were not injured. I also kept the *Book of Common Prayer* and the *Holy Bible* in mine.

The Trimotor, having deposited the first crew, approached our resting spot with its three engines whining.

"All right fellas," Paperlegs finally shouted, "this is it. Let's show the other squads how to parachute."

"Tighten up your harness, get your static-line snaps out and line up. This flight's coming just for you," he said.

We loaded into the plane in opposite jump order. My number on the jump roster was seven, a sacred number for seminarians, so I was the second man into the plane. Tex would jump first, so he entered last.

No one said a word as we taxied toward the runway. We were airborne in half the length of the gravel runway. Bob gained elevation circling over the lake. Soon I would make my first parachute jump if I didn't freeze in the door.

Flying 1,500 feet over the drop zone, I looked at the townspeople surrounding the yellow target, which was 10 feet square and appeared as a little yellow dot. The wind had subsided, so we would jump directly over the spot, able to spiral to the target without compensating for drift.

Tex hunkered down in the oval door with a huge, nervous grin.

"I'm ready!" he said.

After three leisurely passes precisely over the target, Paper shouted, "Go,

Tex!" and slapped his leg hard. We were trained to exit only on that slap because the Trimotor could be as noisy as a threshing machine operating full steam.

Tex leaped out the door like a high diver. After the chute opened, he circled around and around and missed the target by about 50 feet. A cheer went up in the plane.

Kent, the hard-rock miner, was next. He had told us stories about how he broke wild mustangs and rode Brahma bulls as the toughest kid in town, but when it was time to jump, he froze in the door. He was more at home inside the earth than 1,500 feet above it.

Bob, the patient bush pilot, made a second pass. When we got over the target, Kent still had reservations getting into the oval door. Everyone was surprised that this tough guy was finding it so difficult.

Paperlegs shouted above the noise, "Sometimes this happens, Kent, and the best thing is to get in the door, sit on the edge and put your right foot on the step and simply relax. Once you feel the fresh air, you will feel more like stepping off. Picture yourself in the chute at a rodeo. We have lots of time to make another pass, so relax."

"Could I be last if I don't feel good about it now?" Kent asked.

"First, give it a try," Paperlegs said.

The man behind Kent checked his static line and riser hooks again. Kent carefully crouched in the door, sat on the metal edge of the floor and placed his right leg outside the plane on the step. The old Ford slowly approached the spot for Kent's exit. Paperlegs got behind him, sporting the cynical grin of the "Grinch Who Stole Christmas," and at the proper time, "helped" Kent make up his mind.

I remembered Paperlegs saying he'd help us, but this was not what I envisioned. Kent flew out the door like a fighter plane catapulted off the end of an aircraft carrier. He was airborne whether he liked it or not. His legs churned in the air under his canopy.

Kent hit the ground running, and his legs kept moving. He got a ride back to the barracks, picked up his gear and left town. We never saw the man with the ruthless tongue and weak knees again. Perhaps he acted on his talk about exchanging toughness for gentleness.

Finally, it was my turn. I sat in the door on my left leg with my right one on the metal step. Fifteen hundred feet above the marker, Paper yelled "OK , preacher!" and slapped my leg. In a split second, I experienced the exhilaration of space travel.

I shouted "Geronimo" and counted three, which was the time in which my main chute should pop open. There was no doubt when it did. The opening shock hit me like a freight train, turning me upside down, jerking me around like a ball at the end of a rubber string.

In spite of the instant pain, I was thankful my chute was working, and I felt freer than I had ever been. When the noise of the Trimotor departed, there was absolutely no sound. Complete silence. I could fly in any direction I wanted. I tried the right guidelines and the chute gracefully turned to the right. I began to spiral slowly toward the crowd below. With the dark blue lake to my left and forest green mountains to my right, I was centered in a transcendent state, upheld by sky, pure Idaho sky.

I wanted this moment to last forever.

Reality cut swiftly into my transcendent bliss. There was no way I could maneuver enough to hit the yellow marker. Landing about 40 feet from the target was better than Don, but he closed his eyes most of the way down. He ended his first jump in a distant meadow, away too many steps to count.

As a result of Kent leaving camp, we were named the "Seven Squad," since regular squads had eight men. We would earn smokejumper wings only after a fire jump and seven training jumps are required before the first fire jump. Paperlegs guided us through them all, and as the intense training was completed, I experienced a camaraderie that transcended other friendships. I began to know that the real basis of unique smokejumper cohesion is spiritual.

IT IS IMPOSSIBLE TO DESCRIBE THE ANXIETY LEVEL OF MY FIRST FIRE, one week after training ended.

A lightning bust stormed through Central Idaho on the Fourth of July, hurling many strikes at the timber-dry forests. Trees instantly burst into giant torches. Other strikes produced "sleeper fires," which awoke several days later.

There were 44 men in camp, and my number on the jump roster was 43. I would have to cool my heels until nearly every jumper in camp was dispatched. By noon over half were on their way and more fires were being reported every hour. Most reports were coming out of the Krassel Ranger District, respected for its perpendicular terrain. It was not my preference for any fire jump, especially my first.

Shortly after a dinner of two T-bone steaks, baked potatoes, and several helpings of cherry pie smothered with vanilla ice cream, the buzzer on top of the parachute loft began shrieking. The 50-foot loft is like a tall silo where chutes are hung up to dry. First a long blast sounded to get everyone's attention. Then short, crisp buzzes indicated how many men ought to race toward the staging area.

The buzzer rang for eight jumpers, but there were only three left in camp, Paperlegs, Ken Shuler and me.

Ken was playing with a group of children whose dads were off fighting fires. Ken loved kids and always gave their happiness the highest priority. He surprised us once when he held up little Eric and Anna Hovdey and said, "Here; look at these kids, 'cause they're greater than any of us."

Ken reluctantly gave up "hide and seek" and began suiting up for his first fire.

I felt good because Paperlegs and Ken would be with me. After only a few weeks, I cherished any time I might have with Ken. He was strong physically, but sensitive emotionally.

The sun was setting, every minute counted. I was a nervous wreck and it didn't help to hear we would jump onto the rocky ridges in the Lick Creek drainage in the Payette National Forest. As we were loading into Travelaire, I tripped twice — once over the cargo chutes and then over my own helmet; not a good sign.

With only three jumpers and spotter Wayne Weber, the little aircraft bounced off the runway like a ballerina dancing into the sunset. The fire was very close to McCall and by the time we had gained proper elevation, we were almost over the fire.

There is no comparison between practice parachuting on flat terrain and leaping into the unbelievably rugged batholith of Central Idaho. We located the blazing fire by dense smoke hovering over a rocky ridge. There was very little wind drift, but choices for a jump spot were limited. We could land in subalpine trees to the north or near a tributary stream pouring ice cold water into an alpine lake below the fire. As we circled to make the decision, flames spurted high into the evening air. Had we not been there to jump, it would have been a gorgeous scene.

A very small, green clearing paralleled the canyon. On one side were knife-like shards from dead snags in a field of boulders the size of compact cars. A stream beside a steep mountainside with small windswept trees among rock slides was on the other. To the north was a little lake with downed logs along the edges. To the south, a clump of alpine firs stood in wet soil covered with small bushes. If we missed the spot we were to try to reach the soggy area with the alpine firs.

The taunting of new men vanished. The two seasoned fire fighters with us, were sensitive to our nervous expectations. Paperlegs was to be the first man out the door. He was relaxed, and I wondered if I would ever achieve his composed state of mind before jumping.

Ken looked down at the rugged terrain. "I can't believe they would ask us to parachute into this. I wonder why I ever signed up."

The three engines were hushed, and for a few seconds we glided quietly in the sunset. Then, "Jump, Paper!" and a swift slap on his leg. We heard Paper's "Geronimo" in descending crescendo.

"A piece of cake," Weber said, as he reeled in the static line.

"Now," he said to me, "do exactly what Paper did. Spiral right over the jump spot and get a feel for the drift 700 feet below. Then go for the spot over the dead trees. On your last pass, sail over the end of the lake and plunk right down where he landed."

As the Trimotor made its final pass, I felt a sense of immense accomplishment. In a few minutes I would actually be a smokejumper, the

15

completion of a dream. While studying the glowing peaks in the Payette Range, my dream became reality when Weber shouted, "Go, Mark !"

I stepped into the evening as if I was walking on the gold rays from the setting sun. Suddenly, existentially, I was part of God's wild creation, fluttering momentarily toward His green abbey. I circled and spiraled and was proud of doing exactly what I was told. Too soon, I was below the top of the sunlit ridges, heading toward the clearing.

I distinctly heard Paperlegs yelling from the ground, "Turn to the right and plane with all you have, or you'll be in the water. Plane, plane, and get in here Mark!"

The chute slid directly toward the safe spot. I reached as far as I could on my front lines, pulling an airborne chin up, increasing my forward speed. I flew over the water and landed less than 30 feet from Paperlegs

The sensation was like emerging from a car wreck without a scratch. I bounced up and began a spontaneous dance. Paper, who was casually folding up his chute, wondered if I had hit my head on a rock. Spiritually, I was jumping skyward.

I took my helmet off in time to see Ken land right beside us. Our intensive training paid off in the sense we both hit the target earning our smokejumper wings. We felt accepted when Paperlegs said, "Nice jump, fellas — you're smokejumpers."

It had become so dark Ken had to signal he was OK by blinking a flashlight toward the airplane. Weber dropped our fire fighting tools up hill near the beautiful but destructive fire, and we made our way up to the fire in darkness.

THE MOST DANGEROUS TIME TO WORK A FIRE IS IN THE HOT AFTERNOONS when perilous winds fan the flames. Forests are cool at night, so we fight fires then, catching a little sleep during the day. We went right to work after we located our packs, building fire lines until 3 a.m. in the cold night air. I was totally exhausted.

I threw my sleeping bag near thick underbrush sheltered under a large alpine fir whose branches were 12 feet above the ground. In minutes I was sound asleep.

A few hours later, I awoke to movement in the branches overhead. I pointed my flashlight upward and saw two large yellow eyes staring down upon me. I thought it was a large owl, and I hooted gently toward him, but received no reply.

I heard the "owl" moving around again before daybreak, crawling from branch to branch. Since owls feed at night, I decided he had probably coming back from hunting and was settling into the branches for the day, but as I turned over to get a little more rest, something bounced off my sleeping bag. The imagined yellow-eyed owl turned out to be a wiry bobcat.

What a blessing! What a pleasant surprise! Here was one of the wildlife characters I admire most; a wild bobcat. I wanted to get a better look at her, but it was still dark and she scampered away, racing into the woods.

I awoke later in awesome splendor, and brewed a pot of coffee on a burning log. The morning star began to fade. After two steaming cups, I picked up my pocket Bible and wandered off in the direction taken by the bobcat. When I found a place to contemplate this untamed ambiance, I selected a description of God from Isaiah:

> *"Who has measured the waters in the hollow of his hand and marked off the heavens with a span, enclosed the dust of the earth in a measure and weighed the mountains in the scales and the hills in a balance?"*

Massive mountains as mere dust? Only the Lord God could envision this. For the construction of the Salisbury Cathedral, 120,000 tons of stone were used. Compare that to the weight of the natural stones comprising His wilderness cathedral. Imagine weighing one of these gigantic mountains and balancing it on a gigantic scale. What universal fulcrum could balance the weight of one enormous granite mountain?

Did Jesus consider mountains this immense when He said, "If you have faith the size of a mustard seed, you will say, 'move from here to there', and the mountain will move."?

As I prayed, I lamented some of my failures. They felt as heavy as these stone mountains, but the Gaelics have a saying: "Even the Lord can't make two mountains without a valley in between." If God, our empathic holy companion, created these soaring peaks and deep valleys, He no doubt understands our ups and downs. When our mistakes appear hopelessly heavy on the ethical scale of life, God balances them with the enormous counterweight of forgiveness, offsetting failures with greater love than we can comprehend.

Resting on a gray rock with its mossy tip extended into the alpine lake, with crystal water lapping against the rock, I felt I was with Jesus on Lake Galilee. A half submerged log floated up and down on gentle, almost imperceptible, waves. At the other end of the lake, the sun lit razor-edge peaks with reddish light high above shadowed valleys. A few hearty trees grew on the north sides of the peaks, each revealing imperfections. Deep winter snow had bent them to point out this hidden lake. None would be selected for a Christmas tree, but with broken branches and uneven tops, they had character. Wilderness ambiance transcends mere appearance.

Biodiversity surrounded me as an extension of my physical body and inner self. The glowing peaks reflected on the water enriched my contemplation. God was all around me ... beside me, beyond me and within me.

The human body is composed of lively waves of molecules and cells spiraling in microcosms nearly too small for detection. The human spirit also spirals harmoniously to cosmic melodies, melodies perceptible in the wilderness. My mind swayed to a rhythm God set in constant motion billions of years ago. The little waves on the lake, hardly perceptible, complemented the galactic rhythms of my body, mind and soul. Spiritually, I was totally immersed in a vortex of wholeness.

I hoped the bobcat might be attracted to my meditation, but I never saw her again. Occasionally a fish jumped, but I don't think it had much to do with my meditation, though the apostles did catch 153 fish when the great Fisherman spoke. I had a strange feeling that the great Fisherman was present.

When I completed meditating, I was pleasantly surprised to see Ken walking my way. The hillside was bright with wildflowers, but Ken had his own aura of brightness. A red-tailed hawk spiraled high above him.

"I see we've both been meditating, Mark," he said.

"I didn't know you were religious," I said.

"Not so much religious as spiritual," he said.

"What theme did you choose for your meditation?" I asked.

"Just being embraced by the wilderness is prayer, but Psalm 62 was composed for this very place.

> *For God alone my soul waits in silence;*
> *from him comes my salvation.*
> *He only is my rock and my salvation,*
> *my fortress; I shall not be greatly moved ...*
>
> *Men of low estate are but a breath,*
> *men of high estate are a delusion;*
> *in the balances they go up;*
> *they are together lighter than a breath.*

"God is the Rock of humility," he continued, "a symbolic rock larger than the greatest granite mountain. God's compassion balances our heavy burdens for spiritual renewal. Whether we are of high or low estate, our flaws and achievements are balanced by His infinite love."

In natural communion with Ken in that splendid setting, I recalled the Great Fisherman teaching from a boat. I read to him from the *Book of Common Prayer*.

> *Give us all a reverence for the earth as your own creation, that*
> *we may use its resources rightly in the service of others and to your*
> *honor and glory.*
> *At your command all things came to be: the vast expanse of*
> *interstellar space, galaxies, suns, the planets in their courses, and*

this fragile earth, our island home . . .

Your mighty works reveal your wisdom and love. You formed us in your image, giving the whole world into our care, so that, in obedience to you, our Creator, we might rule and serve all your creatures.

"The Eucharist liturgy is just as appropriate for this natural church as for The Washington Cathedral," Ken said.

Peace from God percolated into the valleys of our friendship, and we ended our meditation with a verse from Psalm 19:

"Let the words of my mouth and the meditation of my heart be acceptable to you, O LORD, my rock and my redeemer."

Ending our communion, we walked together toward breakfast.

So ended my first forest fire as a smokejumper.

IN THAT FIRST SUMMER, I sensed something unique about Ken Shuler, but was unable to pinpoint it. Unlike the rest of us, he had it all together. He could laugh and he could cry with everyone . . . top brass, lowly neds and all the rest. He never looked religious but embodied fresh faith and new hope.

WHETHER IT WAS THE PIKA NIBBLING ON MY BOOT or the roar of the Trimotor dropping cargo, something jolted me out of reminiscing about my parachute training and first fire. I found myself again, perched high on the mountain beside the Kinnickinnick Fire.

Our fire fighting goals are the same, but in the Selway-Bitterroots, there is a different element of spirit. Clouds circling the high peaks to the north gave me the impression I was moving in a liturgical procession toward a natural sanctuary of goodness. To my left, a chorus of wild birds declared the glory of God in their melodic anthems. Spirituality lurked in this durable granite forest.

High upon the Selways, I was apart from the ordinary and part of the extraordinary. God spoke to Moses on rocky Mt. Sinai. Jesus communicated with the Holy when he retreated to rocky mountains. Nez Perce Indians climbed these peaks to experience the extraordinary, sometimes piling rocks as altars.

The ordinary returned abruptly as the Trimotor swooped over me like a dive bomber. Caldwell pushed our fire-fighting tools out the door and they plummeted to the ground not far from my perch. The little birds scattered and the pikas darted back into their rocky homes. Ken reminded me we had work to do, and we swung into back-breaking work to control the fire.

"Get up here, Mark, and help carry the cargo. We'll have to take Tex and Phil's packs to the fire line since they won't get here before dark."

Several trips were necessary. We hauled the packs containing food, bedding and other essentials to a clearing beside a huge red cedar. We separated the fire tools — pulaskis, shovels and helmets — and headed for the fire.

Pulaskis are a combined ax and hoe invented by and named after an Idaho hero who fought the monumental North Idaho fire of 1910. When a part of that huge complex of fires blew up in the Coeur d' Alene Mountains in August, Pulaski led 42 men and two horses to a prospect tunnel between the Coeur d' Alene and St. Joe river drainages. One of the men fell behind the rest and perished before he reached the tunnel.

In the tunnel, Pulaski used his pistol to make his men lay face down on the floor of the tunnel while the leading edge of the fire passed by. He himself stood at the portal and used his hat to throw water on the mine timbers that caught fire from the intense heat until he passed out from lack of oxygen. Pulaski and the rest of his crew and the horses lived by his courage and quick thinking.

Fire's personality has not changed since Pulaski's time. Ken and Nick walked the fire line and decided how to attack it. Ken was the first smokejumper on the fire, landing close to the lower fire line. His jump partner, Larry, opted for a safer spot and arrived at the tool drop site later.

Larry was late because he disliked Ken being our choice for leader. Larry was tall and wiry, with an endurance that outclassed the rest of us, but Ken was respected for always being fair.

It was easy to see why Ken was a successful noseguard for his football team. He was a leader in the fellowship for Christian Athletes. The concept of fear was a stranger to him. His solid body embraced a strong heart which pumped compassion into all his human relationships. His rugged, square face sat upon an 18-inch neck.

Since Ken was the first man on the fire, he was boss. The men Pulaski led to safety survived because they listened to their leader. The 13 young jumpers who burned to death in the Mann Gulch fire four years earlier in Montana might have survived if they had followed the orders of their boss. No one objected to Ken's orders.

"The hottest section is over by that exposed granite rock slide," Ken told us. "Don, you and Mark push off and try to slow it down. Nick, go below the fire and build a deep catch trench," Ken said. "I'll check the top and throw dirt on the hot spots. When Tex and Phil show up, if they ever do, have them start trenching up the cooler north side."

Ken chose the most dangerous place for himself. Dense smoke, fumes, and intense heat create a most dangerous area at the top of the fire.

Larry worked safely near the bottom line.

I began hacking a fire trail through the rocks, two feet wide and deep into unburnable soil. Gaps between large basalt rocks had collected pine needles over the years which made it hard to chisel a durable line.

Lewis and Clark found traveling through this region very difficult in 1805. Conditions haven't changed much in a century and a half. Few white men traversed the Selway until gold was discovered in 1860. The area's only residents were Sheepeater Indians who lived off wild berries and bighorn sheep. Nez Perce Indians hunted up here but lived in a warmer climate on the banks of the Clearwater River.

Native Americans didn't suppress forest fires. They understood the important cycle of allowing fires to create new life — relinquishing the past to acquire a better future.

In the 1950s, the policy was to suppress every forest fire.

As Don and I began building line, there were places where roots had burned between rocks and the intense heat caused them to crack. This gave rise to a peculiar "burned rock" odor where extreme heat shattered solid stone. When we tossed cool dirt at the searing flames near the rocks, pieces of vegetation sizzled.

The fire had now grown to six acres and was burning brush and trees rooted in deep, soft dirt. It was relatively easy to shovel a deep trench around them, except at the rock slide. We pitched dirt on scorched branches ignited from superheated air. We mixed smoldering duff with clean dirt, then removed our gloves to feel and be sure it was out.

After three hours, the fire began to cool down and Don and I shared a can of pineapple juice and army-surplus crackers. At sundown the fire began to sleep and Ken said it was safe to pack up our tools and return to the base camp for dinner.

Nick was usually the first for dinner and last to appear for breakfast. He liked to talk about women, and while he thought of himself as the world's greatest lover, most of us thought of him as hopelessly addicted.

Don had him almost convinced there was a college woman on Rattlesnake Point Lookout, five miles to the south. Nick would walk 10 miles if he saw her through the binoculars.

"Stand over here, Nick," Don said, "and you can see a beautiful woman in that lookout over on Rattlesnake."

Larry, miffed that Ken was boss, didn't put much time in fighting fire, but he appeared eagerly for chow. When he showed up, Nick told him to go up to the fire line and tell everyone dinner was ready.

"I'll go on one condition, Nick. Hold your conquest stories until we've enjoyed dinner. I've heard your stories so many times I want ear plugs."

As Larry headed uphill, an embarrassed Tex and Phil dragged their tired bodies into camp. A glance at Tex told me we had best shut up or risk a swift fist in the stomach. This was no time to kid them about missing the jump spot. Tex was blessed with powerful arms, if not a tolerant spirit.

Soon the seven of us were sitting around the yellow glow of a wilderness fire, enjoying beef stew, fresh bread, and fresh apple pie, baked that morning in the McCall kitchen. Imagine a San Francisco restaurant perched on top of the world and you can envision our naturally elegant dining room.

The dinner conversation hushed when a full moon rose like a huge altar candle burning in a dimly lit monastery. Row upon row of ridges like reredos behind a blazing altar. The only sound was a sublime breeze sifting through the tops of the evergreens.

"Smokejumpers made the first fire jump in history right over there; less than 50 miles northwest of this peak," I said, pointing toward the moonlit Bitterroot Valley.

"In 1940, Earl Cooley and Rufus Robinson made timber jumps near Martin Creek on the Nez Perce Forest. They jumped out of a Travelaire just like ours. They didn't judge the wind very well and were carried over a ridge and a rock slide before a rough upwind landing.

"That jump was memorable in more ways than one. They used ripcords in those days and Earl's main chute failed to open. He managed to force his reserve chute open by cutting away tangled lines. His reserve opened 250 feet above some dead needle-topped lodge pole pines. A giant spruce broke his fall. He survived and that's how it began.

"Those were World War II years and smokejumpers used chutes rejected by the military. Discarded football helmets with wire mesh over their faces protected them. Some were leather helmets that still had the high school names and numbers on the sides.

"Many of the jumpers were conscientious objectors ordered to the fire fighting corps by the government. A contentious objector might object in taking another's life but they were no objectors to hard work. They jumped out of older military aircraft. Some of them couldn't afford logger boots or 'frisco jeans and lacked protective padding. Without exception, forest rangers and local fire fighters were impressed with their good work. They took extraordinary risks to protect the national wilderness during the war.

"In 1944, Japan launched 10,000 balloon-bombs toward the Pacific Northwest. They were expected to be carried by the jet stream at 30,000 feet over the Pacific Ocean. As a result, manpower was diverted from the war effort to controlling forest fires. Only 300 of the balloons were known to have reached America, but what would have happened if they began igniting trees in a tinder-dry fire season?

"One of the first smokejumper units was Operation Firefly of the 555th Parachute Battalion from Pendleton, Oregon. It was composed of black infantrymen who were skilled in both parachuting and fire fighting. Some of them were stationed in Missoula in 1944, jumping out of military aircraft. They earned the praise of the forest service for helping to control fires in 1944 and 1945.

"While I was attending seminary at Princeton, I was assistant chaplain at

New Jersey Maximum Security Prison, and I befriended a former black infantryman named Eugene Williams who would fit into that 555th Battalion. He is energetic and exemplifies courage.

"He and his brother Bland were convicted of the same murder. Both men are in the death house where they stare daily at the room containing the electric chair. They knew I got nervous visiting them in that dingy place, and made every effort to comfort me in the prison. I believe they are innocent, though we are having trouble proving it. I wish they could come out and join us."

"I don't want any criminals in the jumpers." Larry said. "They wouldn't be in prison if they weren't guilty. They have to pay for their sins."

He lived in a black and white house in which there was no room built for compassion.

"I believe that Eugene and Bland Williams are innocent," I said. "I'm going to convince someone of that, if it takes me the rest of my life … if they don't get burned in the electric chair first."

"What do they say those fellows did?" asked Ken

"The Williams brothers are in prison for the murder of a night watchman near Perth Woodbridge, New Jersey. The problem is, they didn't do it! They were prosecuted by an ambitious politician who wanted a feather in his political cap. It's a terrible injustice. Every time I go back to visit them in their concrete death house I am more convinced of their innocence."

"Why are you so interested in someone across the country?" Don asked.

"I believe everyone has the right to enjoy a family and home, and they have been denied this happiness by injustice.

"There is also an intriguing, perplexing paradox here."

"What's that?" Don asked.

"Sometimes the Williams brothers sound more at home in prison than my relatives do in their enormous houses. Can a prison cell be a home as much as this vast expanse of beautiful forest? What is a spiritual home?

"Freedom and liberty present another dilemma. They often come to my attention when I'm out here bounded only by sky and miles of horizons. The Williams brothers are confined by concrete, armed guards, and steel doors, yet when I communicate with them, they express a deeper experience of being free than some backpackers out here in the wide open forests."

"Maybe they wouldn't enjoy our wilderness type of freedom."

"I wouldn't want to change homes with them, but I'd love to have their inner freedom. Jesus said the truth would set us free. I'd like to know how humans can enjoy the freedom of the expansive wilderness and at the same time relinquish inner compulsions and addictions, and injustices. Freedom is more than surroundings."

23

THE SEVEN OF US WATCHED the bright glow of the homey campfire fade into orange embers.

Tex took out the book he always carried in his jump pocket, then carefully unwrapped his chanter and opened his book; *Beginning Bagpipe Practice Book,* by Pipe Major Sandy Jones.

"Oh no. Not here!" Don muttered.

"You guys don't know good music when you hear it. If you insist, I'll take my chanter and books and go over the hill. Maybe a cougar or a black bear will appreciate *Bonnie Charley*," Tex muttered as he strolled off into the moonlit night. In McCall, Tex always practiced outside the barracks and never after 10 p.m.

Shortly after, Tex began playing, and we heard a creature howling several ridges to the East. It may have been a cougar screaming or it may have been a wolf responding to Wolfgang Lewis. The screams did not deter the bagpiper's serenade. The truth was we enjoyed his music, but no one dared tell Tex.

With or without bagpipes it was a splendid moonlit night on the top of the Kinnikinnick ridge in the Nez Perce National Forest.

THE NEXT MORNING, AT THE CRACK OF DAWN, the orange and black Travelaire roared full bore, barely 25 feet above us, while we were still in sleeping bags. Skip, a former Navy pilot, dropped a message on a long orange streamer that almost hit Ken's bed. Without getting out of his bag, he leaned over and picked it up. He read it quickly and started laughing.

"There's been a delay with the Selway packer and his pack string. One of his mules took off. Weber says to wait two more days. Skip will drop more supplies in the clearing. There's a hot-springs toward Kinniki trail. P.S. Have fun."

We were free to do as we liked.

I walked to the campfire site to start a fire and get the morning coffee brewing.

"What you going to do today?" I asked Don.

"I promised myself I would begin studying causes of violence so I can understand kids on probation," he said. "Kids in trouble are balancing on a tight wire on the verge of violent behavior. When they lose their balance, they fall off society's norms. I'd like help them develop equilibrium. I'm headed over to those pine trees to study counseling techniques. What you going to do, Mark?"

"You've talked about communicating with Indian spirits here, and other smokejumpers have sensed a mysterious presence in the Selway. Jesus said those who are not against us are for us. I'm going to see if it's possible for a Seminarian to communicate with your Indian Spirit, 'Wey-ya-ki'. Where would you suggest beginning?"

We were facing a steep incline toward the Lochsa River drainage. Slivers of the river appeared as small strips of blue and silver between layers of blue-green mountains, like ribbons stretched out on a Christmas tree.

Don pointed north and said, "First, locate an old Indian trail straight north of the large granite peaks on your left. Drop down past them a few hundred feet and you'll pass lots of dead snags beyond a grassy knoll. When you observe old blazes on trees you're entering the Indian Chapter House of Wakan Tanka.

"It will take you all day, so take your flashlight."

A T A DISTANCE A FOREST APPEARS TO BE COMPOSED of flawless trees, but there are few without major imperfections. Timbermen often log the tallest, healthiest, best adapted trees. A better approach might be to cull the smaller, diseased, over-crowded trees for lumber and allow them rebirth as homes for families, encouraging the bioscathedral to renewal through her healthiest members.

As I danced down the trail, I looked back toward the fire ridge and the silhouettes of trees. Some stood out from others, like people on crowded streets in New York City. Some were broken at the top, while others were missing branches. Others suffered from insects or wind damage and were stunted from severe winter storms. Few approached perfection, but each wild tree was distinct.

There may be a similarity concerning parishioners in magnificent cathedrals built by human hands. When the nave of a church is filled with people, at a distance, they look healthy. A closer examination will reveal broken bodies, diseased trunks, damage from emotional storms ... all the problems which accompany being human.

At a distance, we seven smokejumpers might look alike, but each personality is different. Every member of that seven-man crew struggled with personal problems. Only God knows each person's inner wilderness.

Occasionally, there's a near-perfect specimen of character among the masses of imperfect, like the spiritual connection to nature I see in Ken. But there's a lot of good in ordinary people too. As each wild tree has its own inherent, imperfect beauty, each person becomes more beautiful by their unique imperfections. St. Paul said, "forget what lies behind and strain for what lies ahead." This gives an opportunity to develop courage in accepting and working through the imperfection.

Wandering through the roadless country strengthened the focus on my own inner-wilderness. I asked the Holy Spirit to bless my contact with local spirits, and if not in my best interest, help me deal fruitfully with their mysterious attraction. I found myself euphoric.

Running down dusty hillsides despite the sharp rocks, I was thankful for my logger boots. Indians wore soft moccasins over these hills, but they didn't weigh 200 pounds.

I was traveling though historic country. Several miles to the east, Nez Perce Indians established a trail through the Macgruder Corridor into the Selway wilderness. It was on this trail that they communicated with their guardian spirit,

Way-ya-kin. This is sacred country for the Nez Perce. Chief Joseph led his moccasined Nez Perce over the Lolo Trail through these Bitterroots, away from heavy-footed soldiers.

The trail dates back beyond Lewis and Clark's 1805 expedition and was less than 10 miles away. The trail was so difficult to follow even Indian guides lost their way.

The clear morning was giving way to clouds in the West. I walked around two tall red cedars whose trunks were five feet thick. With sunlight vaulting from above, I felt as if I was stepping into Westminster Abbey. I wondered where the trees would be more beautiful; in that natural cathedral or manufactured into giant spires for a Gothic church?

The hushed atmosphere was interrupted by a red-tailed hawk swishing through the nave. Beyond the cedars, the natural abbey, paintbrush, balsam root and lomatium replaced the red and yellows placed on high altars.

I visualized a processional choir singing a Mozart introit as I entered the sanctuary. I hummed Mozart's *La ci darem la mano* and *Give Me Your Hand, Zerlina,* from the opera *Don Giovanni.* It is not proper to hum upon entering an abbey, but Mozart seems to belong to the lofty cedars in this evergreen cloister.

Wild things extended their hands to me.

A few raindrops fell on a bed of trillium on the forest floor. Each leaf held its raindrop momentarily, then relinquished it to the next leaf. I concentrated on one trillium, relishing its triune petals.

Is there some special meaning in its turning purple as the summer fades away? White is the liturgical color for resurrection and purple stands for suffering. I wondered if there was to be suffering for me or my smokejumper friends similar to the young men at Mann Gulch. Whatever the future, there was one symbol that would not be denied: the delicate trillium was pushing new life through the dead accumulation of the brown forest floor. Life is stronger than death.

Ahead I saw a Douglas fir nearly 70 feet high. Approaching, I noticed a blaze that was probably cut into its trunk 50 years ago. I knew I was on the Indian path.

The trail bordered a creek with water splashing over rocks on one side and a rain forest on the other. Rain was falling on Idaho syringa and mountain ash, and ferns grew everywhere.

The trail widened into a meadow covered with white four-petaled flowers of Canadian dogwood, which local people call puddingberry or blazing day-stars. I stooped to pick one of the blossoms among some poison oak, whose shiny symmetrical leaves have a beauty all their own. It reminded me that good and bad are separated by a thin line in nature or in human relationships. Rain falls indiscriminately on poison oak or dogwood as well as on just and unjust persons.

I carried the little day-star flower as a symbol of spiritual guidance. Dark clouds were forming over the treetops but couldn't dim its glow. Its aura symbolized that someday God would allow me to see His bright Morning Star face

26

to face.

My trail became narrower and broke into a grove of tall cedars. A blaze on the thick red bark of one of the trees resembled the threefold-pointed poison oak leaf. Were there hidden meanings in these blazes?

How do Christians discern blazes given to guide their lives? Where does God carve benchmarks? Are some blazes cut so deeply into lives that inner guidance systems cannot operate properly until corrected by spiritual surgery?

The warm summer rain fell steadily, wetting trees first, then falling upon large syringa and finally reaching trillium before being absorbed into the ground for eventual recycling. This is symbolic; water loses its own life in order to offer rebirth to something else.

Ahead of me, something darted through a grove of white birch. It was too small for a bear, and though I hoped to see a cougar in the wilderness, this animal was too small for a mountain lion. Perhaps it was a spotted bobcat going after a rabbit or rodent. Bobcats are nearly impossible to see, due to their intelligence and exotic camouflage. They are one of nature's most exciting paradoxes — 30 pounds of flesh but a thousand pounds of courage.

The warm air produced a mist in a meadow where less than 300 feet away a family of whitetail deer grazed. They ignored me as I passed by.

Then, on the trail, hoof tracks appeared as large as the Trojan Horse might leave. It didn't take me long to realize the tracks came from one of the strangest creatures ever created by God. Splashing down the creek came a female moose. With shoulders six feet high, she resembled an oil derrick, or a living Thidwick, the good-hearted, moss-munching moose.

Only a moose could love another moose. They look like they've been created entirely from leftovers. Their parts don't seem to match. The smokejumper manual states a female moose may be unpredictable and belligerent, but she ignored my intrusion into her baptistry. I didn't feel a need to climb a tree to avoid her.

Past the birch trees, I came upon five large hot pools hidden among round boulders near the mossy stream. In the first pool a half-submerged human was soaking his weary bones. A leather belt with a USFS buckle lay on top of a thread-bare ranger outfit. He had come in sandals rather than logger boots and wore a reed hat made in Mexico. He had been eating crackers frosted with wild honey.

When he finally looked up, he said, "Don't need to be afraid of that old moose. She comes here every summer and thinks she owns these hot springs. She's more interested in chewing moss than chasing you."

"I've never encountered a moss-loving moose before," I said. "I've heard she's more belligerent than a male. What if she decides to chew the moss in the bottom of the hot pool where you're soaking?"

"If you worry about things like that, you don't belong out here. If you respect nature's autonomy, she will respect yours. If you are looking for trouble, you'll probably find more than you want with that old moose," he said.

Only his head appeared above the steaming hot water. Then he sat up chest-high in the steaming water and became very serious.

"What you young people ought to worry about is creating a world where all people value love and integrity. Humans ought to cherish God's creation as an end, not a means. The human family needs a leader of flawless character who treats others as sacred ends; a hero, you might say, who is willing to sacrifice his life for those who are lost."

"Where in this violent world will we find such a person?"

"God is preparing us for that divine embodiment of truth right here in the Idaho forests," he said. "Go prepare the way for Him!"

A whitetail doe began drinking water from the pool where he was relaxing. I guess deer prefer mineral water flavored with old retired forest rangers. The old ranger began talking with the doe as a farmer might talk to a cow in the background. Backing away carefully, I continued my journey, hoping to communicate with Indian spirits.

Pondering the words of the prophetic ranger, I was reminded of a story about a carload of hog farmers who visited Yellowstone Park. Observing the steaming hot waters of the incredibly beautiful Morning Glory pool, one shouted, "What a great place to scald hogs."

Despite the concern of the old ranger, I suppose someone will possess these springs some day, dam up their hot water and sell tickets, using nature as a means, a sort of cheap way to scald hogs.

Above the hot springs, beneath a steep rock outcropping, I reached a roaring tributary of the main stream. The winter before, in St. John's Cathedral in Spokane, I listened to the organist play Percy Whitlock's *Fanfare* and Bach's *Toccata and Fugue in D Minor,* processional and recessional. I heard strains of those masterpieces reverberating in the tributary's rumbling and cascading falls.

It had become late afternoon and it was a long way back to the ridge, but on a granite boulder near the stream where I was to enjoy the food I'd been carrying in my back pack, I first meditated.

The boulder was grand enough to be a bishop's throne but it settled for a servant priest. It fit me perfectly, physically and spiritually.

I read Psalm 8 for a meditation:

> *O Lord, our Sovereign,*
> *how majestic is your name*
> *in all the earth! . . .*
> *When I look at your heavens,*
> *the work of your fingers,*
> *the moon and the stars*
> *that you have established;*

what are human beings
that you are mindful of them,
mortals that you care for them?

With the song of water falling in the creek for a pipe organ and the still point of forest silence for a choir, I was in perfect harmony with God. I felt profound gratitude, the fountain of all virtues, for a God who is mindful of me.

It is almost impossible to pray outdoors without the litany of birds reinforcing the aura of peace. Their songs in many keys touch me, and my childlike nature leaps out in ecstasy. A raven settled into the Douglas fir beside me amid the flapping of tiny bluebird wings as they fluttered through my contemplation. Unconsciously I hummed Alexander's hymn,

Each little flower that opens, Each little bird that sings,
He made their glowing colors, He made their tiny wings.

Psalm 8 evoked new appreciation for Kant's philosophy of respect, which I wanted to share with the other jumpers back on the crest of the hill. Meditating in this pristine chapel, I peered through the same old glasses, but God replaced their lenses with a greater love for all living creatures.

New lenses nurtured in Christian meditation consist of three major elements: One's authentic self, inspirited by the Holy Spirit; God the Creator; and Christ the King. The elements are as distinct as the three radial engines of the Trimotor. Each engine of the Trimotor works independently, but they operate in harmony. Christian meditation blends these sacred elements in a variety of spiraling sequences.

Much like the Holy Trinity, three basic mantras harmonize in various combinations throughout Christian meditation.

The first perception centers on our selves. We hum *Shaéem*. This is our private time to enjoy being authentic, for better or worse. After a period of relaxation, we begin to feel the inner movement of the Holy Spirit, reminiscent of God's Spirit brooding over creation. The Holy Spirit pumps Life into our weary selves.

Relaxed, accepting myself as I am, I endorsed the beautiful authenticity of nature surrounding me in the forests. There was no need to be anything but what I am, and I'm exalted in my forest home.

We advance toward the perfect splendor of the heavens, the galaxies, spiraling in their infinite beauty, from the exalted self. We hum *Eloheem*, an ancient name for Almighty God. Our spiritual awareness is heightened by glimpses of the presence of God expressed so eloquently in the Psalms.

The vortex of this refreshing meditation spirals in harmony with the gravitation forces in circular motion. There are spiritual circular patterns from heaven which harmonize with patterns of the subatomic cellular structure deep within our physical bodies.

The celestial vortex descended as spiraling galaxies from the heavenly realms to enlighten my biospirituality. I sat upright on solid rock, hands extended toward the untamed universe, breathing deeply of Idaho's sanctified air. A summer breeze swayed bushes and small trees near my granite prayer-bench. The music of the stream gently spiraled within me until I was united with the rhythm of the little birds darting in and out of my prayer.

A yellow warbler, apparently nesting nearby, spun around my head, enhancing the spiritual song ringing deep within.

Meditation has a lot in common with parachuting. Parachutists float high above the mountains and streams, then spiral to earth in solitude. Meditation is the same spiral-spiritual movement, gliding among elements of the Holy Trinity.

At this point I begin the third component of meditation. I reduced the phrase "Jesu Christu" to *Christeem*, elevating Christ's supremacy. Now deeply aware of Jesus, whose home on earth is in the heart of his followers, my thoughts move closer and closer to the spiritual center of life. There may have been no room for Him in the inn, but meditation creates a durable home for Him in my heart. I feel the peace of a Savior born in a barn and at home in the Idaho forests. I feel peace, His peace.

First I communicated with my Christian God. Afterwards I communicated with the Native American Spirits of the Selway through living things. A great horned owl drifted silently overhead. A chipmunk stood on his hind legs a few feet from my rocky chapel, as if in prayer. When he noticed the owl, he hid under a mossy log. Spirituality attracted them both. When adoration of Christ has top priority, it is good to commune with the lively spirits in the wilderness. Jesus said forces who are not working against us are really for us.

I was feeling very close to the animals I met that day, especially the deer and moose, when my meditation was interrupted. Something I assumed was a back packer thrashing around my chapel 10 feet above me. The noisy hiker even kicked rocks toward my prayer bench.

"Next time," I thought, "I'll post a solitude sign on the giant cedar."

In spite of the thoughtless intrusion, I was totally renewed by prayer and ready to start the long hike back to the Kinnikinnick ridge. Shouldering my backpack, I headed for the trail on higher ground when the rowdy being stopped smack dab in front of me, less than 15 feet away. Six feet tall, weighing 2,000 pounds, my noisy prayer partner was a full-grown bull moose with a five-foot rack.

St. Francis of Assisi attracted little birds when he prayed, but I don't remember any moose dropping in. I was awestruck by his rugged sovereignty. I had no doubt we were communicating. The message seemed to be respect.

The huge moose respected my autonomy during meditation and I hoped he would not invade my privacy now. In case he did, I picked out a 40-foot lodgepole to climb — a recommended move in the smokejumper manual.

We stood staring at one another until I began laughing. I hoped his puffy chin and pendulous muzzle reflected good humor. Without warning, he politely turned and marched directly away, crossing the stream. He was so tall he hardly wet his belly. I watched him scratch his antlers against a 40-foot tree. He almost pushed it down with his massive strength.

During the encounter, I was so occupied with the extraordinary, I had no fear, but when he had strolled away through the brush, I trembled for a few minutes.

I wouldn't trade that moment for a million dollars. How many persons meditate with a moose? I could hardly wait to share this with Don.

This was the beginning of my appreciation for Indian spirituality.

When I returned to the hot springs, the ranger had disappeared, but not the deer. They ignored me as I put my clothes on a rock and hopped into the largest pool. My tired muscles welcomed the massage of the soothing mineral water.

The sun was sinking low, and I knew I couldn't stay in the hot water very long or my legs would give out later. Twenty minutes later, my tired legs began the steep climb homeward. A full moon broke over the mountain peaks.

"Am I leaving home or going home?" I wondered. I mused over the idea that home might be portable and go wherever we go.

Moving up the mountain in the bright moonlight, Jupiter and Saturn blessed my inner home. It has been a beautiful day and my spiritual journey has been richer than expected. God loves to surprise prayerful people. Happy voices of ancient Christians expressed this in the *Phos Hilarion*:

> *O gracious Light,*
> *pure brightness of the everliving Father in heaven,*
> *O Jesus Christ, holy and blessed !*
> *Now as we come to the setting of the sun,*
> *and our eyes behold the vespers light,*
> *we sing your praises O God: Father, Son, and Holy Spirit.*
> *You are worthy at all times to be praised by happy voices,*
> *O Son of God, O Giver of life,*
> *and to be glorified through all the worlds.*

As I climbed higher and higher, approaching the ridge, I clutched my glowing evening stars, humming a Charles Wesley hymn:

> *Christ, whose glory fills the skies,*
> *Christ, the true, the only Light,*
> *Sun of Righteousness, arise !*
> *Triumph o'er the shades of night:*
> *Dayspring from on high, be near;*

Daystar, in my heart appear.

THE NEXT MORNING, KEN WOKE US UP UNDER A RED SKY. "Get your gear packed. We're hiking down the Kinniki trail. The packer will meet us at the Lochsa River."

We estimated the trek out would take five hours. We cleaned the campground and buried the trash so thoroughly, a stranger would never know it had been our home. We helped one another set the 90-pound packs onto our backs. Phil, who didn't weigh much more than that, looked like an overloaded pack mule.

We followed a pattern set in similar packouts, marching 10 feet apart so branches didn't snap the next person's face.

"You know to follow the jumper standard of improving trails as we walk, don't you?" Ken asked as we started the packout.

Phil couldn't resist. "Don't litter, right?"

Everyone laughed.

Ken reminded us of the smokejumper nickname, "rock-kickers." We kicked rocks and small obstacles off the trail as we walked. Some Idaho rangers had been rumored to start fires near neglected trails in order to bring smokejumpers in to kick junk off the trail. We cleaned everything off the trail, even taking time to remove large barriers like downed logs.

Ken said his coach might offer us a position with the Hawkeyes if our kicking skills looked promising.

Phil jumped in to lead what he proclaimed the "Hawkeye Obstacle Removal Service" down the cluttered trail.

As we traveled the old path, Don said, "Blackfeet Indians have a saying: 'Don't let grass grow on the path of friendship.' We're making it easier for others to increase their friendship with the wilderness."

Kicking away the debris encouraged me to boot some emotional sticks and stones from my personal life as we hiked. A person has to kick junk out of his life to be happy.

I wanted to tell Don I communicated with Indian spirits, but he was up front kicking debris, and I usually walked in last place, keeping well behind the others so I could savor the fresh wildness of the forests. Also, no one could stash a heavy rock in my back-pack when I wasn't looking.

Ahead of me, my six fellow jumpers scuffed their leather toes kicking rocks aside. By the time I came along, the clogged trail had been cleared. When we unpacked at smokejumper camp, I was embarrassed that my boots were scuff-free. There's something good about people who clear difficult trails so others have an easier walk in life.

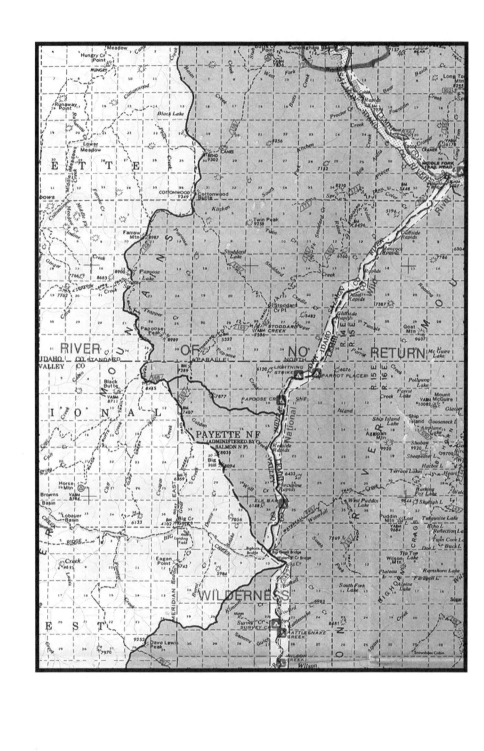

THE RIVER OF NO RETURN

The Good That You Do
Will Come On Back To You

I SPENT THE WINTER IN A CATTLE TOWN on the Yellowstone River in Montana, serving a Presbyterian parish. It was not easy transforming Jesus' sheep parables into cattle stories for ranchers, but I became a good hand in branding Herefords.

When summer arrived, I migrated back to my McCall smokejumper family. The first week was 90 degrees in the shade in smokejumper camp. Payette Lake rippled enticingly in Idaho's midsummer sun. Twelve jumpers were on call a few blocks away, but we were among the next 12, relaxing on the beach, swimming, water skiing, and picnicking. We couldn't resist the cool pleasures of the lake.

My wife, Lynn, and I, ready to grill hamburgers, couldn't persuade the charcoal to light.

"Hey, Davis!" Ken Shuler yelled. "You wanna take that charcoal with you if the buzzer goes off? Maybe you can throw it in the fire and bring it back lit!"

"That's a good idea, Ken!" I retorted. "How about carrying it in your leg pocket?"

Ken had a comeback, but his sister Sharon asked him to open a pickle jar. Sharon and her husband, Jeff, were expecting a baby soon, and she was uncomfortable in the heat.

Distracted, I squirted too much fluid over the charcoal, tossed a match on it and flames shot up explosively. I jumped back. I looked at Lynn and caught a sly smirk before she turned her attention to unpacking the rest of the picnic lunch.

Then, the fire buzzer on the smokejumper tower sounded with a series of blasts. The on-call crew was on their way. But the blasts didn't end at 12., ringing for eight additional jumpers.

Ken and I would miss the rest of the beach party. Lynn knew I had to go. We hugged each other and I hurried toward the loft. I felt a moment of regret as the aroma of beef sizzling on our grill drifted after us. Our next meal would be military-type rations.

Climbing into my jump gear had me sweating profusely by the time I squeezed my body into the heavy, canvas jumpsuit.

At the airstrip, the Ford Trimotor was ready for takeoff. Dean Davis, a calm and experienced jumper, was our spotter. We valued his keen perception in selecting safe jump spots and detecting rocks, downed trees, stumps and logs that are a smokejumper's biggest worry. He made a precise check of every jumper's canvas suit, harness, buckles, rope and parachutes as we climbed aboard.

"Where are we headed, Dean?" I asked.

"Little Five Mile Creek on the Main Salmon. Nasty jump country. Easy work, though … several small fires. Don't drift over the jump spot, or you'll end up in the river. The air is so thin today, you'll drop like rocks, anyway."

The rest of us, sticky and uncomfortable, didn't respond.

The thought of landing in a cool river was almost pleasant, since our protective suits were buoyant, but the Salmon, River of No Return, is such a wild torrent that its white water could be as perilous as the jagged rocks lining its banks.

Ken, whose muscular arms were thicker than my thighs, was my jump partner. Ken stayed pretty much to himself, but always took time to listen.

"Hey, Mark!" he said, "The last time we were partners, it was hotter than you-know-where. Remember? You took the easy way out and landed in a nice jack pine. Today I get the tree, you get the rocks."

I told him I was hoping to stay in the plane.

Fifteen minutes after the fire buzzer sounded, we were airborne. Making our ascent over Payette Lake, Phil pointed. "Mark, isn't that your wife down there water skiing?"

I looked, and Lynn was executing a turn with precision and grace. Phil whispered in the pilot's ear, and the next thing I knew, a drift chute — a miniature parachute with a weight attached to it used to test wind currents — left our plane.

Lynn looked up, and over she went, with yellow skis sticking out of the lake at awkward angles. When I saw her head come up out of the water, I figured it had better be a long fire.

We gained altitude and headed toward the heart of Idaho's wilderness area. Soon, the breathtaking, jagged crowns of God's natural altars rose before us among the rough Idaho terrain. They were infinitely more intricate than man-made steeples of concrete and steel, but could be deadly to parachutists.

A silence descended as it always did when the time to parachute was at hand. Each man was alone with his thoughts. "If my chute opens all right, can I land safely? Can I miss the deadly cliffs?"

I tried preventing these existential questions from entering my mind.

Dean Davis was the first to see the smoke boiling up near the edge of the canyon, drifting away from it. The pilot circled the fire a time or two, holding a steady pattern at 1,400 feet.

"There's a little clearing here, between those two tall ponderosas." Dean pointed to the green speck from the window of the plane. "Do you think you can get in there? There's another larger spot quite a ways downhill."

Ken and I studied the meager jump spot with the surrounding landmarks. It was rocky and the ponderosas appeared as green giants, but we opted for it.

Dean released a drift chute to determine where the wind would likely carry us. Its path indicated the river would be directly below us when we jumped. We had to trust the wind to carry us about a quarter of a mile to the edge of the canyon. I prayed the wind wouldn't shift.

"Davis and Shuler, get ready! Hook up! Take your positions!" he shouted above the drone of the three engines. We hooked up our static lines, connecting us to the plane. When we hit the end of that line, it would yank the chute open.

As we made the last turn of the final pass, I gazed at the white-foamed line of river. There were white water rafters down there, their rafts like tiny dots floating down a churning, pulsating blue pathway. I wondered if they were watching our free air show.

"The idea is to stay out of the river," Ken yelled. "If you don't, at least land on a raft with a pretty woman!"

I couldn't respond. I felt more like fainting than joking.

The pilot cut the engines. The roar embracing us ceased, leaving us vulnerable to the empty space between the silent plane and busy river. Ken squatted in the door of the plane. My knees bent by some will of their own and I crouched behind him. Deep concentration separated us from the other men. I felt alone. My heart pounded like a jackhammer. The plane descended rapidly.

Dean smacked Ken's leg with a sharp slap and shouted, "Hit it!"

Ken leaped without hesitation, and I jumped right behind him, too eager and too close. I got tangled in his deploying canopy, completely enveloped in orange and white silk, falling toward the river.

"Is this it, Lord?" I asked, though my lips were frozen shut. "Is this how I'm going to die?"

At that instant, my own chute burst open, unfurling like Old Glory waving in the endless sky, jerking me out of Ken's canopy, an answer to prayer. When my chute opened, the incomparable freedom of soaring had never been so rapturous or the exquisite mountains more beautiful.

Then, I committed a second blunder. I was enjoying flying so much I forgot to keep track of Ken.

Once the parachute opens, the first thing is to look for your jump partner. I felt my chute collapsing and realized I was directly above Ken. His parachute was catching my air. My chute, being directly over his, lost its loft, fluttering in the breeze like a dead mainsail.

I jerked my right guide line, which normally would steer me away but it was too late. Like a rock with no guidance system, I was free-falling toward the top of Ken's canopy. I thought of grabbing one of his lines as I slid by him and he and I riding down together. This maneuver once allowed Bob Rawlins and Rob Graves to land safely.

I bounced on the front section of Ken's canopy feet first, and I was amazed to find that it was a hard surface like a trampoline. Taking a risk which may have saved our lives, I bolted across his chute and leapt away as far as I could, clearing the skirt of his canopy. As I whizzed by him, I caught a glimpse of his expression. His eyes flashed alarm and his mouth sputtered angry words which I was glad I couldn't understand. I would have preferred not to rile this airborne linebacker.

In a few seconds, my chute reopened. I had good air, but I was underneath Ken. Would I steal his air now, causing him to crash into me?

No. He correctly turned away from my position toward the fire. I heaved an atmospheric sigh of relief.

Our zig-zags suggested an airborne square dance with the caller on break. I turned as quickly as possible toward the edge of the canyon and landed a half-mile downhill from the jump spot, a safe half-hour away from the big guy. I hoped he would cool down before we went after our fire fighting tools.

I wound my way up the hill and located Ken by an old ponderosa pine which held our cargo 25 feet above the ground. He was waiting for me.

"Davis, you sight-seeing Socrates! The Creator should place traffic signals in the heavens for absent-minded people like you! What the Sam Hill were you day dreaming about? You just about ended it for both of us!"

I couldn't blame him for being angry. I didn't know what to say, so I said nothing. He accepted my silence as an apology.

"Let's get up that tree and fetch the cargo," he mumbled.

Ken handed me the climber's spikes, and I buckled them onto my boots. I slowly climbed up the towering pine to salvage the equipment, using crevices between large outcroppings of bark for handholds.

Our cargo had made a direct hit on the ancient tree, smashing the contents. A broken limb supported what remained of our axes and shovels. Using my knife, I cut the lines of the cargo chute, hopelessly tangled in the branch. The bags fell to the ground with a heavy thud, exposing the ax and shovel handles. They were splintered into long shards directly beneath me, pointing upward like the tines of a pitchfork.

Ken was preparing to slide the battered cargo bags out of the way when the bark supporting my climber's spikes suddenly tore loose. I fell helplessly down the tree trunk, tumbling toward those surgically sharp spears, screaming. I felt the solid shoulder of my friend's body thrown against me with a force that knocked me far downhill, preventing me from being impaled on the surgery-sharp handles.

When he blocked me, one of my climber spikes ripped a huge gash in his right arm. Blood began spurting from his wound in a terrifying red shower. I scrambled to my feet, grabbed a stick, pulled a cloth from the cargo pack and made a tourniquet. As I twisted it on his arm, I realized how alone we were.

We had signaled Dean in the plane that we were well. It might be two days before they would fly over again. Ken could lose too much blood before helicopters could come pick him up, and we didn't have a radio, anyway.

My first aid training proved invaluable and with the first aid kit, I managed to repair the serious cut. Finally, the bleeding stopped. I felt he would make it. Then Ken said, "It's time to hit the fire before we lose a chance to control it."

"You'll have to stay right here and rest while I go up to the fire."

"OK, I really don't have the strength right now to help, but give me a little time and I'll join you," Ken said.

I unpacked our chutes, making him a comfortable bed. I helped him lie down to give his body's depleted condition time to recover.

"You saved my life, Ken, and the best I could do was rip a hole in your arm."

"Mark, this isn't exactly your day with smacking into my canopy and then slashing my arm, so be extra careful, and please don't surprise me anymore."

"Yeah, it's one of those days I'd like to keep plenty of distance from everything including myself. I'll check on you in an hour."

I went over our broken tools. The shovel handles were splintered beyond repair. I managed to make one pulaski usable by whittling the broken handle with my jump knife.

Ken rested and slept, trying not to move his painful arm. I saw him wince when he shifted positions. There was nothing more I could do, so I concentrated all my energy on suppressing the fire.

Using what was left of a pulaski, I began chopping roots, clearing brush away from the fire area. After checking on Ken, I worked through the night, separating small trees and dry undergrowth from my fire line, digging a shallow trench around most of the perimeter. At times it seemed I was not making much progress, and I was grateful for the cool evening air.

B Y THE SECOND EVENING, I had managed to contain the fire in less than half an acre. When it burned itself out, I was also burned out.

That evening, I contemplated our three brushes with death and their corresponding miraculous escapes. First, I got tangled in Ken's canopy. Then, my chute collapsed above his, which might have forced us both helplessly to the ground. Then, I jammed a climber spike into his arm while he saved my life. Perhaps because I'd spent my life caring for others, it was difficult to accept someone helping me more than I could ever repay.

I was exhausted. Working through two nights had expended my energy. I desperately needed rest. It was so warm, I didn't want a sleeping bag. Instead, I heaped some bunchgrass for a bed. The high, padded, canvas collar on my jumper jacket which protects us from branches jabbing us between our shoulders and helmet made a fairly good pillow.

When I settled down on my natural mattress, I felt some creature crawling under me. It may have been a mouse or pika, or it could have been a snake wanting to rest beside a warm body. I was too tired to worry about it. I fell off into a heavy trance, and whatever it was it stopped scratching and went back down its hole.

I awoke after three or four hours' rest. The first rays of sunlight graced the highest ridges of the surrounding mountain ranges. Ken was stirring and would soon have "one-armed" coffee brewing, but I wanted to begin the day with meditation. We meditate better on empty stomachs and blank minds, being more open to the refreshment of God.

The crest of the hill a hundred yards above the fire was a good setting for an early meditation. One of the benefits of smokejumping is that we always land near the top of the mountains so we always had an unsurpassed view of God's bioscathedral.

As I walked up the mountain, I studied the Master Sculptor's work, the vast Salmon River canyon, illuminated by a rising sun. It was a phenomenon only God could have designed.

At the crest was a clearing surrounded by five giant yellow pines. The grass was two feet high near the trunks where old fires had left their signatures years ago. Nature provided flowers — dogtooth violets and wild hyacinths — for a chapel peaked on the summit of glory. Their aroma blended with the morning breeze, enriching prayer. The first red-gold rays of sun massaged new life into my sore body. I was truly at home.

I had seen bighorn sheep from the Trimotor when we approved the jump site, and prayed I might communicate with them on this fire. I was not disappointed. Searching for a prayer bench, I encountered 15 sheep gathered under the protection of the largest bighorn ram I've ever imagined. His powerful curl formed a complete circle. His weathered horns were scratched with deep gashes and the end of the left curl had broken off.

The other sheep were not threatened by my visit to their home. It was their leader's task to protect them. He was a regal sentinel if I ever saw one. The ram didn't seem bothered by my presence, but his golden-brown eyes with long black slits never left me.

I knew if I threatened the wild sheep the ram might launch me into the next mountain range. He stood taller than domestic sheep. He had a little white strip on top of his head, between the horns, and a clean white area around his nose and mouth. The white hair of his rump distinguished him from the rest of the herd. I longed for a camera but had smashed mine in a cargo drop on the Wangedoodle fire.

The prayer bench I selected was 25 feet away from the sheep family. The ewes had delicate, little, curved horns, unlike the powerful, coiled horns of the rams. The sheep and I relaxed together in their church.

I delight in St. Francis because animals flocked to him during prayer like the massive moose attracted to me in the Selway. The sheep came closer to me for group meditation. I was blessed to have this rare opportunity, therefore I focused on sheep for my meditation. I closed my eyes and concentrated on the Lord's illustrations of good sheep and compassionate shepherds, repeating Psalm 23.

Why does the term "sheep herder" sound less sophisticated than "shepherd" to our American culture? Do Bishops, the "shepherds of the church," realize sheep herders get dirty and struggle against harsh adversaries? Jesus was a sheep herder who loved both sheep and goats.

The Risen Christ lives in various degrees in authentic persons in every generation and may resemble working sheep herders. The men walking on the road to Emmaus after the Resurrection didn't know they were traveling with a Man risen from the grave. We long to walk with Him ourselves, but how will we know Him?

Just as the bighorn ram was one with his flock, Jesus is one of us. No sheep herder could protect his flock better. I didn't see any lambs with the bighorns. Jesus, the lamb of God, may also have been a ram sent by God to promote justice.

I began my meditation by humming *Sheep May Safely Graze* by J. S. Bach. As I became more relaxed, I hummed *Sha'eem*, which resembles a Hebrew word for peace.

The wilderness produces primal trust, an ethic ignored in the modern world. It encourages persons to be themselves without pretense marring the natural atmosphere. Relaxing on this altar-peak I had no need to prove anything. I simply enjoyed being. I didn't have to do anything for Idaho's untamed residents.

> *The Lord is my Shepherd, I shall not want.*
> *He allows me to rest in green pastures.*

The aura of meditation attracted the ram, and we enjoyed sanctified communication. I put my fear of being butted down the hill aside in gratitude for our wild friendship. I considered a metaphor of this friendly ram and his family and Jesus' love for His people in an Easter Collect:

> *O God, whose Son Jesus is the good shepherd of your people: Grant that when we hear His voice we may know Him who calls us each by name, and follow where He leads; who, with you and the Holy Spirit, lives and reigns, one God, for ever and ever. Amen.*

Prayer is thanksgiving and surrender to God, not protection from a congregation of wild animals, or a host of vexing dragons in a troubled society.

Humming *Christeem*, I drifted deeper into meditation, focusing on Jesus as the Lamb of God. God usually reveals himself in gentle ways, not by butting sinners into submission, but Jesus, the King, might also be symbolized by a ram with a full curl.

I was meditating these thoughts when I was swept into the presence of the great Servant of Souls, who lives in isolated wildernesses as well as in big cities. Whether Jesus was a ram or lamb, He didn't take divinity for granted.

St. Paul said: "Let the same mind be in you that was in Christ Jesus, who, though He was in the form of God, did not regard equality with God as something to be exploited, but emptied himself ..."

Ken had emptied himself by saving my life, personifying a servant shepherd.

Ending my meditation, I thanked God for everything — especially my jump partner; the pastoral love with my flock in Montana; my smokejumper friends; and mountain sheep on the Salmon River drainage.

With a complete joy that comes from the silence of the holy, I returned to our campsite for fresh morning coffee. Ken was feeling better, although his arm was very swollen.

"I can help today by feeling for hot spots with my good hand," Ken said. He was worried the fire might flare up, though no smoke was visible. In the hot sun, some blazes were likely to appear.

I related my close encounter with the sheep. He said he was going to take his coffee and communicate with them for awhile before joining me at the fire.

We spent the third day in Idaho sunshine snuffing out the last few smokes. After supper, we knew the fire was absolutely dead and we could return to McCall. What we didn't know was how Ken's goodness would come back to him.

EARLY ON THE FOURTH DAY, Packer John showed up with three mules and one very thin, tired-looking horse to escort us back to the trail head. Packer John was aloof and didn't enjoy his time with firefighters, but when he took a look at Ken's arm, he decided he'd better make haste. He loaded up the splintered handles and the rest of our gear.

He gave Ken the horse. Riding a mountain mule, I turned and waved to the bighorns as we headed down the steep mountainside. As we rode together, I explained to the packer how Ken had received the ugly wound. He began to philosophize:

"Sometimes in life, ya gotta leap before thinkin' or stoppin' to size up the situation," he said. "Now, I remember this ol' mule here you're ridin' - she came up on a rattlesnake near a creek last year while carryin' a jumper. She jumped backwards so fast the smokejumper ridin' her darn near fell on the snake. That ol' mule jumped first and thought about it later. Sure glad that slitherin' viper didn't bite my mule. Good mules are hard to come by these days."

I couldn't decide which I enjoy more: parachuting into or recessing out of this splendid cathedral splashed with untamed beauty. As we traveled the roadless backcountry in solitude, Packer John and his mule string had a communication all their own.

That evening, when we arrived at McCall, I took Ken to the hospital. Dr. John Moser said his arm was healing just fine and he could go on another fire in a week. The physician marveled on how quickly it was healing.

THREE DAYS LATER, Lynn and I were traveling toward Burgdorf Hot Springs for some "R & R." We had driven five miles when Lynn said, "We ought to turn back to McCall. Maybe the kids need us."

"Oh, you're acting like a mother. Getting away is so foreign to you that you're just not used to having time to yourself."

Lynn reluctantly agreed. She turned on the radio and as western music flooded our car, it was interrupted by an urgent announcement by Dr. Jay Hunter at McCall Hospital.

"We have immediate need of B-negative blood. A patient's life depends on this. Anyone with B-negative blood, please call the emergency room as soon as possible. We repeat ... "

This was my first day off fire duty for a month, but we both knew Lynn's blood was B-negative. It only took one glance from my wife, and I knew what we would do. We spun the car around without a word, turned on our headlights, and sped for the McCall Memorial Hospital. We hurried into the hospital ten minutes later. Dr. Hunter and a nurse named Grandy took Lynn to a bed near a quiet form on a bed hidden behind a curtain. Soon, blood was flowing out of Lynn's arm into a system that would give new life to a person unknown to me.

As I stood outside the emergency room, I noticed a familiar figure sitting in a chair by a window, staring out at the lake. Ken had been coming to the hospital to have his arm treated since our return from the bighorn sheep fire, but as I approached him, I could see he needed something resembling a transfusion of spirit.

"What's up, Ken. Your arm not healing ?"

He turned to face me, and I was struck by how perplexed he looked. Ken was not a person to show emotion, but I sensed deep compassion. Then, his eyes lit up.

"My sister Sharon's in there," he said softly. It was a voice I barely recognized.

"I prayed to God for someone with the proper type of blood to come and help her. And thank God, someone with the right type has come to donate blood. They said it was just in time to sustain her life until more can be flown in. God always answers prayers, but this was coming right down to the line."

I was bewildered with joy, knowing Lynn was the donor.

"We almost lost her," Ken murmured, his voice breaking. "They almost lost their baby, too. Now they will live."

He turned away from me, unable to say anything more, tumult inside him, his shoulders taut and his breathing heavy. At last, he relaxed and turned to me once more.

"What you doing here?" he asked.

I slid into a chair near him and explained that Lynn was the donor.

"That's Lynn sharing her life? I'm overwhelmed and very thankful," he said, sounding almost like himself again.

Dr. Allen appeared and told us the Twin Beech was at the airport with more blood and we could go in. We entered together, and found the curtain drawn back. Lynn and Sharon were almost asleep, gazing at each other. Sharon looked very pale, but had a glow about her. We knew she was going to make it.

Ken's eyes embraced Sharon with an expression that was both tender and healing. After bending down and giving Lynn a kiss, Ken offered a short prayer of gratitude.

Several hours later, Lynn and I were relaxing in the Burgdorf Hot Springs. She was very tired and extremely happy. As the warm water soothed our bodies, another kind of warmth soothed our souls. I asked Lynn if she remembered Turk Murphy's gospel song, *The Good that You Do Will Come On Back To You.*

"Yes," she said, knowing the Lord had guided her to "shepherd" another person in need. "Ken saved your life. It's exciting to think God used me to help save the life of his sister and her baby."

"Yes, I think we have entertained Angels unawares. Let's meditate on God's goodness. You must be glowing with satisfaction that God spoke directly to you today."

"To me? When?"

"Remember when you felt we should return to McCall? Wasn't that the voice of God responding to Ken's urgent prayer?"

In the solitude of the steamy water, we were thankful for the goodness shared, and for it coming back to the giver this time, one-hundred-fold.

"What's the difference between prayer and meditation?" Lynn asked.

"Ken was asking God for a specific outcome. That's called intercessory prayer; petitioning God, as Christ Himself would, on behalf of a person or situation. Jesus said 'Ask, and it shall be given unto you.' "

"But what is meditation?"

"More of a silent, mental prayer; enjoying God and being in His presence without an agenda. I like to apply my mind to a passage of Scripture in a free and easy way and just let it soak in, like the healing warmth of this pool. Meditation can prepare us for prayer. Today, it follows Ken's prayer for help. They intermingle and pull us closer to God."

"Where does contemplation come in?"

"Perhaps it's the sum of meditation and prayer. It is simply a time to express wholeheartedly one's gratitude to God for His goodness."

"That's what we're doing right now," Lynn said, "relaxing in a pool of God's goodness."

JESUS SAID, "The measure you give will be the measure you get, and still more will be given you."

Ken's goodness had come back, with love.

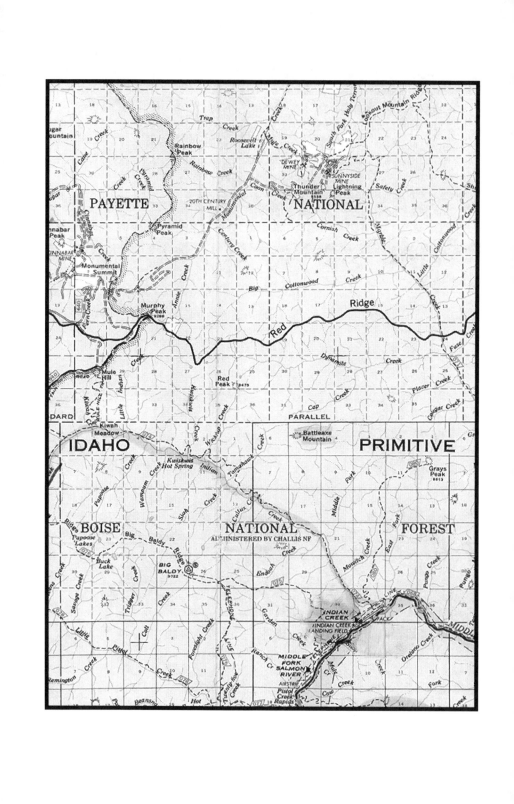

THE IDAHO PRIMITIVE AREA

DANTE'S INFERNO

WINTER CAME AND KEN RETURNED TO THE UNIVERSITY OF IOWA preparing to become a high school coach. I spent another winter as pastor in Hysham, Montana.

When we drove through Yellowstone Park on our way to smokejumper camp in Idaho the following summer, we noticed masses of visitors. We appreciated the fact that the Idaho primitive forests were far from the maddening crowds.

I began the summer fighting two small blazes on the Payette National Forest. Then a once-in-a-lifetime wildfire swept our elite corps of airborne firefighters into an Idaho version of Dante's *Inferno*.

On the Fourth of July, I was drawing double pay as designated cargo dropper. Before dawn, Matt Beasley knocked on my door shouting, "Get some breakfast and whip out to the airport. You're delivering food and supplies to the outbreak at Marble Creek."

In a matter of minutes I consumed a steak, two eggs, three muffins and a cup of coffee. Matt drove a Dodge six-by-six out to the hanger with a cargo of hot breakfast. Johnson Airlines dispatched their trustworthy Travelaire for the firefighters'buffet. It was an old plane with a fabric covering almost as reliable as metal. I loaded eight metal cans containing the steaming food into the Travelaire and hooked cargo chutes to them.

Standing with Beasley beside the black and orange, single-engine plane was a woman I assumed to be a reporter doing a story on Idaho forest fires.

"Mark, I want you to meet Mary Kay Clark from Missoula," Matt said. "She's going to be piloting the Travelaire for the rest of the season."

"I'm delighted to fly with you, Mary Kay," I said, wondering if she understood down drafts.

"You look worried, Mark. I started my career as a surgical nurse. If I can handle surgical instruments in the operating room, I can manage the Travelaire."

She checked out the airplane before stepping inside.

"Been jumping long?" she asked.

"I've been jumping a few years, but I'm new at dropping cargo."

I put on the emergency chute every spotter had to wear. Matt, who knew I'd never flown with a female pilot, much less a good-looking one, was grinning.

"She may be young," he said, "but she's been flying the NC 8112 in Montana for three years. She knows how to fly the backcountry as well as anyone. Well, maybe not as well as Bob Fogg, but then nobody's as expert as Bob."

If there was any doubt about her proficiency, it vanished with the blue exhaust from the radial engine as we taxied down the gravel runway. Dawn was in the east, painting a few high clouds silver and white. In minutes we were part of the crisp sunrise, guided by the morning star. Mary Kay set the heading directly into this splendor which exploded across the horizon, defying description.

Marble Creek drains into the Middle Fork of the Salmon River, between the Boise and the Salmon National Forests. Pilots often locate Shell Rock Peak, almost 10,000 feet elevation, for a guidepost. The Marble Creek drainage is below Whitehawk Lookout, another popular communication point for backcountry pilots.

Two teams of jumpers had been dispatched to Marble Creek a week earlier, but couldn't contain the fire. It burned in heavy grass and dense brush with dead trees, explosive fuel. After working feverishly, the crew had retreated and radioed for more help.

Three "Hotshot" ground crews trooped in by foot. Hotshots work much like jumpers, forming competitive teams of 25 skilled persons who take great pride in their work.

We were to drop their breakfast at the head of Norton Creek, where they had set up a subcamp. Mary Kay had made previous cargo drops to them, flying out of Salmon, Idaho, farther north. She said all three teams were made up of Native Americans, among the best forest fire fighters in the nation.

"This is my fifth trip over here," she said. "Each time the fire doubles in size. The first time I flew over it was only eight acres and not going anywhere. Now look down there — several thousand acres. You can hardly see any wisps of smoke, but by 10 a.m., the smoke will be billowing out, making it hard to fly."

I spotted fire fighters waving bright orange banners below the lookout.

"Are they our target?"

"They'll be getting a hot breakfast," Mary Kay said. "Hook yourself up and get the cargo ready. Don't push it out until I scream 'drop'and wave my right hand. I don't like to miss the mark."

I worked my way back to the door and hooked a nylon line around my waist so I wouldn't slip out. Then Mary Kay plummeted the old Travelaire downward to deliver the savory food.

This "dive-bombing" was the type of flying I enjoyed the most. Fortunately I was securely fastened to the plane. She banked it over on its right side so far I had to hold the cargo from sliding out the door with one hand and grip the shroud cable with the other. I worried about being in a fabric-covered dive bomber. She leveled out a hundred feet above the tree tops, allowing only seconds to get everything ready. I shoved two units out exactly at her command. Both cargo chutes popped open and hit the spot. We flew downhill below the drop zone, then gained altitude in a wide circle for the next drop.

On the way back to McCall, we went sight-seeing in the fresh summer air. Mary Kay had spotted three elk the day before by Ruffneck Peak and wanted to see if they were still around. Then, she flew over the landing strip at Indian Creek, where float trips begin for rafters on the Middle Fork of the Salmon.

" ' This is the day the Lord hath made,' " I said, " 'let us rejoice in it.' "

"Are you the pastor that spends his summers smokejumping?" she asked.

"I don't say much about being a minister. Frankly, I just love being part of the mystery dwelling in the wilderness. And, I really appreciate being included as one of the boys. They don't treat me differently because I turn my collar around the rest of the year. Out here, I'm just plain Mark."

"I find most people are just plain 'whoevers'in the wilderness," Mary Kay said. "It brings out the healthy urge to just be simple selves. Out here character counts. It's the same feeling I get listening to Bach."

"How many talents do you have?" I asked.

"I play the pipe organ for my church when I'm not flying, but horse training is my greatest talent," she said.

"I suppose you say there's a similarity between flying and riding a horse."

She smiled but didn't answer. We swooped down low for a look at mountain goats running almost perpendicularly up a rocky cliff.

I made several cargo runs with her in the next three days. She added a dimension to smokejumping that was missing from our "men only" mentality. I supposed someday there would be women smokejumpers.

Early on July 9, Red Jackson, the smokejumper foreman, told Larry to get the Seven Squad suited up. There had been an ominous blow-up on the edge of the Marble Creek fire. It could become a terrible danger to others. Seven Squad was going to jump on the north side of Mahoney Ridge and suppress a spot fire boiling up on a heavily timbered slope near Prospect Creek. We were to keep the fire from spreading onto a hogback with sparse timber but high dry grass. The fire might reach the ridge near Battle Ax Mountain if we didn't stop it.

In minutes we were airborne, heading for the area I had dropped cargo into earlier. When the Ford drifted over the battle area, the smoke was so thick it was difficult to distinguish Whitehawk Lookout.

We were to parachute on the north side of a ridge running up from the Middle Fork River. We made three passes and the spotter decided on a grassy slope on the southern exposure of Marble Creek, a quarter of a mile from the energetic new fire.

The smoke trailing away from the spot fire indicated a mild uphill wind. The spotter dropped us directly over the valley, and all seven of us drifted into soft soil under a grassy area. It was like jumping onto a mattress, and no one complained.

By the time we got our gear and stacked it on some rocks, it was almost 9 a.m. We took a couple cans of cold stew and fruit, filled our canteens, picked up the fire tools and headed toward the swiftly moving flames.

The fire was less than three acres, but air currents were churning up and visibility decreased dramatically. The fire spewed Olympic-size balls of fire hundreds of feet into the air. I remembered the young men killed at Mann Gulch. They landed above the fire and none of them except my friend Walt Rumsey and two others lived to tell about it.

Larry was boss.

"Bring plenty of water and follow me. We'll wind around the hillside through the sparse timber and cross Marble Creek. Then we'll be parallel to the heart of it and attack it above and below."

Adrenaline was flowing, and we were confident we could tame this hot spot in a few hours and polish off a good dinner before sunset. When we reached the fire, Larry directed Don, Phil and I to the bottom to build a deep trench designed to catch rolling, burning debris that could start new fires far below. We worked both sides of our pulaskis, using the grub hoe to cut the trench and the ax blade to cut away small trees and roots. Larry led the rest through thick underbrush to the hottest side on the north and began digging two-foot wide trenches.

Our hope for quick control ended abruptly. Intense winds pounded us and the fire spread to the Sunflower drainage on our south. The fire torched the sparsely timbered hillside with a vengeance we had never encountered.

My anxiety leaped into the chromosphere in awe of this inferno. Trees burned like patio torches, spouting live ashes for hundreds of yards. The crowns of green trees ignited as though they had been doused with high-octane gasoline.

The fire howled like military jets roaring off the deck of a carrier. The smoke trail was dense and black, which was a bad sign. Flames shot a hundred feet skyward.

We heard trees exploding on the other drainage. The trinity of fuel, heat and oxygen was igniting the subalpine forest, torching an entire hillside. We were witnessing a fire storm with the intensity of a tornado.

Fires do not generally ignite everything in their path. Instead, they prance around like Indian dancers. Sometimes they pass over areas of green lush growth and explode on other flanks. This was one of those unpredictable fires, but by good planning, we were safely to one side. It danced away from us momentarily.

We were dog tired. Our eyes watered. Sore back muscles throbbed. Our bodies twitched so severely, the ubiquitous dust separated from our clothing. Dense, smoky air cluttered up our lungs. Burning fragments landed on our arms, tattooing minor holes in our clothing.

This was the moment we had trained for. Now, courage was not an ethical theory but the existential means for survival. Larry led us to the lower section, closer to the Salmon River, to start a new trench. We spaced ourselves about 10 feet apart, each man digging with all his strength. We continued working our line until we reached the trench the man ahead of us had completed. Then we'd yell "Move up," and take over where he had been.

If there are ground crews on the same fire, jumpers get a little crazy trying to outwork them. Prometheus, the Titan, stole fire from the gods to share with humans. He unleashed immeasurable power to mankind. Jumpers take Promethean pride in building fire-proof lines to contain that power. We had a reputation that we could control the destructive disposition of fire. This was our test. Our muscles ached. Our arms were exhausted. But, we had no choice but to continue the effort and battle this fiery dragon until evening came and the fever of the fire subsided.

We started a new line on a mild slope around a few tall pines and aspens. Our progress was discouraging in the face of the force we were confronting. It was literally hotter than blazes.

Around three in the afternoon, Nick, who was the last man down the hill, shouted, "She's gone under us!"

Thick black smoke was ascending from our right. Burning pine cones had rolled down the mountain from the main fire, igniting new blazes below us as they rolled. Our best effort had been futile, and it was time to think about our safety.

We sprinted down to join Nick. The smoke was much heavier than we anticipated. A thousand yards below us, underbrush and young saplings were burning. Devastating flames were crowning in the tree-tops. Dry superheated evergreens exploded propelling burning splinters in all directions. The dragon was now threatening our lives, not just helpless timber, and the noise level was intolerable. We communicated by shouting.

Out of the thick, smoky air, we heard the piercing engine of the Travelaire. I took a small mirror and reflected what sunlight there was so they could locate us. With surgical precision, at treetop level, they dropped a two-way radio bound by long orange streamers. Ken raced up the hill and grabbed the radio, already turned on and tuned in.

Yensen, somewhere in the smoke above us, shouted into his radio. "The fire below you has spread sideways and is spreading rapidly on both your flanks. The southern fire is moving slower toward a rocky area. The fire to the north is in heavy fuel. You can't outrun it."

"How far's the rock slide?" Ken yelled.

"At your level, it's directly south about 150 yards," he answered. "There's an Apache Hotshot crew somewhere on the other side of the rock slide who don't have a radio. Get your crew into the rock safely; then see if you can guide that crew safely into the slide. OK?"

"Roger! Roger!" Ken yelled, with his mouth filled with dust

Yensen's voice came on again. "We have a TBM slurry bomber coming. It will be here in a few minutes. We'll clear your way to the slide."

"No! We're going to make it all right to the clearing. Most of the trees have already burned and we can stand the heat. Tell the TBM to bomb the other side for those Hotshots. It looks terrible over that way," Ken said. "Over and out!"

"If you insist. Good luck down there."

"Follow me!" Ken shouted above the raging storm. "Toss your tools. You might have to crawl over burned logs and hot rocks. Save your water and let's go."

Larry moved in, angry Ken had volunteered the retardant to the Hotshots.

"That slurry-drop might save our lives. You threw it away without asking me. I am the boss on this section, you know."

"Keep your legs moving and save your breath and do unto others as you want them to do for you. Come on fellas; move!" Ken said.

Slithering through an outcropping of smooth rocks in the old burned area, we were thankful stone couldn't ignite. There were searing hot spots. It was important to watch where we placed our hands. It was too smoky to gulp air. Below us, fingers of flame ignited any flammable matter, but this particular rocky area was pretty much burned out. Charred tree trunks stood as reminders of 50 years before, when they may have been through a firestorm like this. We hoped we would survive better than they did.

We fought our way toward the rock slide, breathing hot air. Once there, we would have to live on the whirling terms set down by the firestorm after we secured crevices with good air. A superheated wind from the fire might destroy our squad at any time. Struggling for each yard, we reached the boulders in the rock slide totally exhausted.

Above the deafening roar of the fire, we heard the powerful whine of a TBM slurry bomber making its pass on the other side of the rock slide.

"I feel like we're in the Battle of Midway," Don shouted.

The single-engine bomber cleared the tree tops and delivered gallons of thick, red ammonium sulfate in the vicinity of the Hotshots. The heavy mixture of water and retardant hit a large fir and toppled it over. We hoped the Hotshots were not near that tree.

When we were all present and accounted for, Larry told us to get into crevasses between the large rocks close to the ground. "Don't get into caves. The superheated air will consume the oxygen and you'll suffocate. Now everyone quickly find a safe place and get ready for the monster to blow over us. Good luck."

"What about the Hotshots?" Ken asked.

"They're on their own. It is too risky for anyone to go past the slide," Larry said.

"That's not right! We ought to go for them immediately," Ken argued. "I'm going over there and look for them. Anyone want to come with me?"

"Not me," Larry said. "I'm married with two children."

"Let's go for it, Ken," Don shouted. "Anyone want to give me some water to share with them?"

We shared what water we had, and Ken and Don were off into the smoky unknown. I decided I was safer with them than hiding between rocks and hard places and tagged along. The rest looked for safe crevices, knowing they might never see us again.

There was less smoke to the south and more space between the green trees. The underbrush was less profuse and easier to move through. After five minutes of moving sideways on the rocky hillside, Don thought he heard voices. In smokejumper fashion, he "hooted" three times like a great horned owl. Smokejumpers learn to communicate long distances by hooting. A high-pitched voice squealed back. By exchanging hoots and squeals, we found the Hotshots.

In the midst of rocks and downed logs appeared 18 of the most beautiful persons to ever grace a fire line, even when resembling mud wrestlers. These retardant-covered firefighters were the Apache women of the famous all-female 209th San Carlos Hotshots from McNary, Arizona.

"Over this way!" Don shouted. "We've come from a rock clearing that's safer and we'll lead you back to it."

"Thank God you found us! We got disoriented with the crown fire and didn't know where to go. We couldn't have made it without the slurry bomber. Do you have any water? We lost ours, and I don't think some of us can make it without water."

I watched Ken share the water in his canteen with most of the Hotshots and I don't think it ever got empty.

"Here, take all we have and get moving toward the rocks," he said. "We don't have much time. This is no place to be when it blows up again."

Dry needles were beginning to crackle in the tree tops high above. A wall of flame was about to devour us. Exploding trees created bursts of flame as if shot by cannons, sucking the good air up and away from the ground. Violent air was swirling in every direction. It was hard for Ken to stay ahead of the tired but physically fit fire fighters from San Carlos. Moving quickly we soon located the cherished rock slide.

A cheer drowned out the terrible fire-roar when we appeared, and a louder cheer followed when it was clear they were women. Nick, somewhere among the huge boulders, would have been a one-jumper greeting committee for the slurry-stained women, but he was in hiding.

Crew leader Della Warrior gave quick instructions to her crew members.

"Lie face down as close to the ground as possible and wait for the fire to pass."

In a few minutes, the wall of destruction enveloped us. The heat was so intense that the shirts on our backs felt scorched. Oxygen was at a premium. A terrifying wind blew, replenishing the sickening smoke. We were baptized with fire.

In baptism, going under the water symbolizes dying and being buried with Christ. Then the person comes out of the water, alive, symbolizing new life in the Resurrection. After the fire passed, one by one, exhausted bodies surfaced, sitting up and peering to see what remained. We had been reborn from above, arising from a sea of smoke.

We became euphoric. We had lived one lifetime in a few fleeting seconds. The will to live had proven stronger than the fire. We were united in a common bond that went beyond gender or race or religion. Both crews got up and hugged everyone in sight. I thought I heard the refreshing music of *Dance of the Blessed Spirits*. I even hugged Larry. When Nick crept out of his crevice and saw lovely women dancing among the rocks, he decided he had actually died in the crown fire and gone to heaven.

Larry got the radio working and sent an elated self-congratulations for the Seven Squad and the 18 women from Arizona.

"We found the Hotshots and brought them here to safety, and we all made it safely down here. Watch out above us. This fire has terrific velocity and destructive powers."

He didn't say Ken rescued the Hotshots. He was afraid Ken's heroic act would be noticed and that he would become squad leader.

Ken shook the dust off of himself and declared that we ought to celebrate being alive. "I lost most of my food crawling over the rocks, but I've got a can of tuna fish. Let's share. Does anyone else have anything for a celebration?"

Della reached into her pack and produced a can of pink salmon. A Hotshot named Marie pulled out five small bags of large crackers. Phil located several cans of beans and one of pineapple. Soon, upon a large flat boulder which served as a wildland altar, appeared a mound of edibles like the original Thanksgiving in the New England forest.

"Before we begin our jubilation," Phil said, "we ought to thank God for our lives and that we are all one in this beautiful life. There are no barriers in the forests to becoming what God wants us to. I feel like a brother to all living things, and especially all of you."

Without a word, the men and women joined arms, forming a tight circle around the table, glowing red from the fluorescence of the surrounding fires. It was the eye of the hurricane, an intimate place of sacred solitude, and for several minutes everyone just held each other, which, in itself, is a form of prayerfulness.

Della, speaking in the Apache language, thanked God for being one with the earth, and for the fire, which would renew the deadfall on the forest floor. Others joined in chanting Indian prayers. Don was lost in reflection and surrounded by Native American love.

Phil, a Mormon who had just returned from a mission, surprised me by borrowing my battered prayerbook for prayer. He chose a prayer of thanksgiving to complement the incredibly beautiful Apache prayers:

> *"Almighty and everlasting God, you made the universe with all its marvelous order, its atoms, world, and galaxies, and the infinite complexity of living creatures: Grant that, as we probe the mysteries of your creation, we may come to know you more truly, and more surely fulfill our role in your eternal purpose; in the name of Jesus Christ our Lord. Amen."*

"The fire spiralling around us and whirling out fingers of flame reminds me of the supernova Crab Nebula," Phil added. He dabbled in astronomy. "I feel like we are spiralling in Andromeda, and God has heard our prayers."

Ken then asked God to bless the food piled on the granite table, and the hungry firefighters shared a sacred meal. When everyone was satisfied and ready to walk to the ridge, there were leftovers of fish and crackers.

Marie said the ladies wanted to take Ken out to the fanciest dinner in town and dance the night away for guiding them to the rock slide. There were no objections. We began the ascent toward the main camp, drawing up plans for a combined celebration in Salmon City.

Neither crew had flashlights, but the glow of the red Idaho skies lit our way to the ridge near Whitehawk lookout. I thought of Moses, following the fires of God by night and the smoke by day, toward the promised land. God had been good to us, and gratitude glowed like the light guiding Moses.

We reached the summit of Whitehawk Mountain shortly before sunrise. There were sleeping bodies everywhere, except in the cook's shack, which offered fast food service around the clock. Bacon and eggs never tasted so good.

A few hours earlier, we had confronted Hell. Now we dined together as we will someday at the Lord's Table in heaven, reminiscing about our close encounter with death, comparing it to the new dawn. Breakfast was served on two long tables interspersed with men and women on a high ridge overlooking the wilderness. The view was magnificent, as if we were peering through a living rose window in a cathedral.

As the sunlight said "good morning," the courageous crews said "good night," clutching sleeping bags from a stack six feet high and going our separate ways to clean up and rest.

In late afternoon, after a good rest, we reported to the fire boss, a hundred feet below the lookout. We had flown over it many times, and seen the 77 on the roof. For the couple manning the lookout, this had been paradise a month earlier. Now it was more like the center of the inferno. Most vegetation had been consumed by the Marble Creek Fire. Only the roof on the lookout building was still green.

The fire boss chose the lookout as headquarters since the other sites had been conceded to the unstoppable, flaming dragon.

I asked the lookout, Nancy Zahn, what caused the big fire.

She said, "It started from an afternoon lightning strike about a hundred yards below us. We saw the flash and heard the thunder. It was like a nuclear bomb. It splintered a large dead fir tree and set it on fire. There was so little moisture that the flying splinters set off fires around the tree in the dry grasses. By the time we called it in and went down to contain it, things were beyond our control. Jumpers were here in an hour or so, but it was too late. Too much grass and wind."

Weary fighters filed by grabbing up C-rations for lunch. I sipped the ice-cold water the Zahns were sharing.

"Last year I jumped a fire to your north in the Selway-Bitterroots," I said. "We parachuted into a heavenly sacristy, and here we've confronted Hell. What a contrast."

"I remember hiking off another fire last summer and going right by here," Ken said. Everything was green and beautifully alive. What a shocking difference, but if I return in a few years it will be restored to its original sparkle. Patience is needed to allow God to produce new hope out of old ashes."

THE NEXT DAY, THE FICKLE FIRE-DRAGON CHANGED PERSONALITIES and became gentle as a lamb. World War II torpedo bombers continued dropping retardant on the hottest spots. We watched them making their dangerous runs eating lunch near the lookout.

"If people in England owe their existence to Spitfire pilots," Tex commented, "Americans should forever honor the pilots and gunners of the TBM's who defeated the Japanese Navy at Midway."

Nature has a way of recycling deadwood into greenery. The green and white lookout loomed high above grey ashes like a phoenix arising out of debris, but with the underbrush consumed, new grass and young shrubs will become good browse for elk and deer. Lush groves of lodgepoles were reduced to black trunks without needles standing in thick dust. In the natural cycle, lodgepole seeds germinate only after the intense heat of fire.

One of the most difficult truths humans must learn is that in order to grow, one must relinquish deadwood, give up the impenetrable underbrush of significant failures and successes. Forgiveness is more than forgetting — it is letting go and moving ahead.

I was settling down for a good nap in the shade of the lookout's porch when fire boss Thomas Scott awakened me.

"Pick up your gear and this power saw and come with me," Scott said. "We're going to set up a helipad a quarter mile down the ridge. Helicopters will be unloading supplies and shuttling men to various parts of the fire from here. If we don't get this fire under control soon, there may be two choppers on the pad so make it big. You and Ken have managed a heliport before, so you're in charge."

We walked a few hundred yards along the summit, enjoying a unique view of the heart of Idaho's wildest country. In the wilderness you feel as if you are the only person in the entire world, visualizing an unbounded universe. Moses and Jesus often experienced the similar spiritual highs from smaller peaks in the Holy Land. To the west, we could see Rainbow peak, 10,000 feet high, emerging above the other grandiose peaks. To our south, we recognized the Challis Forest and Sawtooth Wilderness Area. The Whiteclouds Mountains look like they were snow-covered, but their composition is white stone. Indians named them after clouds, which often symbolize the presence of mystical spirits. Looking east we could see into Montana and the ridges of the Beaverhead National Forest. Salmon City, Idaho was to our north.

"Stop gazing and get moving," Ken said. "We're lucky to be on this project. Let's not lose it. Larry won't be here directing things. You bring food and I'll carry the saw."

I didn't argue. The chainsaw was very heavy. It was typical of Ken to offer to do more than anyone else. He'd go an extra mile if someone needed him, while the rest of us would grudgingly move across the room. I rationalized that heavy work like that would make him stronger for Hawkeye football.

We came upon Scott halfway down the ridge. He was carrying a radio and a yellow tarp for the heliport, but had sat down for a short rest, absorbing magnificence.

We watched smoke trailing into the vast blue sky, trying to determine the best approach for the choppers. The best helipad site was above a large cliff on the west side. We would have to cut two 45-foot trees which had been spared from the raging fire.

How ironic for that pair of trees, I thought.

"Ken, you carried that machine up here. I'll take the first turn," I said.

"If we had a 'misery whip'we would both have to work, but since you offered, you're on," he said.

A 'misery whip'was a two man cross-cut saw, which we had used in the past. Power machines, with a few exceptions, were outlawed in the roadless areas.

Ken stood watching for falling branches known as "widow makers" while I fell both trees. Fortunately they didn't fall over the cliffs. This saved us from having to tug them up a steep incline. I began slicing the trunks into four-foot sections for a retaining wall.

Ken wasn't one to rest. He was busy moving small boulders with almost a supernatural strength. It was like watching a Caterpillar tractor dozing things around. I pitied the quarterbacks in the Big Ten the next fall.

By evening, we had the pad ready for the first helicopter. A light, nippy breeze flowed across the site, causing the orange flag to flutter. We welcomed the coolness by stretching out on our sleeping bags, enjoying the mountain fresh air.

After a short rest, we put on our jump coats and began the walk back to the lookout for dinner. Ken wanted to race me to the chow line, but I signalled him to run ahead. I took my own sweet time. The truth was, I could hardly move.

Somewhere far across the Western ridges I could hear the synchronized whine of the triple-engine Ford. Straining my eyes into the sunset, crimson red from all the smoke, I observed what appeared to be a lumbering whale playing in the ocean of eternity. The props from the three engines glistened in the sunlight.

The pilot made the first pass count, releasing T-bone steaks for the hungry congregation in the outdoor chapel. On the second swoop, he dropped 5 gallons of strawberry ice cream. With dinner for 60 men was on the ground, the "waiter from the sky" droned off toward the evening star. That old airplane nurtured us like children.

We spent the chilly evening sitting on the high lookout deck, talking with Frank and Nancy Zahn. Both were school teachers who had been lookouts for a number of years. They were shocked by the scorched landscape. Much of their eastern view was completely stripped of shrubs, or grass or flowers. Most trees had been cremated. One perfect evergreen was untouched beside the lookout.

At 10 p.m., we started back down the ridge to our helipad. The aura of a half-moon transformed the peaks into mysterious sentinels. I've never been afraid in the wilderness at night, although in cities I become very nervous.

At the helipad, Ken said,"Listen."

Far to the west, we heard the cry of a mountain lion. Jumpers dream of seeing mountain lions in their home territory. It seldom happens since lions avoid humans, and I've never been privileged to see one. Unlike the typical "woman screaming" style of cougar screams, this solo sounded forlorn, like a mating call echoing something sacred in wild animal relationships.

Most hunters are not irresponsible, and hold great respect for wild creatures, but there are ill-advised hunters who intrude into the wilderness with assault rifles and hounds. Wild lions have little chance to escape their warfare. Listening to this wild cry in the night amplified my contempt for thoughtless people who get high by destroying these awesome animals.

The eco-system needs good hunters who help balance animal populations in the forests. Many gifted hunters consider deer and elk as sacred brothers, a concept shared by Native Americans. Thank God for hunters who respect the cougar's art of hiding in trees and play fair.

The wild chant was replaced by the silent music of forests, but I was wide awake now.

"Last summer, Tex and I heard a cougar screaming for three nights on a small fire at Little Soldier Mountain. We packed out of there on the McNaughton trail. A few days later Scott and Dan were packing out on the same trail. They saw our bootprints with wildcat paw prints clearly on top of them. Apparently a cougar had been following us at a safe distance.

"He'd been playing his chanter and believed the lion was enchanted by his performance. Tex is still upset that he was shadowed by a mountain lion and didn't get to take her picture. He said folks in Texas would never believe him without a picture."

"I'm going to sleep before you get going on your bobcat stories," Ken said. "Good night, Mark."

I lay awake for as long as I could, hoping to hear more from our lion chanter and wishing bobcats could also sing. In my opinion, bobcats have more courage per pound than any animal in the world. I fell asleep before the wild cat blessed the moonlit night again, singing evening prayer in the silent transcept of trees.

IN THE DAYS FOLLOWING, the helipad resembled a Spokane train station in the '40s. We unloaded men and equipment; ladyfinger shovels, power saws, and even wool socks moving through our shopping center. It seemed we had enough aviation fuel to keep United Airlines flying for a week. There was more daily activity on the helipad than at the lookout, and nights were even more eventful.

Jeff Clemson, the Bell helicopter pilot, flew into Salmon City each night, preferring motels to sleeping bags. He invited us to accompany him, but there was only room for one passenger inside. The other man had to lie on the rescue stretcher attached to the struts on the righthand side. That looked like fun, so I talked Ken into letting me ride outside.

If you ever get the chance to ride a basket through the wilderness at treetop level, take it. It was wild. I sampled the mountains from an unequalled existential perspective. On our first flight into town, Jeff spotted an elk with huge antlers and circled back to see him better. He banked so steeply that I almost rolled off my perch, and he flew so close over tree tops I could have reached out and touched them.

Salmon City airport looked as if there was a World War II reunion of old planes — B 25s, B 17s, Avenger TBMs, B 24s and C 47s.

Jeff flew over the airport and down Main Street, looking for a "Vacancy" sign. After several passes, we found one near a convenient cow pasture; the Big Dipper Motel. Jeff said to Ken, "There's one that looks reasonable ... with free parking. Let's go for it."

Jeff whipped that machine around on an airborne dime and landed less than 200 feet from the motel, next to a herd of Holsteins. Bystanders appeared a bit nervous. It was hard to be inconspicuous. We hadn't had a bath or shave for a week.

We approached the old man at the motel desk, whose eyes were the size of pizza platters, "We noticed your vacancy sign and would like a couple of rooms. Don't need a parking space just a place to sleep for the night."

Jeff filled out the registration forms and entered the chopper's licence number, Z8305. The old man perked up.

"What state's your rig registered in? I've never seen a number like that. Of course I don't get helicopters very often. But after this summer I'd believe anything."

A shower never felt so good.

Looking semi-civilized, we headed for Salmon City, Idaho, a favorite rendezvous of smokejumpers everywhere. Townspeople, however, would rather see almost anyone else visit their town. Fights between jumpers and local loggers had torn the town up in the past, so I stayed close to Ken just in case loggers didn't like my smokejumper hat. One look at Ken and most loggers became friendlier. We meandered into the Branding Iron Tavern looking for a tall Pepsi.

Jeff pulled up a chair with veteran pilot friends, as if the Air Force was on a training mission in Central Idaho. They swapped stories about dropping retardant, supplies, and jumpers, in that order, which concerned me.

I thought of returning to the motel after dinner and sacking out in a clean bed with a mattress, but it was more fun to explore Salmon City. We stayed until the bars closed and then returned to the Big Dipper.

In the morning, since I was riding shotgun in the basket, it was my job to shoo a few Holsteins away from the helicopter. Once the engines started roaring, the cows streaked to the far end of the field. Several became airborne themselves, attempting to jump the fence, and may have been utterly ruined.

When we showed for breakfast, fire boss Scott asked where we had been. Ken told him about Salmon City and ended the conversation with an old smokejumper slogan, "It all pays the same."

SHORTLY AFTER LUNCH THE NEXT DAY, Tom Scott came to the helipad.
"This dragon is calling it quits. He's destroyed about 17,000 acres, but it looks like we have him by the tail. The entire fire is lined and it's mop-up time. You guys can go back to smokejumping," he said.

"That's OK by me," Ken said. "I'm ready to get back on the jump roster."

"Me too," I said, "I've enjoyed managing an airport, but my heart is in parachuting and working on the line."

After Tom left, there were no helicopters, so we found a quiet place under one of the few trees left.

"Ken, you often wander away from the rest of us, and I've been thinking it might be to pray. I'd enjoy praying with you and asking a few questions. Would you mind?"

To my surprise, Ken was delighted.

"Remember the trinity of combustion?" he asked. "Fuel, heat and oxygen. When wood is heated to 800 degrees, it bursts into flame, releasing burnable gasses. There is also a trinity for prayer ignition which harmonizes like the three engines of the Trimotor.

"First, prayer demands time. That may be its most difficult aspect. 'Take time to be holy,'the ancient hymn proclaims. It requires 20 minutes every day devoted to being quiet and listening to what God might have to say.

"The second important factor is content, the fuel which produces the flame of prayer. When you see candles burning on the altars of churches you're observing another trinity. First there is the vaporized invisible gas near the wick, then the yellow glow made up of glowing carbon particles. The heat or combustion area is the bluish glow that surrounds everything else."

"May I assume prayer-fuel comes from the Bible?" I asked, "Remember Eugene Williams in the deathhouse at the New Jersey prison? One day he shared a Scripture from Colossians which served as fuel for his prayer. It was, 'Pray for us … that God will open for us a door for the word, that we may declare the mystery of Christ, for which I am in prison.'Can you imagine how that influenced the 'combustion'of hope for a murder he didn't commit?"

"Yes," he said. "Before Christian prayer, I read a short passage of Scripture for fuel. What I select is important. I might consider the entire book of Nahum and Nineveh's destruction, and not find much burnable fuel. On the other hand, every verse in the Gospels has great substance."

"What is the third essential element?"

"Take a guess," he said.

"It has something to do with the person, right?

"Go to the front of the class. The third element is the proper attitude toward God and one's innermost self. To quote a familiar hymn, 'Prayer is the soul's sincere desire, unuttered or unexpressed, the motion of a hidden fire that trembles in the breast.' When we hear Almighty God, this hidden fire — like a spot fire — begins glowing within us."

"People often ask me if I get bored with praying written prayers from *The Book of Common Prayer*," I said. "I tell them no two parachute jumps or prayers are alike. In praying them, I spiral to the highest heavens and glide back to the sacred earth, never knowing where I'll land. It's like jumping skyward.

"Remember that huge pine tree down the ridge hit by lightning? That strike of lightning burnt a spiral path down the trunk from top to bottom. Sometimes, when I'm praying, the Spirit of God spirals right down my trunk and lights a fire in my soul."

"Balance is important," Ken said, "just like in parachuting. In the midst of problems, unless I can find at least one thing to be thankful for, prayer is nearly impossible. As each parachute jump is new and exciting, so is the outcome of 20 minutes with God."

Ken asked for a verse for meditation. I thought of "How great a forest is set ablaze by a small fire," but offered a verse from I John.

" 'Everyone who loves is born of God and knows God.' Let's use that for fuel."

"People ask how we can know God, and it is this simple — learn to love. And if everyone is born of the same spiritual parent, then we ought to love equally," Ken said.

High on the mountain, we meditated quietly together on God's love, physically silent but spiritually talkative. When we were finished, a hawk, spiraled 30 or 40 feet beside us, riding a warm air current. Studying his movements Ken said, "Look at that beautiful red-tail. I'd love to be a hawk soaring on warm air flows.

"Birds of prey have incredible eyesight," I said. "They observe minute things which humans may never see. I'd like perceiving everything, even little things, clearly, without distortion. Ken, you've been given a new name today. I'm going to call you 'Hawk' from now on."

The red-tail ascended several hundred feet above us and gave a loud screech, adding to our conversation. Ken was more like a Swainson's hawk. Swainson's have extraordinary vision but don't say much.

D URING THE LAST AFTERNOON ON THE FIRE, Nick made a deal with the chopper pilots so the entire Seven Squad could spend a night living it up in Salmon City. Seats in cockpits or beds in the baskets were determined in smokejumper coin-flipping tradition. Most jumpers wanted a basket.

We could hardly wait to get off the fire for a party. The motel operator thought he was under attack when three helicopters landed nearby. This trip we avoided the pasture with the dairy cattle, settling our machines across the street on a vacant lot.

62

The Seven Squad didn't lose any time and were shortly jogging down Main Street. If there was any action, it would be at the Jersey Lilly, a Salmon City tavern that created a place of honor for smokejumpers. Tex set a table for the squad and ordered Cokes and other refreshments. Nick was first to join him, and after half the crew showed up, managed to stick a Budweiser label on the ceiling.

A tough-looking logger jumped up on the bar and tore it down. Soon there was an old fashioned brawl between jumpers and loggers. I tried to do my part, but it was no place for a preacher. I grabbed a logger's hat and stomped it on the floor and took a hit from a local Paul Bunyon which convinced me I was not a fighter. A fellow in a red plaid shirt grabbed me and threw me out an open door in one motion. I landed flat on my face on the wooden sidewalk, humiliated and not anxious to go back in.

The rest of Seven Squad arrived at the Jersey Lilly, and a burly forester made the mistake of jerking Ken's glasses off. Without his glasses, he couldn't distinguish friend from foe. From previous encounters, we knew to shout our identity when we entered his vicinity.

It didn't take the loggers long to realize that Ken was a champion college wrestler as well as a football player. The loggers were rather rugged themselves, but the most serious damage was inflicted on our pocketbooks; 45 bucks each for physical damages. The encounter ended like an ice hockey match with each group shaking hands and picking up the pieces together. It was raw, wild fun, Salmon City style.

We offered to buy a round of drinks for the loggers, but the owner said the place was now off-limits to smokejumpers, so we moved our operation to the Silverado Bar.

Nick was a self-destructive genius with a drinking problem. He fancied himself a conqueror, and he couldn't resist the compulsion to draw the undivided attention of every attractive woman around. He was good at playing the little-boy-in-need for women who liked to rescue men, and a friendly brunette was ready to fall for it. The rest of the jumpers ignored him. They didn't care if Nick was chasing women as long as he reported sober the next morning for the demanding work of fire suppression.

I had my own addictions. I left the Silverado to play hymns on the pipe organ in the Salmon Presbyterian Church.

The pastor was not available, but the front door was unlocked. The pipe organ keyboard was locked tighter than a bank vault. I expected this, so I asked God if it would be all right to play, and waited three minutes for a reply. I didn't hear anything to the contrary, and I began hunting for the key.

It generally takes one minute to locate an organ key. It is almost always under the seat or beside the foot pedals. This time, it was not in the ordinary place. Locating it took two full minutes. It was hidden in the hymnal under Hymn 43; "I danced in the morning when the world was begun ... "

After playing familiar hymns, I left a small contribution on middle C, gratefully closed the lid and headed back to the Silverado.

Halfway back to the bar, I ran into an angry, obnoxious group of men who had been drinking too much. Nick and two other McCall jumpers were involved in a dispute and outnumbered by the locals two to one, which doesn't normally matter for jumpers, but this time they were outmuscled as well.

I was caught in an ethical dilemma. Being a coward by nature, I hesitated to enter the conflict, but the jumper code states never back away from duty and always help other jumpers at any cost to your own welfare.

It didn't look good. As a Vicar, I could try negotiating, but my clerical collar was in McCall. I would have to stand up and be counted instead of retreating behind my collar.

Taking the middle ground, I darted around the shouting match to the Silverado. Thankfully Ken, with his unbroken glasses, was still there. I relayed the problem to him, and he casually finished his drink and put on his jumper cap.

He moved toward the wild scene like a linebacker who didn't know if the offense would pass or run. Either way, he'd be in the middle of things. I arrived five feet safely behind Hawk, and there was a sudden calm. Maybe his reputation as a wrestler had come to Salmon City. I stood on a flat rock so I was taller than the loggers.

"What's the problem, boys?" Ken said with half a grin. "This is the only clean shirt I have on this fire and I don't want to get it all messed up unless I have to."

An angry, muscular woodsman pointed at Nick. "This ugly guy made a pass at my girl and won't apologize. Everyone stand back and let me at him 'til he does."

"Nick, is that true?" Hawk asked quietly.

"This sawman was nowhere near her when I spoke to her. If he was with her, he was sure ignoring her. I was ... "

Ken cut Nick off instantly."Did you or did you not make a pass?"

"I guess you could call it that," Nick said. Looking the man in the face, he said, "I'm sorry my friend, it won't happen again."

The tension broke instantly. A smile from the angry man replaced his bitter glare, and most of us were relieved. A few were disappointed, but not me or Ken, who wanted to go peaceably ... with a clean shirt.

Hawk was a philosophical fighter. He told me later, "Sometimes it's better to turn the other cheek. You have to balance each situation by weighing the good and bad, the benefits and the risks."

Back at the Silverado, Larry joined us at the bar which was inlaid with hundreds of silver dollars. "Nick had it coming. He embarrasses me and is a disgrace to the rest of us. He doesn't even know what a mess he's making of his life."

"The problem is that we can't talk sense with him while he's drinking," I said. "When he's sober he's one of the most likable guys I've met. I'm going to get him to talk with Bishop Foote."

"Nick has a real problem," Hawk said. "I hope he gets some help before someone knocks his head off. We best go find him and bring him home."

"He found his way into town. Let him find his way back," Larry said.

As far as he was concerned, the jumpers would be better off if Nick never came back.

"Nobody's perfect, except maybe yourself. He'll come around someday," Hawk said. "There'll be a turning point. He'll wake up."

After finishing the refreshments, Larry suggested we call it a night. It was almost midnight, and I agreed. Heading for the door, I looked back at Hawk.

"Aren't you coming?"

"You guys go ahead, I'll catch up with you later."

Larry and I were fed up with Nick. We couldn't imagine what event would ever change his miserable life. We hightailed it toward Helicopter Inn.

Later, we pieced together what happened after that.

HAWK SET OUT LOOKING FOR NICK and found him lying in a yard near the river, not only drunk, but beaten up. After Hawk helped him out of the scrape with the sawyer, he offended a rancher who rode saddlebroncs. This time no one rode in on a white charger and Nick took a good licking.

Hawk helped him to his feet and cleaned his wounds with his clean hankerchief.

"Thanks for coming back. I'll make it up to you someday," Nick said. He was struggling to stay upright, brushing dirt and grass off his shirt.

"I don't want to see the rest of the crew tonight."

"You're in no shape to walk back, anyway. Come on, I'll put you up in the hotel across the street. You can meet us in the morning for breakfast before we fly back,"

Hawk put his shoulder under Nick's arm and helped him across the street to the hotel. Nick had no money and looked terrible, and the hotel clerk hesitated to take him in. Hawk reached for his own wallet.

"I'll pay you to take my friend for the night. If you need more, I'll be back in the morning and give you whatever you need. He's had a hard night."

Getting Nick up the narrow stairs and into bed was no easy task, but Ken did that, walked back to our motel and went to bed. He never told anyone what he had done.

At breakfast, Nick didn't mentioned a thing. Only God knew Nick would someday fulfill Hawk's prediction and "wake up" ... not far from Whitehawk Lookout.

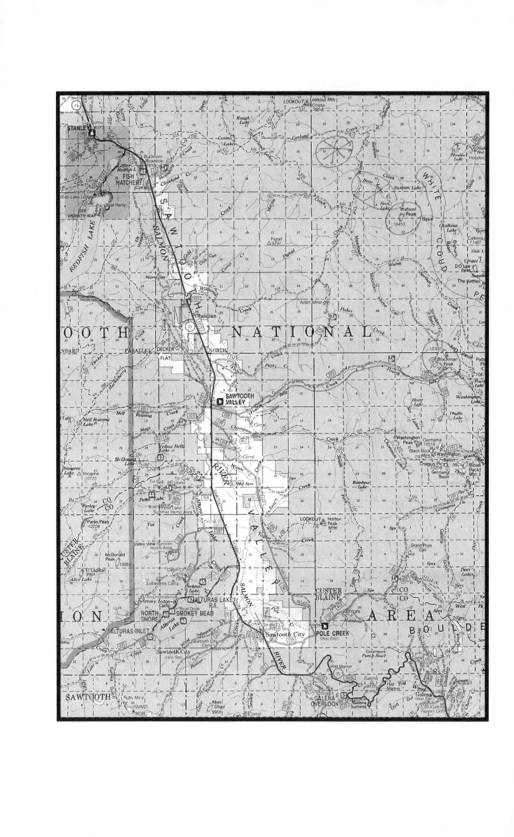

THE WHITE CLOUD MOUNTAINS

RESPECT FOR THE UNTAMED

THIS WAS MY LAST YEAR AS PASTOR FOR THE COMMUNITY CHURCH in Hysham on the Yellowstone River near Miles City, Montana. We moved to Montana with two children and left with a lovely girl and two lively boys. I also left with Ordinations in both the Presbyterian and Episcopal Churches. The church doctrines were complementary and fit my ecumenical ministry better.

Summer came. It felt good to return to smokejumping in the robust mountain ranges of central Idaho, though it could be my last season. I had inherited a beautiful white home with black shutters nestled in two acres of trees, grass and shrubs. It awaited me when I "came home." I could show my kids where the Oregon Trail went through our farm, and exactly where my great-grandparents' covered wagon broke down. That's why they settled in Idaho.

Upon our return to McCall, Ken Shuler reminded me that I'd named him "Hawk" during the previous fire season.

"If I come up with a name for you before the summer's over, it ought to have something to do with parties. I hear you guys got in a bit of trouble."

Ken had returned to Iowa before our DC-3 Party Express ended the fire season. The Missoula jumpers invited us to their termination party at the end of the season. We accepted and chartered the DC-3 for a champagne flight. I told my version of the party.

"We loaded all the jumpers left in camp and flew to Missoula. They'd decorated the high school gym for the farewell party, but that afternoon almost half of them were dispatched to fires, so there we were with all the food, refreshments and music and the nurses from a large hospital."

"Did you dance it up?" he asked.

"I was having a good time when Earl Cooley tapped me on the shoulder and insisted I sit with the chaperones. He introduced me as 'Reverend Davis, pastor of the McCall Crew,' and I ended up as a bored observer for the rest of the evening. I guess parties are not my thing."

"I understand this may be your last summer smokejumping. We'll have to have a termination party at the end of August," he said.

Normally the rainy season ends in July and fires begin exploding after every July thunderstorm, but this year was an exception. The first month of the fire fighting season featured one rainy day after another. Forest Supervisor Sam Defler had been thinking up one "busy-work" project after another for us and he was running out of ideas. Forest fire suppression is like fire fighting anywhere; boredom or crisis.

One Saturday in mid August, the Seven Squad was assigned to standby. I had fought only four fires all summer, and we knew it was more an incentive to lure us back next year rather than a real fire danger. It was a pleasant day with no wind and the temperature a balmy 75 degrees.

Nick and I hooked a dart board to an aspen sapling not far from the kitchen, and we were taking opening throws when, to our amazement, the fire buzzer sounded a long blast. The short blasts ended at eight; enough to fill the Trimotor.

In minutes we were suited and loaded in an old World War II troop carrier speeding down Main Street toward the airport, fire fighting cargo on a trailer behind. Tex had asked to paint the troop carrier bright red, but Carl Catlin, our boss, preferred camouflage green. People on the streets cheered like we were football champions.

When we arrived, Bob Fogg, the backcountry flying virtuoso, had the three engines on the Trimotor synchronized. We loaded our fire fighting packs first, and used them for seats. While weight was no problem for the Ford workhorse, leg room was at a premium. The jumpers fortunate enough to be near the door enjoyed fresh air.

In a matter of minutes we were bouncing down the gravel runway with the tail section airborne. Fogg usually taxied to the paved runway but he was in a hurry. The rugged plane didn't know the difference. It slowly separated itself from the gravel and we headed due east toward the serrated Sawtooth range.

We had attained 2,000 feet of elevation when Hawk shouted, "Great Scott! It looks like an atomic bomb went off. Look at that mushroom cloud. It must be 10,000 feet high. No wind, and its going straight up."

"The fire's in the White Clouds," Wayne said, "and into heavy, dry fuel and you fellows can rescue thousands of acres if you get it controlled right away. You're the first ones on it. We have already requested a Doug load of Missoula jumpers."

As we approached the towering gray mushroom, I enjoyed the spectacular scenery of the Sawtooth Mountains with Stanley Basin on one side and the White Clouds on the other. It was like a double take on the Swiss Alps. On both sides, sculptured meadows surrounding crystal lakes glimmered below us. The grandeur of huge granite upthrusts, unspoiled by mankind, rose sharply from the Idaho batholith.

We were flying near Sun Valley, Ernest Hemingway's favorite country. Aloft in his "high, blue, windless skies," we soared high above Stanley Basin where old rail fences kept Black Angus cattle from mixing with the Herefords.

We were fast approaching the huge funnel of dense smoke, but gazing at the chiseled basalt peaks below us, aware of their infinite beauty, I thought of a discussion I'd had with Don earlier that day about the philosopher, Immanuel Kant.

"I was talking philosophy with Caldwell this morning," Don had told me. "He said Kant's philosophy has some similarities to my Nez Perce religion. He said to ask you what we have in common."

"For one thing," I told him, "Kant said to treat all persons as ends in themselves and not as means only. I know Native American religion teaches respect for other people."

"That's one similarity," Don agreed. "But we go beyond respect for humans. We believe all living creatures, not just human beings, ought to be seen as ends for their own intrinsic value. Rivers, trees ... they're all sacred."

Don agreed with Kant that there are universal values to guide civilization toward peace, if people would just follow them. Don spoke of the "Wakan-Tanka" spirit within persons.

"In this mystery, all persons are related."

"One problem with your ancestors is they believed humans could exploit the earth. They treated nature as a means, not an end. Native people believe in respecting all nature, which includes people."

Don concluded, grinning, that if Kant could change his name from Immanual to something like Doctor Coyote, he'd probably fit right into his religion.

BOB CIRCLED THE TRIMOTOR. The fire was racing up a heavily timbered north slope. Orange flames shot hundreds of feet into the clear mountain air. There were no spot fires below the main conflagration. Large rocky cliffs and outcroppings of stone prevented it from spreading downhill. Instead, it was burning upward into the alpine area on one of the most beautiful peaks in North America. That was where we had to get a line around it.

We chose a jump spot about a quarter of a mile from the flaming trees. Hawk and Tex got ready to be the first stick. Hawk crouched on his left leg in the door with his right foot on the step with Tex close behind. We flew directly over the place the streamers had settled, and then proceeded exactly that distance across the spot. Wayne slapped Hawk's leg. The response was as if he had released a bow string. He watched Hawk fly an arrow trajectory toward the fire.

It was a good jump site, a large landing area void of rocks and downed timber. Hawk and Tex landed off to the right side in some forty feet high, wind-blown pines. Treeing up in those limber pines was like bouncing into a haystack.

I was the last man out, which gave me time to enjoy the incredible view of Mt. Castle. I thought of it as church steeple constructed with 11,000 feet of granite blocks. Behind it, I recognized Mt. Borah, like a rood screen, rising almost 13,000 feet, the highest peak in Idaho.

My pleasure in the grandeur below ended abruptly when my canopy fouled and didn't open properly. The lines twisted together in the middle of the canopy, forming what we called a "Mae West." In this configuration, the nylon lines cut through the apex of the chute, forming two equal parts which continue to give adequate support, but eliminates the ability to guide it.

I couldn't steer it, and I feared opening my reserve chute would only make matters worse, so I rode it out. I hit the ground hard, but not hard enough to break any bones. I was knocked out momentarily but by the time Don came over, I was staggering around, still hooked to the chute.

"Where am I?" I gasped.

"Mark's all right!" Don shouted to the others. "He's just learning respect for *all* things."

I soon stopped seeing stars.

We collected our gear and carried it to the camp area. Hawk took charge, directing us to flank some whitebark pines by following the natural terrain and utilizing rock patches. The gear dropped to us included only one chain saw but we were able to slice a dead line alongside the hottest area and stop it from spreading sideways.

Hawk called for a short rest during the hot period in late afternoon. Don and I chose to rest under a wind-bent spruce jutting out on a ridge offering a perfect view of the majestic Sawtooths. The tenacious spruce literally grew out of solid rock. The flat stone had stored up heat from the brilliant sun, creating comfortable lounges. We rested silently in awe of the luster of the land held sacred by Native Idahoans for hundreds of years.

We dozed in the rarefied mountain air as if drugged by pure peace of mind. When I awoke, Don was sitting in the shade contemplating the Sawtooth peaks. On the horizon we could see the Trinity Peaks, which I pointed out. I assumed it referred to the Christian Trinity.

Don asked about that and the Christian Spirit.

"Is It living out here or confined to downtown buildings?"

I pulled my battered New Testament from my back pocket. Don looked nervous — like a rabbit ready to bolt if I read too much.

"My understanding of Christian biospirituality is explained in the Prologue to St. John. John 1:1 says, 'In the beginning was the Word, and the Word was with God, and the Word was God ... all things came into being through him ... in him was life, and the life was the light of all people.' "

I explained that in Greek "the Word" is *Logos,* which accompanied creation.

"Is *Logos* one of many spirits?" Don asked.

"No, *Logos* existed before the world began and will survive when it wears down through entropy. The personification of *Logos* is the life, death, and resurrection of Jesus Christ. He is the Light that enlightens all spirituality, including unconfined spirits in the White Clouds."

Watching the fire burn briskly to our south, Don said, "Native Americans believe there are different kinds of spirits in the White Clouds. While most of them protect us as guardians, there are also destructive and rather mischievous spirits. I can easily see the four elements of existence ... water, earth, air and fire. What I can't see are the spiritual dwellers in these mountains."

"Why do you suppose the peaks in the Hells Canyon area are referred to as the Seven Devils?" I asked.

"Chief Joseph and his people experienced unfriendly spirits there, labeling them devils. I hope we never have to jump anywhere near them.

"Native spirits are becoming silent and harder to discern. White man destroyed the buffalo and other wild animals which shared spiritual strength with us. I've never seen a spirit. Can you see Christian Spirits?"

"No. That is why God sent his Son to be born a human and live as one of us. Jesus became the most authentic human to ever walk the wilderness. Jesus is the embodiment of spirituality. His Spirit can be seen throughout the world in quite ordinary people."

"He was the oldest child in the family of a working carpenter. Is that correct? And the Queen of England is the head of your Anglican Church, right?"

"Yes."

"What happened in the meantime? The Queen is the richest woman in the world. As head of your church, why doesn't she give her money to the poor?

Indian spiritual leaders never accumulate wealth other than being richly loved. Love is more than a word, it's being generous."

"In universal values, love and generosity must be near the top of the list," I said. "The Risen Christ returns to our world in loving persons, but most people don't recognize Him. Jesus could appear right here among the jumpers, if you can believe that!"

"Love is one of our highest values," Don said." Our most respected spirit is Tam Sogobia or Mother Earth. Every good thing we do is in thanksgiving for Mother Earth. We communicate with her wildlife because they are divine and we are one with them."

"St. Paul told Timothy that everything created by God was good if received with thanksgiving," I said. "In the story of Noah, God expressed affinity with all forms of animal life. There may be grizzlies in Montana because of Noah."

"I listen to messages through nature," Don said, "especially from winged creatures and four-leggeds. Bears are our brothers. We discover what it means to be human by listening to the wild songs.

"The Idaho Primitive Area has been our home but there's nothing primitive about our values. We don't talk much about values, we just live by them. Native Americans have lived by them for hundreds of years, predating Columbus's visit.

"We migrated to Alaska after originating near China. Our spiritual traditions may have originated in Tibet, influenced by Lao Tsu's Tao.

"Some Indians believe the first living creature was a human being and from that human came the animals. An important symbol for us is the circle with a cross inside. The cross represents humans as the center of life with everything moving in circles around them."

"Christians believe fish, birds and animals preceded creation of human beings," I said. "At the appropriate time, God created humans with divine spirits. People mistake human priority as an excuse to exploit earlier creatures. When carried to extremes, it becomes harmful."

"Excessive behavior in anything is not good," Don said.

Our break itself was becoming a little excessive and it was time to join the other firefighters, eat and assault the fire.

After we had been working a few hours, the Trimotor returned with eight more McCall jumpers. They landed much higher on the mountain, attempting to stop the upward thrust toward the ridge. According to Phil's radio, a ground crew was keeping the fire contained below to prevent a firestorm like the Mann Gulch fire.

We expected 16 more Missoula firefighters, but they never arrived. After three days and nights of back-breaking work, the fire was controlled. Ground crews hiked up the hill, taking charge of smoldering areas that might flare up again.

The Seven Squad had become known as the Hawkeye Squad in recognition of Hawk's heroic service at White Hawk. After dinner all seven Hawkeyes were lying around a glowing campfire built near the top of Watson Peak above Hoodoo Lakes, overlooking the White Cloud Range. Only Mt. Borah on the eastern horizon still retained sunlight. Mt. Watson and Mt. Blackman, each rising more than 10,000 feet, were fading into the night sky. The peaks of the White Clouds in the west were already ghostlike.

I finished brewing a large pot of steaming hot coffee and found enough metal cups for each man. Don held his coffee in both hands, and gazed to the north.

"There are many spirits in these hills, and when the inner spirit is nourished, it's possible to feel the spirits in these mountains. The beauty of the White Clouds shows that some great spirit continues re-creating beauty."

Larry referred to God as the Father of spirits.

"Is our God the same as yours, Don?" he asked.

"Indians believe God is fire ... fire is not merely a symbol of God ... but God is the fire. God is the sun. Once a year we dance with God in the Sun Dance. God is too holy to be addressed just any time we feel like it. There must be sacrifice, suffering and purification before we speak to God at the Sun Dance. We call God, 'Wakan Tanka,' 'the Great Mysterious.' "

"Christ has been called the 'Sun of Righteousness,' s-u-n," Phil pointed out, "and in the same chapter in Hebrews Larry mentioned, God is referred to as a consuming fire. Christians believe we are baptized by the Holy Spirit and with fire. Jesus said he was the Light. He didn't say He reflected light."

"Do you communicate personally with Wakan Tanka?" Larry asked.

"Do you communicate with angels as messengers of God ?" Don asked.

"Yes, angels are intermediaries sent from God," I said. "However, we also communicate directly with God."

"When we spend three days on a vision quest, praying the Great Spirit will speak to us," Don said, "we receive messages from the Great Spirit through animals and birds beside quiet mountains and restful rivers."

I said, "After one of His miracles, Jesus went up into the mountains to pray, not to the temple. St. Francis prayed among the birds and animals. St. Bernard found the Divine Master among the beeches and oaks. He said he learned as much from trees and stones as spiritual masters."

"I can't imagine learning much from a stone, other than how to stub a toe," Nick said, tired of the whole conversation.

One by one, as the stars began replacing the evening's pink — almost white — clouds, the crew disappeared into the hills. There had been other occasions when the subject for evening discussion zeroed in on the religious, but tonight had been special.

NICK WAS A DIFFERENT PERSON AFTER THREE DAYS WITHOUT ALCOHOL. He was first one out of bed the next morning, pouring fresh coffee and handing out packages of whole wheat toast. Perhaps just being immersed in the White Clouds reformed his outlook.

Feeling a little guilty for being so surly the night before, he said to Don, "We learned the Nicene Creed when we were kids and what we ought to believe. Do Indians have doctrine?"

"Our doctrine is summed up in reverence for all life. Everything is sacred," Don answered. "Our creed is taught when hawks, eagles, bears, bobcats, winds, rivers, rocks communicate with us. They help us feel whole. We believe individuals are 'unfinished beings' until they become one with these universal life forces.

"Another spiritual value we share is humility. In this Sawtooth basilica, how can anyone not be humbled by God's exalted splendor?"

"I feel at home here," Phil said. "The whole earth is our home and we need to take care of it. I used to be afraid in the wilderness. Pioneers thought they needed to be protected from it. Now my wilderness home needs protection from the unscrupulous who break in and vandalize it."

Hawk joined the conversation.

"Communicating with nature crafts completeness to our splintered day-by-day living. A key to understanding life's mystery is knowing we are imperfect pieces in the puzzle of life. We realize only a fraction of our potential. Friendships are fragmented, and love goes unfinished. Life's incompleteness, whether you call it sin, evil or suffering, haunts us throughout life. Wounded hearts have been restored to wholeness out here for centuries."

I was surprised Hawk's concept of suffering related to unfinishedness. I wondered where he uncovered such profound insight into human suffering.

"It's not too late for you guys to become part of our heritage," Don said. "Dr. Brown from the University of Montana said, 'Indians have a pervasive sense for the sacred.' Life's so beautiful we can't express it with words, so we dance it,

"Before a child can become an adult, he must go on a vision quest. At the top of a mountain, alone and naked, with just a blanket, he seeks divine communication through some living thing — mine was a great horned owl — through prayer and fasting. If one does not receive a vision, a dream may occur. Either way, the searching person may receive guidance for the future."

"Christian spiritual exercises begin with purification and end with union with God. How does this compare with a vision quest?" I asked.

"Our sequence also begins with purification and ends with unity. However, the middle stage is very important. We call this 'expansion.' We expand the awareness of our incompleteness. As we expand, we are joined to the universe, like a new fragment of cloth woven into a limitless quilt."

"Is the key to spiritual expansion listening?" Tex asked.

Hawk chose to answer.

"Listening helps us experience contentment, but that isn't everything. When we are alone in this peaceful country, we relax and become awakened from within. When we wake up spiritually, God weaves fragments of meaning like beautiful rivers and trees into His plan for our lives. Individual incompleteness encounters divine completion. It's a gift and can't be forced."

As the unclouded sun peeked across the shimmering peaks, Larry said it was time to hit the fire lines. He looked at Hawk and said, "It wouldn't hurt if you worked a little harder today. You spend too much time contemplating wild flowers and listening to birds."

With Larry leading the way and Hawk bringing up the rear, we took our places on the fire line.

"Hey, Bob and his Trimotor are headed this way. Let's hope he's dropping off breakfast," Phil yelled.

What a magnificent sight. The Ford Trimotor was almost parallel to our elevation on the mountain, glistening in the sunlight, flying directly from Trinity Peaks. To me, its three radial engines symbolized vital balance. It flew over us like a soaring eagle returning to nourish its young. The rugged basalt background complemented the super strength of the corrugated airplane. They belonged together.

Less than 30 feet above us, Ron Yergenson pushed the hot meal out the door. It landed between Phil and Tex. Opening the package, they found enough breakfast steaks for an army, plus three fresh apple pies from the kitchen crew.

After several helpings, we returned to the fire line, toiling steadily until 3 p.m., when Larry authorized a break. No one objected.

We found a lofty place to sit in the shade of a Western white pine. Enthralled by the view, no one spoke, but I was thinking about our fireside discussion the night before.

Don was as well. He reminded me we had compared the philosophies of Immanuel Kant with the Nez Perce before we left for the fire. Having never studied philosophy, he asked if all philosophers taught respect as the foundation to ethics.

"More or less, but not as thoroughly as Kant," I said. "Basically there are two major trends in philosophy. The first is deontology, that is, duty ethics, where the rules justify the rightness of the act. For example, 'We ought to love one another because God loves us and we ought to imitate God.'

"The other major approach is teleology, often called utilitarian ethics. In teleology theory, action is judged right or wrong by its consequence or outcome. The greatest good for the greatest number of people is the bottom line to utilitarian philosophers."

"Where does Kant come into this? Is he duty oriented or more concerned about consequences?" Don asked.

"Definitely duty oriented," I said. "He values universal maxims such as the Golden Rule or the Silver Rule."

"I know the Golden Rule by heart," Phil said, "but I've never heard of a silver one."

"The Golden Rule says to treat others as you want to be treated," I said. "This is called beneficence. The Silver Rule is the opposite side of the ethical coin; nonmaleficence. That is, do not treat others as you do not want to be treated. Hippocrates said, 'Above all, do no harm.' A person needs both principles to do good."

"Now we're talking universals," Don said. "That is more like Indian ethics. Peace and unity are possible within everyone."

"Kant insisted that the highest values should be universalized," I said.

"Is there a long list of values?" Phil asked.

"There are several. One goes something like this: 'Act only according to a maxim which you want to become a universal law.' Think about that. How often do we act universally?"

"Hawk seems to act that way," Don said. "I don't think he does it consciously. It's just part of him."

"Kant and Native Americans stress the intrinsic worth of persons. His second maxim is one Hawk lives by also. 'Treat yourself and others as ends and never as means only.' "

"Power-famished cults think they're so special that everyone else is only a means in their grasp for power," Phil said. "In Central America, I saw aggressive cultures murder others as means instead of respecting them as ends."

"A truly successful person is one who combines elevating his or her situation and, at the same time, helping the less fortunate. They both benefit," Hawk said.

Larry found us under the tree, like Buddhas meditating on ethics. "Get up the hill and help. We've been shoveling dirt for 30 minutes. Get with it!"

It's a traditional American notion that unless you're doing something physical, you're not working, but all work and no philosophy makes a dull boy, and they don't come any duller than Larry. Good and dull, the traditional religious model for sincerity.

THE NEXT DAY, THE HAWKEYE SQUAD LEFT THE FIRE for the ground crews to mop up. The packer met us at the fire, so we didn't have to carry the heavy packs. He assigned each of us to a horse. Don and Phil were given Appaloosas and pranced off like ballet dancers. My transport was more like riding a John Deere tractor. The heavier men got stronger horses. He fixed me up with a big, stout horse that could easily be mistaken for a Clydesdale.

We toured Idaho for four and a half hours before arriving in Stanley Basin, where we were met by a large Forest Service truck. We threw our packs into the back of the truck, using them for seats. It was a near-perfect day, and we tired firefighters slept as we trucked over dusty trails to the Stanley Ranger Station.

When we arrived at the station, a handsome, lanky ranger welcomed us but wouldn't let us go in.

"You guys need to clean up. Make your beds out back in the barn." He pointed to an old log building behind his house. "There's a shower and lots of hot water there. They will fly in for you in the morning. Go into town and get yourselves a good meal at the Red Rooster Cafe. Charge it to my district. Anyone who doesn't get enough to eat has only himself to blame."

As we found places for our sleeping bags and showered off layers of fire dust, I made the mistake of telling my friends it might be my last summer. When we got back to McCall, I planned to exchange my chute for an alb and my shovel for a stole.

Immediately, a howl went up for a farewell party for the "Reverend Rancher;" a party to end all parties. Plans were made to carry as much food and refreshments as we could back to the barn.

Tex said he was going to be "barn again," and talked the ranger out of a truck to get to the Red Rooster. Phil did the driving since he wouldn't be drinking, and as soon as Phil hit the brakes, we headed for dinner.

We landed in Stanley, Idaho on a Saturday night at one of the famous Stanley Stomps. Every weekend, the little town hosted hundreds of Western dancers; men and women dressed in their best Western finery. Three bars featured live music and people danced everywhere. The single street became an extension of barroom floors.

Nick was off to the largest dance hall without taking time for a thick steak dinner.

An attractive waitress fed our egos and our bodies, telling us townspeople watched the plume of smoke and our jumping demonstration. She even saw the "Mae West" malfunction and asked if the jumper was hurt. Don, usually calm and reserved, became a bold Native American and rose to the occasion, embellishing parachuting dangers.

After dinner, we wandered over to the festivities. It wasn't hard to recognize jumpers in the crowd. In the midst of expensive cowboy hats, it was easy to distinguish our baseball caps with smokejumper emblems. We looked pretty grubby, but no one in that part of Idaho ever said much about smokejumpers. Motorcycle gangs have been known to hit the road when two or three jumpers appear angry.

Phil headed for the Cliffhanger. He was a talented pianist, and heard they needed a player for the piano. He didn't leave the upright all evening.

Complimentary drinks lined the top of his piano, but Phil gave them to others and continued playing. During one of the breaks he played a couple of semi-classical tunes, and the crowd loved it. When he sang a Spanish song he had written for his people in Central America, a noisy, boisterous crowd stopped dancing and listened intently.

Dancing fit our exuberant mood perfectly, but we wore logger boots and had to be careful we didn't crush toes. Dancers couldn't move around much anyway. It was so crowded you danced with everyone there just by walking across the floor.

One rhinestone wrangler type, 6 foot, 3 inches tall, had too much to drink, and thought Don didn't belong on the dance floor. He made a couple of bitter remarks about Native Americans. The tough-talking guy, dressed up in a white Western suit with a big, silver belt buckle, pushed Don against the wall and held him about a foot off the floor.

"You a dancer or a fighter?" he asked.

Don stood only 5 feet, 10 inches, but he was the tallest person in Stanley, if you measure courage. "I'm a dancer and not a fighter and I'll give you to three to gently lower me while I'm still the dancer."

Hawk and Tex appeared on each side of the glittering cowboy.

"I'll do the counting," Hawk said. "One, two ..."

The big cowboy gently lowered Don to the floor, dusted off his shirt, and started to walk away.

"We're not finished, buddy," Tex said, grabbing the fellow's trembling right arm. "You owe someone a big apology. I'll start counting again. One, two ... "

"I am very sorry I said what I did," he said to Don, who by this time was amused. He had been quite annoyed, but he was determined not to make a scene.

Don bought drinks for Tex and Hawk, and interestingly, several glittering trouble-makers slipped out into the crisp night air, not to return.

The regular Stanley Stompers would not halt the dancing 'til breakfast, but Tex rounded up the jumpers, and we agreed to return to the barn. No one had seen Nick all night, but he could find his way back by himself and hopefully without his latest admirer.

There was room for everyone in the back of the truck, even after refreshments were loaded. Phil enjoyed driving, but from the time he started the engine, Larry was brooding. He seemed upset that Davis, a minister, was partying with the rowdy jumpers.

"Why don't we take this bottle and shove it down his throat?" Tex said, irritated at having our fun dampened.

"Jesus said 'We played the flute for you and you did not dance,' " I said. "Some people become angry when others are having fun, but it doesn't bother me. The Lord of the Jordan wilderness was called a drunkard and glutton by the same sort."

SMOKEJUMPERS ARE ESPECIALLY SKILLED IN TWO THINGS; fighting fires and playing games. No one can devise better games than a group of jumpers. Back at the old log barn, we sat in a circle on the rough wooden floor. Hawk decided we would have a gong show and found an old anvil and hammer to gong the losers.

Each of us had to tell the best jump story of his career. Anyone who didn't exaggerate a bit might be automatically gonged, so the stories became quite colorful.

Hawk gave everyone a few minutes to form a circle then spun a bottle to see who would be first. It pointed directly at Larry. He thought a minute and then said the rest of us were too rude to listen. "Gong!" Larry was out.

Tex Lewis told about the time he and Larry Clark got lost in the Challis forests. For three days, local radios broadcast that Lewis and Clark were lost in the woods.

"Gong!"

Phil told about the time he checked out a 32-foot chute instead of the usual 28-footer. His ankles were sore and he wanted to land easily. The jump was near a rock slide and it was very windy. Jumpers who weighed 200 pounds wanted to trade chutes but he wouldn't, and when he jumped, the wind carried him far into the hills.

"Gong!"

I shared the experience of landing on top of Hawk's chute, which prevented my own from catching air. "It was like jumping on a firm mattress; the surface was so solid that I used it for a platform and leaped off like a diving platform."

"Gong!"

The winner was a McCall jumper not from the Hawkeye Squad. Al Rossini, a World War II veteran, told of wanting to land right beside a fire because the jump spot selected was at the bottom of the hill and he didn't want to walk up the mountain.

When the spotter finally agreed, Rossini jumped and the wind shifted and he got caught in updrafts from the heat of the fire. He almost reached the ground three times before the updrafts pushed him back above the edge of the fire. He almost died of smoke inhalation before he managed to fold his canopy and drop like a rock landing outside the fire on safe ground.

There were no gongs for Al's story. The game was over.

Then, Don rolled a 55-gallon oil drum in through the barn door, dressed it up a bit and invited me to use it for a pulpit. He allowed me only five minutes to preach my final sermon on what being a smokejumper had meant to me.

The mood of the evening changed dramatically. There was a hushed atmosphere. I mounted the friendliest pulpit I had even known and asked them to go around the room again, only this time each man was to say briefly what jumping into the wilderness meant.

An hour later they were still talking. I never got a chance to express my thoughts. Tex said it was a great group sermon and that I could preach the five-minute smokejumper sermon to my congregation.

Giving up my summer home in the wilderness would not be easy. Part of my future plans included helping my family changing our farm into a residential development. I'd always enjoyed building things, and looked forward to helping shape a planned community. I had plans for a community counseling center which emphasized biospirituality, but deep in my heart I wondered if I would be happy spending my summers as a minister-farmer.

Men were beginning to drop off and go to bed, so Hawk produced a few bottles of champagne for the occasion, and poured the contents into plastic glasses brought back from Stanley. Hawk called everyone together and proposed a toast.

"Davis, we think you're making a mistake leaving this fine summer company of men, but we understand you plan to settle down on the old Van Geekherdt family ranch. So here's to the Reverend Stanley Stomp Davis who will give up partying with the boys and become Mr. Straightarrow.

"Seriously, we wish you best. We'll miss you and God bless you and Lynn. And remember this — old smokejumpers never die. They just forget to hookup."

The rowdy congregation shouted "Amen."

"Thank you everyone. You can sleep in the barns on our ranch anytime. Lynn and I are having a barbecue next week and everyone is welcome."

As I dropped off to sleep, I was grateful for having been a jumper, but felt it was time to move into something else. Since the day Lynn and I were married, we had never owned our own place. Now we were going home.

THERE'S NOTHING MEANER THAN A BUNCH OF SMOKEJUMPERS who have been partying the night before. Larry knew we needed time to get it together. When he woke us up, he already had a large pot of coffee brewing with a platter of rolls and oranges. The aroma of the coffee worked miracles and soon everyone was acting like humans and enjoying the morning. No one said anything, but everyone wondered where Nick was.

Larry shouted, "Get this place cleaned up. It looks like a barn."

"It looked like one before we came," Tex yelled, reaching for another cup of coffee.

"All right, let's get moving. I heard the Ford go over Stanley a few minutes ago," Larry said.

We couldn't keep Johnson Airlines waiting. They had a better record than most national lines for prompt arrivals and departures.

When our truck made its way to the top of the hill the airstrip was located on, Bob Fogg was standing beside his favorite plane, N7861, a great combination.

There were two Trimotor loads, so a coin flip would decide which crew got to fly home first. Larry had a silver dollar left from the night before. He flipped it high into the air. Tex grabbed it in the air and put it in his pocket.

"You owed me that from a bet we made last night. Thanks."

Some gentle persuasion by 13 jumpers produced the coin again, and our crew won the first ride home, but there was a problem: Nick was missing. Bob Fogg was willing to wait a little while Phil drove around town to look for him.

Bob looked at his watch, "If your man isn't here in 10 minutes, I'll take the second crew home first."

He knew how important it was to be the first back to camp. The first ones back signed the jump roster and aced the other crew for the next fire.

While he was gone, Bob heard about my farewell party. "Davis isn't the only one to leave at 30 years of age. When N7861 reaches that age, which is only a few years away, they are going to retire my reliable old friend."

Bob reached into his coat pocket and pulled out a neatly folded paper he had carried most of the summer. "Here, I want to read something as a farewell to Davis and, eventually, for N7861. It's the TWA announcement for the Trimotor's first retirement.

" 'Like faithful old fire-horses, unshod and retired to a life of ease and green pasture ... Trimotors were set aside for faster planes.' "

Then Bob began telling the history of his three-engine friend. He spoke affectionately about the Tin Goose as he leaned on the strut stabilizing the wheel and engine assembly.

"Smokejumpers began as an experiment in 1939 with an entirely new concept of suppressing forest fires. They were barnstorming parachuters who developed their own styles. Early equipment and procedures were very primitive. They utilized available resources, old football helmets, canvas suits, with cotton webbing for harness. Innovations came from need. Grasshoppers ate the silk chutes of the parachuting pioneers, so nylon replaced silk. Canvas wings couldn't support the powerful engines needed to safely get over the high peaks, and that's where the Trimotors came in.

"This Ford has many names; 'Fabulous Ford,' 'Flying Washboard' or 'Tin Goose" but whatever you call it was the finest piece of equipment ever made for back country flying. Smokejumpers and their 'Tin Goose' were forerunners of the new age of protecting the forests. It was only right that they develop together.

"In the development of the Ford Trimotor, there is a direct relationship to Ford's 'Tin Lizzie'. Henry Ford didn't invent either one, but he had a vision; to fill the highways with his affordable cars, and stack the sky with these metal cantilevered aircraft.

"Mr. Ford insisted on three, 450-horsepower Wasp radial engines for safety. Its wings are three feet thick where they connect to the fuselage, allowing it to lift almost two tons in mountain air.

"She sold brand new for $42,000. Johnsons bought this one for $10,000. She can be airborne in half the length of the runway. I'd like to see a twin-engine trainer do that."

"The new twin-engine ought to have turbochargers to fly in this thin air," Hawk said. "Bob, you remind me of my dad when he was setting the Model-A aside for a newer model. He knew it would never be the same. The Model-A was dependable, just not very fancy.

"We took some supplies to Boise last week," Hawk continued. "The Ford was filled with all kinds of fire fighting gear. We were unloading it when some wise guys from a Lockheed Electra transport made snide remarks about the old Trimotor. I thought about telling them about the time over Grangeville when one engine went out and shook itself loose from the plane, leaving us with only two engines and how we slipped out the door and landed in a hay field while the pilot simply flew back to the airport. I could tell them how much we love this old condor, but what good would it do?"

"How many years did it take you to learn to synchronize all three engines, Bob?" Tex asked.

"It's still hard. Each one is independent. I throttle the outboard ones in harmony and then synchronize the middle engine. I can't stand to hear them sounding like a threshing machine."

"Niebuhr said that wisdom consists of three parts that need to be synchronized, " I said, "knowledge of God, of companions, and of one's own self, and you can't separate the three engines that drive the Christian faith - Father, Son and Holy Spirit."

"We didn't let Mark give his farewell sermon last night, and now, here it is," Don joked.

It took two men to crank up an engine and Bob was lining up men to crank the port engine when a truck raced into view at the far end of the dirt runway.

"Nick's coming," I said.

We loaded through the oval door and after Bob had the Trimotor lined up for takeoff he looked back to us and shouted, "I told you how strong this aircraft is. Now, in honor of Mark leaving, I'll give you a ride home you will never forget. I've flown this craft like a dive-bomber dropping cargo and it is as solid as corrugated rock. This metal bird can dive like a hawk and soar like an eagle. We'll take a few dips and if the wings don't fall off — don't worry, they won't — you'll have more respect than ever for the Tin Goose. Then go tell the Electra people what real mountain flying is all about."

Parachuting was never like that ride. An hour later, seven light-green jumpers staggered through the oval door and flopped down on solid turf at the McCall airport, while Bob turned the noisy engines back toward Stanley Basin to pick up the other crew. Phil carefully stepped over the bodies who had partied too much to really enjoy their post-champagne flight, whistling the Spanish tune he'd played the night before.

No one ever doubted the power of the rivets that welded the parts of the Tin Goose together or the bonds that united the Hawkeye Squad.

Following that frightening flight, I spent the next day loafing on the front lawn. Toward evening, Hawk walked over to the kitchen and returned with two icy Cokes. We found a place in the shade of a red fir to talk.

"So you're settling down on the farm in the valley. If I had a chance to live anywhere near McCall, I'd consider it."

Hawk often accompanied me to the farm. He enjoyed wandering beside the long white fences and the Van Geekherdt manicured lawns. He never failed to take time to play with our children no matter how busy he might be.

"Enjoy them while you can, now … now is the best time of life."

Hawk lost his father while he was in junior high school. As the oldest child, he worked hard keeping his father's cabinet business productive, helping his mother support the other five children. He didn't fret about the past or the future, easily relinquishing problems that imprison many people.

He was very different than the Van Geekherdts, who were upset that earliest family records were lost in Noah's flood. I never could figure out how the Davis family fell out of the Van Geekherdt family tree, but the Van Geekherdt's never let us forget they came first.

Nevertheless, Lynn and I were excited to settle down with our relatives. Our children were growing up, and we wanted them to enjoy the farm I had loved as a child. Lynn and I had lived in houses provided by the church, and owning our own home was beyond our wildest dream.

While I loved the people in my parish, I wasn't very skilled in church programming,so I had mustered all my nerve and called Dad. I had to tell him I had used up much of my inheritance and wanted to come home.

What I hadn't spent, I had givne away, yet somehow, we always had plenty. Someone was watching over us, but home sounded good. I couldn't figure out how to play church games. However much I enjoyed pastoral care, counseling skills would never move me very far up an ecclesiastical ladder.

I told Hawk about calling my dad.

"What did your dad say?"

"I thought maybe he wasn't planning to be around long, because as I was struggling to organize my confused story, he said he would like me to return home and work part time on the farm and eventually form a community development. He never equivocated."

"Where will you live?" Hawk asked.

"Do you remember the big white house with the black shutters?"

"You're going to move your family in with your parents?"

"Dad said they didn't need the large house anymore. He said they would gift it to us simply because they were happy we were coming home. Is that love or what? They plan to live in a condominium they purchased near the lake. Lynn and I will own the beautiful home that we've always dreamed of."

"I will serve St. Andrews-by-the-Lake as a self-supporting vicar, earning most of my living at the farm. It's the best of all worlds for sure," I said. "Everyone needs a place to call home."

"How does your brother feel about you moving onto the farm?"

"My older brother, Reginald Van Geekherdt Davis is a bit resentful. Dad tried to convince him we had found ourselves, but that didn't impress him or the Van Geekherdts. They don't like sharing ... power and goods."

"Reggie will someday inherit the family farm, insured of a handsome income for life. Milk subsidies have created insurance policies for him, courtesy the taxpayers. He can't lose. An old Van Geekherdt once joked, 'God led the Pilgrim fathers to America to develop milk subsidies for the chosen.' That's humorous, but I don't feel that way."

"Yeah, I've never desired to beat the system, either. I guess we have that in common. Some people are born with the intention of milking the system for all it's worth." Hawk said smiling. "It's ironic that 'self-made' men, while enjoying government support, show such little respect for people on welfare."

"My relatives' idea of success goes back further than special preference from the government," I said. "The belief in special treatment for the oldest male originated in the Torah. Important decisions belong to the oldest male, and that's the end of the matter."

My grandmother, whose father brought the Van Geekherdts to Idaho in a covered wagon with Kansas license plates, died before we returned from Montana. My philosophy, placing a high value on equality, would have been as unwelcome to her as the Indians she feared along the Oregon Trail. In her mind, God predestined the elect to possess the land.

Her cult, the Primogentarians, credited Moses for originating her favorite doctrine, 'primogeniture.' The oldest male child inherited family land and business. The youngest was dispatched to Egypt. I was upsetting their predestinarian cart by returning home.

"The settlers had moral approval to exploit the land for their own profit, and that outdated concept is hard to revise. You can't change all that," Hawk said. "You're the new kid on the block. You've got to learn to negotiate when they have all the power. It takes spirited faith to accept injustice when you don't have any power except love, but love is stronger.

"Everyone is your brother and you must learn to forgive wrongs and move forward. You have many brothers, like myself, from the smokejumper family, so don't look back but press forward."

"You're right, Hawk, I do have lots of brothers ... and sisters. Jesus said 'Whoever does the will of God is my brother.' There are lots of good people in the world. Why dwell on the ones who can't live beyond their own self-interest?"

WHEN SMOKEJUMPER SEASON COOLED TO A CLOSE, I drove an 18-wheel Kenworth to Montana to pick up our belongings. We didn't need all the room in the shiny white dairy truck, but I was embarrassed to tell Dad we hadn't acquired much materially.

When I returned from Montana, Dad sent two farm hands to help unload the huge van. He and Mom had left furnishings, drapes, and carpets in the magnificent white house, and the men unloading our belongings felt our furnishings were unfit for the most beautiful house in Lost Valley. When they lifted two imitation-oak end tables out of the almost-empty van, they asked if I wanted them put in the barn.

We were emptying the van, and Mom was helping us place our sparse furniture where it would look good. She loved her big white house, and moving into a condo would not be easy. But she was delighted she could get to know her grandchildren. Mom, a Methodist, was not bound by the primogeniture tradition.

She walked up the elegant stairway to the yellow bedroom.

"Give this room to your daughter, Teri," she said. "It's the only thing that I am requesting." Tears welled up in her gentle blue eyes.

My sister Elizabeth, whose summers on lookouts began my interest in smokejumping, had died in the yellow bedroom, before our children had a chance to know her. If there was one Davis in whom Christ's Spirit dwelt, it was Elizabeth. Her beautiful spirit exuded a welcome for us in our new home. Our kids would now get to know her.

"Well of course, Mom, this is the perfect room for Teri."

"Elizabeth's lovely spirit still dwells here. I can't explain it, but on her birthday and at Christmas, her presence makes itself felt . . . a warm comfortable love. Cherish her presence and she will bless your home, I know," Mom said.

IT DIDN'T TAKE THE KIDS LONG TO BECOME PART OF THE FARM LIFE. They were too young to drive tractors, but they helped paint the white fences and feed the calves. Their little friends filled the white house.

They especially enjoyed raising pets. Teri, Scott and Flip had so many animals on our two beautiful acres, I began to wonder if my title should be "wildlife manager."

Mom gave Teri a Tennessee Walker named Orange Molly who allowed only Teri to ride her. She bucked older people off. The two of them glided over pastures with perfect timing and grace, as if they were one.

Scott had all sorts of animal friends in, under, over and around the house, including a young red-tailed hawk. The baby hawk rode around the farm on his shoulder until he sensed it was time to say goodbye. Then Scott went up on Jug Handle Mountain, and after a little ceremony, sent his friend to the freedom he deserved.

Scott's closest animal friend, though, was a bobcat named Benjamin. Mike Shank, one of his school friends, brought Ben to Scott while its eyes were still closed. Someone had killed the bobcat's mother for her pelt, and that violent act made Benjamin an orphan.

We knew wild cats should not be domesticated, but what could we do when a helpless kitten needed food and love? Scott fed him enriched milk from baby bottles. Ben gulped the milk and usually ended his meal by chopping the rubber nipple off the bottle.

This first glimpse of Ben's super strength came when his eyes were barely open. There was something profound in the incredible power of this baby kitten!

We concluded bobcats may be the most courageous animals ever assembled by Almighty God. There may be larger and more ferocious species, but none braver. Early one morning a good-sized black bear was poking through our garbage looking for breakfast. In a flash Benjamin went after him. Fortunately, the bear took off before there was contact. We learned to never ... *never* ... challenge Benjamin or mess with his food.

It was Immanuel Kant who taught me to respect other persons as ends and not as means. This respect ought to be extended for all creatures great and small. People whose families include bobcats learn absolutely to live on wildcat terms, not imposing their own.

One of the strange things about bobcats is their love of water. An irrigation ditch two-and-a-half feet deep flowed beside our lawn and one summer evening Scott was irrigating our two-acre yard of the thirsty Kentucky blue grass lawn. We were astounded to see Benjamin in all his glory swimming.

At the same time, Orange Molly was kicking a rubber basketball up and down the irrigation ditch with Brun Hilda, Flip's St. Bernard, chasing her. Only our resident great horned owl, high above in the poplar tree, was not acting crazy in the warm summer air.

Benjamin came into our family as a blind, helpless kitten, and the other animals accepted him, never realizing he was a genuine wild cat. People saw things differently. The number of house guests dropped off drastically after Benjamin became our youngest adopted critter.

The remaining overnight guests received small admonitions. We warned them to close the bathroom door securely when they took a bath. Ben loved a bathtub full of warm water and never missed a chance to jump in. Showers were safe ... he didn't like showers.

Behind the spacious white house was a 75-year-old willow tree that Grandfather Davis planted. The base was 12 feet in circumference. Eight feet up the trunk, huge branches flared out, creating a bowl. I found a set of old stairs at a deserted school and placed them so the kids could walk up to their "tree house." The steps were only visible from the back, so persons driving up to our house never saw the stairway.

The bobcat and Brun Hilda, who had become devoted friends, needed no coaxing to use the steps to join the kids in the tree.

To our surprise, they spent most of their daylight hours together in the tree. The St. Bernard had a huge branch she especially liked, and the bobcat snuggled right below on a smaller limb. Sometimes he drooped all four legs over the branch, looking like a bobcat pelt drying in the sun.

Native Americans had the highest regard for bobcats, and Don loved to play with Ben. He would throw a tennis ball in the air and watch Benjamin catch it on the run. He also was fond of Brun Hilda.

We acquired a little blue Fiat convertible and allowed his jumbo dog in the other front seat. Eventually the right hand seat was flattened out by Hilda's massive weight and no decent person would sit on it.

In harsh winters Flip let Brun Hilda sleep in his bedroom. Scott gave Benjamin permission to sleep on his bed. When we woke the kids up for school, we did it very, very carefully. Bobcats and St. Bernards become unreasonably protective of little boys.

One winter night, both boys had their pets indoors to protect them from the zero weather. About 3 a.m., a great controversy arose between the dog and bobcat in the family room. By 3:15, the room was in shambles.

Lynn was screaming, "Do something ... but be careful!"

Scott was cheering for Ben. Flip was rooting for Hilda.

I flipped on the light and attempted to separate them with a broom. Benjamin destroyed the broom in a second. I opened the door to the patio and they both exited, chasing one another. The harsh zero-degree weather cooled them off.

The dogged dilemma tested the house's ability to weather an internal hurricane. We spent the next morning patching up furniture and family relationships.

In these rare disagreements between the two courageous friends, the St. Bernard would ultimately win. She would get hold of Ben's fur and throw him into the air. When it was over, they didn't nurse any grudges. Ben never once delivered a vicious strike at Hilda or our family. Although our arms looked tattooed, these were only love scratches, never serious bites.

DON WAS ENTHRALLED WITH COMMUNICATING WITH BENJAMIN. Often he would perch beside Benjamin in the willow tree while the rest of us sat around the outdoor fireplace. Don said wildcat and coyote spirits guided brave men and women through difficult struggles. He said to communicate with a bobcat in the wilderness was one of the highest signs of good fortune.

I was stunned when the farm manager, Mordred Wallace, said he did not want "that wild cat" on the place! He told me that if the bobcat got into the barn again, he'd been told to get rid of him. We knew Benjamin was in trouble.

Mordred had a keen ability for sabotaging any good that might happen on the farm. He seemed to create chaos and uncertainty in every important project. There was always one certainty, though — Mordred and his boss would come out smelling like roses.

We avoided the family feuds and threats to our pets, filling our time with happy smokejumper friends. We awoke each day embraced by our new home.

I began building things; reconstructing an old woodshed into an office and chapel. Using stones from an abandoned train depot, I fashioned sandstone prayer gardens and worship centers throughout the yard. When my parents came for Sunday dinner they noticed the various revisions in the family home including a large painting of Benjamin Bobcat over the fireplace.

Norman Foote, my Bishop, was our overnight guest.

"Most churches in Idaho are not much larger than your gorgeous home. Why don't you put a steeple on the east end and hold church services here?" he said, half seriously.

I showed the Bishop the little chapel I was building in what had been a woodshed.

"One of the jumpers, Yergenson, is building a steeple for it, " I said.

"I'm also building," he said. "We're busy with a new dock at church camp, and we could use a helping hand now and then."

He had designed the perfect dock the year before out of styrofoam. Unfortunately it also proved to be a perfect place for otters to chisel winter nests. Those wily creatures spent all winter carving out their condos. In the spring the beach was covered with a foot of styro-snow. The Bishop was making a new dock out of 55-gallon barrels. Without his usual concern for wildlife, he was going to force those pests to bite into solid steel.

"Bishop, I've been praying about going back to smokejumping," I said as we looked at my chapel. "I worship God every time I parachute into His sanctuary. That inspiration helps me hold up around the relatives and offer better pastoral care. I also unearth homilies by listening to the gentle choruses deep within those mountains."

"You quit jumping, but your heart didn't."

"Truthfully, I believe God is calling me to the wilderness, just as He called me to be ordained. Besides, I would love to join my brothers this summer. What do you say?"

"I've seen your close and healthy relationship with God when you're out there, but what about the non-wilderness flock at St. Andrews?" the tall man said in a bishop's tone of voice. "I know smokejumping is also an important ministry for you and for the people you work with. I wouldn't want to see it come to an end, but who's going to care for them when you are out fighting fires?"

"Would you allow me to hire a Curate to care for St. Andrews from June through August?"

I was hoping he would agree that it was a win-win situation.

"Seminarians are always looking for summer parish work. I know several at the Episcopal Seminary at Berkeley who would love living in McCall during the summers. I'll contact my first choice. His dad is the priest at Nampa. He sings his sermons with a guitar. I hope your people will accept your non-musical sermons when you return."

"If he sings well, I may be in trouble. If he's a little flat, they'll be glad in September."

FRIENDS OFTEN STOPPED BY MY LITTLE CHAPEL FOR EVENING PRAYER. One brisk fall day my father arrived just in time for the brief liturgy. He heartily joined in the service, which was quite different from his tradition. He never joined the Primogentarians, and was an elder in the Presbyterian Church.

Afterwards he said, "Don't you ever close your eyes and just pray? What good is it saying the same prayers? Life changes each day."

"What's on your mind, Dad?" I asked, knowing it must be important.

"We're getting pressure to quit farming. There have been complaints about the fresh fertilizer from people in nearby developments. I'm moving the cows to a new place down near the Snake River."

"That must be really hard for you, Dad. You've nurtured this land for the last 50 years," I said, aware of the pain in his expression. "What will happen to it?"

"It's time to start the development I promised you. I'm getting older everyday. I want you and the rest of the family to form that development company to construct residential homes that will retain the beauty of this land we have loved. I want you on the board to be sure it is the most beautiful development in Idaho. The dairy corporation will option off all the land one piece at a time."

"I'm delighted to be asked to be on the board of directors."

Dad explained that he planned to issue shares, so that if everyone worked together no one could misappropriate the land.

"If everyone plays fair, everyone will benefit. At first, it will cost you money. You must invest heavily but when the last parcel is developed, you will make enough profit to put your kids through college."

"How long do you see this working out before it is profitable?"

"The way I see it is, we develop the least desirable land first, like the rocky land for the future school. But, remember your Lord's parable about building on a rock. The final project will be built in the center, on the foundation of the original dairy."

He frowned. The idea of asphalting fields we had cultivated for years was painful.

Then he continued. "In the end, we'll develop the 10 acres around the old Van Geekherdt home and dairy barns. That homestead area will be the most valuable. By that time I'll probably be gone, but you and your children your grandchildren will benefit by its high value."

"I need to talk this over with Lynn, but you know I love building things. I'll tell you tomorrow. Imagine: me on a board of directors that is not planning rummage sales."

THE FAMILY CORPORATION WAS DIRECTED BY DAD, and for once in my life I sat as an equal on a family board which was not dominated by the outrageous "first sons first" tradition. In time, I got my sister elected to the board.

Soon bulldozers were leveling our cherished fields into pastures for people. I borrowed tractors and trucks to build a tall berm with a ponderosa pine in front of our house. It took me back to my childhood when I spent summers on John Deere tractors.

I was glad I had come back to a permanent home, surrounded by all sorts and conditions of relatives. There was a prayer bench under a black walnut tree beside my chapel. One iridescent autumn evening I prayed about the meaning of "home." What did "home" mean?

Jesus did most of His healing in family dwellings. He even cut a hole in the roof of a friend's house to heal someone. He loved "coffee breaks" with Mary and Martha in their modest home. His Last Supper was in a large beautiful home, perhaps like ours.

I selected the first verse of Psalm 91 for meditation; "He that dwelleth in the secret place of the most High shall abide under the shadow of the Almighty."

I centered on the thought that foxes have homes and birds have nests but Jesus never had a place to call home came into my awareness.

Then the familiar words of Holy Communion pulsated within my heart; "to be filled with Christ's grace and made one body with him, that he may dwell in us, and we in him." The Spirit of Christ even dwelt in the concrete "home" of Eugene and Bland Williams in the New Jersey Maximum Security Prison.

The Hebrew root for "dwell" comes from "tent," implying movement. Though I prayed the Williams prison home was temporary, I never wanted to move from my new home.

Two members of our family joined me during the meditation. Benjamin Bobcat curled up on my right foot. Our treetop guest, a great horned owl, softly hooted a series of three clear notes. Benjamin looked nervously upward but didn't dart away.

I meditated on the Psalm, dwelling under the shadow of the Almighty with the owl and bobcat relaxing in their places. The longer I meditated, the more I realized permanent dwelling places are only temporary residences under the shadow of the Lord.

As my meditation unfolded, something within me questioned the quality of the Van Geekherdt's solidarity. I had denied this for a long time, but it was impossible to ignore one unpleasant confrontation after another. Perhaps they were waiting for the time Dad would be gone, then they would "encourage" us to leave our stately home.

I thought of times when Dad was absent for extended periods, how the relatives began dumping stale milk against our back fence. We objected, but it did no good, and the longer we stayed in our elegant home, the more irritations appeared; roofing nails in the driveway, broken glass in the backyard and the mail box blown to pieces.

Happy people are always targets for miserable people. After considering the ecstasy of owning a classy home, and the agony of the hostility of relatives, I was driven to the Gospels for support and guidance.

It's not good to meditate and problem solve at the same time. Now I was problem solving, trying to figure all this out so I could go back to my psalm.

Jesus did not convert his dad's cabinet shop into a counseling office. He did not develop the Upper Room into a permanent chapel. His ministry was always moving. His followers were willing to shift like the desert sands of the wilderness.

My thoughts accelerated with the concept of motion. The Apostolic Church was constantly on the go. St. Paul never opened a permanent center for sinners and saints because the Spirit kept him moving.

Ordination vows imply motion. Jesus said "Come follow me," not, "Come over here and we'll build a permanent dwelling." Enduring security dwells in a person's heart, not in material acquisitions.

This concept was devastating at first, since relinquishments are difficult, but I knew the story of Camelot well enough to know that Mordred destroyed King Arthur's dream. Dad's dream of fair play was under attack.

With that, I quit trying to solve my personal problems. Slowly, peace from my meditation returned and a new vision commenced soaring within me like wild birds confronting a brisk wind ... a wind of change.

Where was God leading?

After being still, the warmth of my meditation communicated, "The Lord himself is my inheritance, my prize. He is my food and drink, my highest joy! He sees that I am given pleasant brooks and meadows that are unbounded and free."

What a wonderful inheritance! I thought.

I felt I could relinquish material goodness for spiritual values which no one could take from me. My spiritual inheritance was more valuable than a handsome home and exotic yard. This inheritance would accompany me beyond the grave.

But could I surrender a beautiful house for a dwelling not made with hands?

Was God preparing me to relinquish my lifelong dream for something better? Scripture described my new journey better than I could.

> *"Indeed I am well content with my inheritance ...*
> *Thou wilt show me the path of life."*

91

When I finished meditating, I walked slowly around and around the beautiful yard and through every room in the house. It would take all my faith to be willing to move into the unknown.

The next day I discussed my meditation briefly with Hawk, who said I ought to chew on some Idaho potatoes. I felt he wasn't listening.

"What do potatoes have to do with my problem with relatives?"

"Your relatives place a high value on their ancestors, and accomplishments like coming over the Oregon Trail, don't they? When anxious people brag about ancestors who are dead, they're talking potatoes. The best part of both are located underground. The genuine joy of living is above ground, in the sky, so move beyond your potato ancestry," Hawk said.

"Hawk, that really helps. Thanks."

He got up and started away.

"What are your plans?" I asked.

He grinned at me and said, "Where I'm going, you cannot come."

I sought God's help later, and a message from Psalm 16 brilliantly presented the solution to my dilemma. God will show me a pathway less traveled. By following His spiritual trail, I will be lead to my true inheritance.

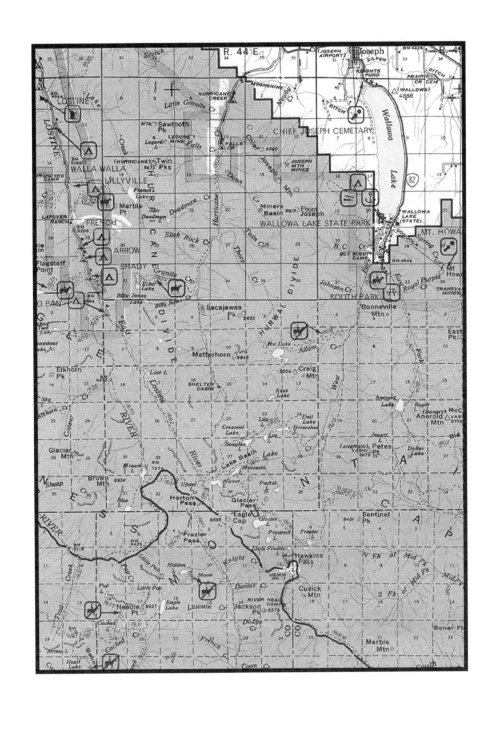

Wallowa Mountains

MALFUNCTION MIRACLE

IN THE WILDERNESS WE ARE ACCESSIBLE TO GOD'S GOODNESS. There, a natural force balances our ups and downs. If we become too euphoric, the immensity of the natural world humbles us. When discouraged, the gentle orderliness lifts our spirits. Out there, we experience what it means to be human without pretenses. The more human we are, the greater our ability to transcend humaness and move beyond old boundaries of stifling tradition and gamesmanship.

In the wilderness we need only conform to our true selves and not to unexamined values of worldly success.

WHILE SINCERELY ATTEMPTING TO BE PART OF A FAMILY BUSINESS and continue my ministry, I made plans to jump smoke again for restoration of my spiritual wholeness. I hoped a summer in the woods might give me positive spiritual direction as I examined my unknown future.

The clear spirit of the wilderness and her wild beings called louder and louder. I had to spend time in my forest office. The solitude might heal my

95

troubles at the farm. My earlier call to the ministry had slipped away trying to play my family's games.

Bishop Foote provided a divinity student for my parish responsibilities, and like the old Trimotor, my fire fighting prescription was reactivated.

My fifth summer as a smokejumper was energizing as the pulsating light of Idaho sunshine. Six men from the Seven Squad were reunited in the rugged spring training, and Hawk was nominated for squad leader.

During the interview with the top dogs, he pleaded for turbochargers on the World War II trainers.

"If you don't beef-up those engines, someone may get hurt."

Ken Shuler was not one to say things to improve his own image, but other than upsetting the management, his plea was ignored.

Ken wasn't a military veteran like some of the older jumpers, but every time vets talked about landing on enemy barracks, we teased Hawk about landing on ours.

During a practice jump to impress Forest Service officials from Washington, D.C., Hawk wanted to electrify them, so he maneuvered over the observers' stand. He couldn't get his chute turned around in time to avoid smashing through the roof of Larry Clark's house trailer. He was not exactly a hero. The next morning we began intensive training for better chute handling.

A few days later we were practicing chute handling, jumping from the DC-3. We packed 20 jumpers in each load, not jumping by squads but by drawing numbers. A damp morning with no wind crested over the yellow crevices of Jughandle Mountain. There could be no excuses today for missing the spot with such favorable conditions.

A wind might come up later, forcing others to make adjustments to land near the target, but I was fortunate and drew number one. With no drift, I could exit right over the spot and pirouette to the big yellow cross for a perfect score.

At the airport, Neal Washam wanted two volunteers to try newly designed experimental chutes. Being number one and close to the new chutes, I grabbed the first one. Rob Yensen yanked the next one from the hands of a more hesitant adventurer.

The new chutes had white and orange panels. Looking up toward the apex, after the chute opened, the jumper would see three colors; orange, white, and through the guidance slots, blue sky. The experimental chute was designed to prevent the massive opening shock which often jolted jumpers harder than the ground. Older canopies opened all at once sounding like the blast of a shot gun, and men were almost knocked unconscious. While it was a good feeling to know the canopy opened, the impact was like jumping off a speeding freight train.

As Rob and I adjusted the novel parachutes on each other's back, Neal explained the innovation.

"We fold it neatly into a deployment bag. The lines come out first so they

96

don't tangle while the canopy opens. Don't expect a strong opening shock. You'll experience a small jerk on your risers when the lines deploy. Finally, a nylon cord will pull the main chute out of the bag by its apex. It will blossom gradually, so don't get impatient."

Neal concluded with an encouraging note.

"The soft opening will spoil you forever."

Jim Larkin fired up the powerful Pratt and Whitneys on the Doug. I was the last one to join the party of happy campers. It was like going to a county fair. There were nervous jokes and lots of pushing and shoving. Crowded together physically and emotionally, we enjoyed bonds of friendship I had never experienced.

The aircraft leap-frogged into the cool morning air, using only three-quarters of the runway to break into the sunshine. After reaching an altitude 1,200 feet above the selected spot, we began circling the drop area. Washam, the spotter, threw two yellow drift streamers directly over the spot.

In the Doug, the spotter lies down on the floor with his head out the door. I was first, so I was standing above him, enjoying the bright reflection of the early sunshine on the blue lake below. It was so breathtaking, I almost forgot to follow the streamers and see there was only a minor drift.

"I'm going to let you jump alone, Stan," Neal shouted. "They're flying beside us to record the new deployment chute."

I'd have a better chance to hit the target if I jumped alone.

We were approaching the jump zone and Jim idled the engines. The air racing by the door pounded my excited body like a hurricane blowing against a sturdy beach house.

In a few seconds I would descend on Slaughterhouse Meadow, less than three miles from McCall. Church groups had brought busloads of observers to the exciting event. Families spread their breakfasts on the tailgates of station wagons like football stadium parties.

My family — Lynn, Teri, Scott and Flip — chose a grassy slope not more than two hundred yards from the canvas target. Through their binoculars, my kids recognized their dad as I poked my head out the door. I wore a bright blue helmet with a Celtic cross painted on the top. They could not see the yellow target because small fir trees blocked their view.

I tried to locate them, but could only see my brown station wagon. I was holding myself in place by gripping each side of the doorway, poised like a football running back before the snap. I kept thinking to myself, "Now don't panic — be patient — it will open in its own sweet time. With no wind and a delayed opening I should be half way to the spot before I even have to guide it."

Then, I heard the command and felt the slap on my leg.

"Get outta here Mark !"

Like a fullback smashing directly through a rowdy defense, my legs thrust my body into the rushing wind. After jolting out the door, everything became silent. I was diving headfirst toward the spot, awaiting the delayed opening.

I immediately felt a tug on my lines, and a slight pull on the deployment bag. It was strong enough to turn my body right-side-up. I could see the plane depart. Everything was going as planned, I patiently reassured myself.

Then, I began spinning uncontrollably. The ground and crowd below me, then blue sky, rotated around and around in my vision. Nothing was happening with my canopy, and I knew there was serious trouble. I managed to look up and see what appeared to be a sleeping bag on the end of the extended nylon lines. The bag, which held life or death for me, wobbled back and forth in the very rapid wind stream.

I was embarrassed to think my final thump would be heard by observers.

I spent the seven or eight seconds accelerating to 120 miles per hour asking myself questions. Would my family hear a terrible thud as I smashed into the turf? Why had I chosen to experiment with a new design? Was my insurance paid up? Would my lovely wife ever forgive me?

Halfway to my death, spinning at immense speed, I began experiencing euphoria. My ordeal didn't seem real, but more like a dream. A complete feeling of serenity enveloped me, like the peaceful spirit I had observed with dying parishioners.

Then, someone, perhaps an angel from God, prompted me to open the reserve chute.

It's not over 'til it's over. I tried reaching for the handle on the reserve chute with my right arm, but those muscles froze and refused to operate. I was falling headfirst so close to the yellow target I saw sagebrush plants looming toward me. There was no chance to tackle an evergreen tree to cushion my fall. Life might be over in a split second.

All I can recall is racing toward sagebrush and rocks, head first. Something — I believe a messenger from God — caused my strong left fist to hit my paralyzed right hand with such force that it pulled the reserve chute open. The good left hand grabbed the reserve white nylon and jerked it into the wind. Within a tenth of a second, the white, 24-foot reserve canopy exploded open, resonating like a cannon. It swung me upright and my feet hit first as I crashed between three fir trees, missing a large boulder by only a few feet.

This split-second miracle happened so fast that neither the men in the plane nor the people on the ground — only a few hundred yards away — saw my reserve chute open. I landed on my feet, and the impact was so formidable my feet drove five inches into the soil. I couldn't roll, but bounced straight up. The compression squashed discs in my back. I've been an inch shorter ever since, but my faith grew a foot taller in my appreciation for what I consider a miracle, God's rescue.

When I hit and bounced, an ironic thing happened. The chute that didn't come out of the bag added insult to injury by falling on my right shoulder like a swift kick. I wanted to kick it back, but I felt I had probably broken my back. I decided to carefully lie down and wait for a stretcher, and thank God for His deliverance.

Miles and Shep Johnson, two brothers, got to me first.

"Great Scott," Shep lamented, "he's dead! Hold back Mrs. Tate and the kids. Everyone stay back. This is terrible."

Half-conscious, I let Shep know I could move. I told him I was stunned but alive. Ron Dunn, a third year medical student from the University of Washington, began checking my bruised body to see what, if anything, wasn't broken. My neck was so swollen I couldn't turn my head. My right arm was still unable to move, but neither of my arms or legs were broken. My back was compressed, but not broken, so I stood up, taking off the my jump suit, slowly determining whether I could walk normally.

"Davis, you never walked normally anyway. Maybe this will straighten your style," Ron joked as I stood up.

A curious ritual followed my escape from death. After hugging my wife and my children, I walked around the circle of smokejumpers, formally shaking hands with each individual. "Nice to see you, Bill. How you doing, Carl? Nice day, Wayne."

I felt the presence of the Lord in that circle of friends. Like Lazarus coming out of the tomb, greeting friends, exchanging grave clothes for living attire.

Events like this completely reshape our values in a matter of seconds. A few minutes earlier I was worried about hitting the spot and winning a steak dinner. Now I was thankful for life itself.

I was taken to the McCall Hospital for X-rays. Dr. Moser told me he was watching our parachuting from his kitchen window and saw me fall. He was raising a spoon full of Wheaties toward his mouth, and his hand followed my rapid descent with the spoon full of Wheaties, crashing on the table. Leaving the spoon where it fell, he told his wife, Marjorie, he was going to see if there was anything left of the smokejumper.

My neck and shoulders were swollen and bruised, but after X-ray examination, Dr. Moser announced that not one bone was broken. I was sore and stiff, but so happy to be alive that I didn't worry about the pain. When we cherish God's most beautiful gift of all, life, we can accept severe pain.

My ordeal with the miraculous ending happened Thursday. Friday morning, I was back in uniform with a regular chute on my back, first in line to get into the Doug for another jump. Neal Washam said I could jump first, last or never. I was the honored guest in a plane load of well-wishers.

In the calm morning air high above the lake, I surmised my true home was with Almighty God, not the forests or the farm. Home is whatever makes each moment of life precious, and God is always there.

99

The sunlight was breaking forth as the plane held her proper altitude. There was no crowd below, only jumpers. Standing in the doorway over the very same spot, I was afraid I might freeze up if I waited too long. I wanted to get it over with. As we flew over a smooth spot near a green hayfield, I asked the spotter if I could jump without drift streamers.

Without saying much he stood up, checked my lines and buckles and said, "Have a good one, Mark."

He radioed Jim to cut the engines. I threw my body and hopes for a good jump into the fresh morning air.

For the first seconds, my heart pounded like a hammer. Then the orange and white canopy popped open like a circus tent. Experiencing a hallowed calm and drifting leisurely in the morning light, I hummed the first line of this hymn:

> *"Morning has broken, like the first morning . . .*
> *black bird has spoken, like the first bird.*
> *Praise for the singing . . . "*

I didn't care where or if I ever landed on planet Earth. Consequently, I plunked down in a hayfield, barely missing a baler.

BENEATH THE TOUGH EXTERIOR OF MOST SMOKEJUMPERS IS A DEEP SENSE OF GRATITUDE. Saturday, fellow jumpers talked about life and death instead of partying. Sunday, my parish was filled with jumpers analyzing the possibility of miracles. My sermon on God's messengers helping us through life was short but authentic.

After church, Bob Fogg spoke of another glimpse into God's Grace for Skip, another Johnson pilot. This miracle occurred 15 miles north of McCall near the north fork of the Payette River.

Skip, an ex-Navy pilot, always attended the early Sunday Eucharist, if possible. The only time he missed church was when his job had to come first. On special days, he attended a later service with his wife and four boys. He teased me about being an Air Force Chaplain for the Idaho 124th Fighter Interceptor Group. I told him there weren't many aircraft carriers in Idaho.

Early one Sunday morning, Skip was flying 50-gallon drums of aviation fuel to the back country in the Travelaire when the plane lost power.

God blessed Skip with only one escape; a curvy dusty road below the dead-stick aircraft. If he had flown another 15 minutes, there would not have even been a salvific roadway. Skip struggled to zig-zag the powerless glider down the dirt road, thankful for no traffic.

He negotiated the first six curves without shearing off the wings, with the barrels of gasoline at the point of breaking their nylon tie-downs. With a straight stretch ahead, he failed to make the last curve, and the pilot, plane, and gasoline tipped over, landing upside down in the north fork of the Payette River.

Skip was pinned inside the plane with ice-cold water rushing over him. Ironically as a Navy pilot, he had never hit the water. With an unbelievable burst of energy, he sprung the door open and floated to the surface. He crawled miraculously out of the water without serious injury. Leaving the aircraft in the water, he hitched a ride back to McCall with a fisherman who had seen him rise out of the swirling water. He surprised the driver by asking to be taken to the Episcopal Church rather than the hospital.

I was just finishing an early celebration of Holy Communion, a Eucharist for sportsmen, when Skip arrived. He burst into St. Andrew's and marched up to the altar rail where I was distributing wine from the chalice. As he approached the Lord's Table I wondered why he hadn't cleaned up for church. He was bloody, as if he'd been fighting, partying or something. It was not Skip's usual demeanor.

"Thank you, Jesus! Thank you Jesus!" he said in a loud voice. Grasping the chalice with both hands, he consumed the entire contents. He limped down the aisle, spoke briefly with an usher and left the church. After the Benediction, I was told by Arlene Shank of the altar guild he wanted me to visit him at McCall Memorial Hospital, immediately.

I hightailed it to the emergency room. Overwhelmed with gratitude, he told the story of his miraculous escape. He wanted to thank God first for sparing his life and then go to the hospital.

Eucharist, by the way, means "thanksgiving" in Greek.

Bob Fogg concluded the story of Skip's miracle with, "Here's a backwoods pilot who has his values in order."

A MONTH AFTER MY DELIVERANCE, I was talking with Skip about his escape from tragedy in the river. One thing Skip and I had in common in the midst of our traumas was the fact we had both asked God and our guardian angels for help. The upheaval of my "malfunction miracle" compelled me to reflect on finishing the tasks I was called to accomplish.

At that moment the fire-buzzer in the tower rang loud and clear — one long and four shorts.

"Here we go Skip. Fly me to a fire with a good view," I said, running toward the ready shack.

The spotter was waiting for me. "Mark, run to your trailer and pick up your stole and communion kit. You're going to an airplane accident in the Wallowa Mountains. We don't know if the occupants are dead or alive. Let's hope for another miracle."

The mood was somber as we rushed headlong down the runway in the twin-engine aircraft. Cargo included stretchers with first aid cases as well as four plastic body bags with a sack of body preservative powder.

As soon as we were airborne, Skip throttled back the engines on the World War II trainer. The plane was similar to an Oregon aircraft known as "Iron Annie,"

101

a Beech E-18 which flew injured people to Portland hospitals. It was this same type of plane that Hawk wanted refurbished with turbochargers for high-altitude flying.

Our primary goal was to render first aid, then build a heliport so the injured could be helicoptered to LaGrande. "Iron Annie" would then fly them to Portland. My role was to offer pastoral first-aid during the ordeal.

The scene of the crash was near Eagle Gap, five miles south of Wallowa Lake. En route, we cruised near Seven Devils Mountains and over Hells Canyon, the deepest gorge in America. I hoped I would never have to jump a fire there.

Eagle Gap rose over 9,000 feet, so Skip maintained a high altitude as we approached the crash site, then dropped a few hundred feet to locate the downed aircraft.

"Over to the right, Skip," the spotter called. "Right down there, on the lower side of the box canyon. I see something bright blue and it doesn't look good."

About a hundred feet below a serrated, rocky ridge were the scattered remains of a silver and blue single-engine plane. The tail section had separated from the battered main fuselage, and the crumpled right wing was torn off. There had been no fire, but the scene offered little hope for survivors.

The box canyon was rimmed on three sides with stone walls several hundred feet high. There was only one place to jump; a green patch in the middle of the horseshoe-shaped canyon below the crash site. It looked like a rodeo arena with granite bleachers on three sides.

This type of jump required split-second timing and only one man could jump on each pass. As the plane flew over the side of the "bleachers," we would count to three, and shove off at the center of the arena, about 1,100 feet up. Skip skimmed over the steep ledge of the rocky canyon, and Hawk leaped out the door directly over a grove of green trees. He circled the spot three turns, and came to rest on the edge of the greenery.

Phil and Tex followed individually, landing safely in the green island surrounded by a sea of rocks. Finally, crouching in the doorway, I took one last glance at the crumpled airplane before I felt the slap and heard, "Go!"

I was out the door like a race horse springing from a starting gate. After a perfect opening, I glanced around to get my bearings. I was over the crash site, but too far south of the jump spot to reach the green area. I was making headway, but falling too rapidly to clear the boulders near the bottom of the canyon wall. I had no choice but to head for the top of a flat boulder about twice the size of my Studebaker station wagon. I wondered if one of the stretchers would be used for me.

As if landing on the deck of an aircraft carrier, I hit the stone deck in the center of a flat platform, then rolled instantly and fell over the side between two large rocks. My metal face mask caused sparks as I skidded along the rock. My right knee throbbed with pain but wasn't broken,

We didn't take time to collect our gear but immediately climbed up a rock slide to the wreckage. Metal parts were scattered over the rocky hillside. The engine had separated from the fuselage. We approached the passenger compartment with hope of hearing pleas for help, but there were none.

A man and woman, dressed in bright green Western attire, lay side by side, strapped into their front seats. Their bodies were mangled almost beyond recognition. A little blonde girl was alone in the back seat with her seat belt on. About 12 years old, she was dressed up for happy times in a fluffy yellow dress with white sneakers. All three passengers had died instantly.

I anointed their bodies with holy oil and Phil offered a prayer before we extracted them from the wreckage.

"Jesus, you raised Jairus' twelve-year-old daughter to life saying 'Talitha Cum.' Please take this little girl and her parents into your eternal home where there will be no more plane crashes or suffering."

Tex asked what the words of Jesus meant

Phil said, "Little girl, get up!"

It took all our courage to gently slide the little girl's body into a plastic bag. I looked the other way as Phil tenderly placed her doll beside her.

I questioned why my life was spared but this precious little child's was not. It wasn't fair. She had a whole life ahead of her for happiness and adventure. The other men entertained questions, too, but no one said anything. I wanted to tell them that parents and child were together in a new celestial church with many rooms. I had listened to enough people who survived near-death experiences to know guardian angels greeted them when they departed and no one dies alone. Believers who die together will live together with the same God who maintains eternal light beyond the global crypt in our bioscathedral.

We made three treks, taking turns carrying their bodies to the top of the ridge. The spotter dropped two chain saws so we could carve out a helipad. We laid the bodies in the shade and then fell five alpine firs to clear a landing spot.

Forest Service helicopters were on the Challis fires and could not respond immediately. We were going to have to wait until early morning to transport them to La Grande. Tex and Phil volunteered to hike back down to the original jump spot for our sleeping bags and food. We would sleep near the departed.

A S TEX AND PHIL TRUDGED BACK UP THE MOUNTAIN WITH DINNER, daylight dimmed and the sun slid between the snow-clad Wallowa peaks. The shadows lengthened around the three bodies temporarily resting under an evergreen. I prayed to God they were experiencing a sacred sunrise beyond the sunset.

Physically and emotionally exhausted, I yearned for solitude and spiritual renewal. At home, I might have listened to the first act of Verdi's *Idomenio* allowing the choral masterpiece to renew my strength. Since this was impossible, I walked to the ridge above our camp in search of a natural prayer chapel.

There was no trail. The mountain was covered with small shrubs among windswept trees deformed by years of harsh weather. Downed logs had brittle, sharp branches protruding like barbed wire. I was grateful for my jumper boots and tough 'frisco jeans.

When efforts to serve others subside, solitude is necessary to restore spiritual balance. I found a restful place on the highest point to contemplate the tragedy, aware of the three bodies not far below. Suffering involves unfinished dreams and unexpected short circuits of our plans.

Surrounded by the timelessness of the Wallowa Mountains, human suffering appeared temporary. My prayer bench was a gnarled alpine fir stump perched above Wallowa Lake and the community of Joseph, Oregon, named for Chief Joseph. The intrepid Nez Perce leader once lived down there near the lake. I pondered whether he ever came up here, admiring the same stars shining over the spectacular Seven Devil Mountains.

The outdoor chapel spanned hundreds of scenic miles with horizons enclosed by clouds like stained glass windows. The stone altar was framed by tall, uneven alpine firs. The windward sides of the rugged trees were almost void of branches. Heavy green moss clung to the protected side. A tree to my left was bent over so far, it pointed to the horizon, like an old man who once stood as a tower of strength before years of suffering bent his tired body.

The busy day made room for the hush of evening. I could hear the wilderness singing softly as evening shadows glided along rectangular patches of green and yellow wheat fields miles below. A solitary eagle soared to the left of the lake, soaring toward me like a hang glider. Paradoxically, he issued a tiny cackle rather than a more vibrant tone, like an owl. I surmised the emblem of American freedom accentuates action over rhetoric.

The awareness of God reverberated within me watching that eagle. Possibly the departed family had been soaring over exactly the same area when they encountered an unexpected down draft. Even the rock foundation of my chapel conveyed the message of the temporality of our existence. The peaks in the Wallowas are enduring altars, sacred places which evoke a merger of our mortality with the external timelessness of God, but they too shall someday return to dust.

Jesus chose to worship God upon stone altars like these, and He is as alive today as He was upon those eroding mountain tops.

In this magnificent setting I chose a passage from Isaiah for meditation; "Those who trust the Lord will rise on wings like eagles and not grow weak." I repeated "Wings of eagles, strong, not weak" silently to myself.

The bio-spiritual wind lifts sacred wings of compassion like mountain air lifting the wings of the Trimotor. In the enormous splendor of my chapel, wild birds soared gently above and below me on the buoyancy of wispy evening breeze. Was the breeze I felt from the soft touch of angel wings?

104

I began slowly humming expressions of wings of God's eagles, along with "Sha'*éem* ... Elo*héem* ... Chris*téem*."

Healing, following vicarious suffering, requires the combined resources of the Trinity; Father, Son and Holy Spirit. The Trimotor requires thrust from three engines ... two will not sustain the aircraft in strenuous flights. A Christian who attempts flying on only one or two engines will never benefit from the balanced force of Christian spirituality.

After a few deep breaths, my spirit ascended among the rugged peaks above the lake like the eagle, circling closer to a spiritual home with many rooms.

I heard a bird in one of the trees behind me. She dislodged a piece of bark which fell on my left shoulder. An eagle? A hawk? An owl? I sensed a mystical, beautiful bird not far away. I thanked God for her and continued meditating.

I N St. John the Divine's in New York City or in St. Francis of the Wallowas, God heals suffering. Persons emerging from households of suffering have a higher quality of character. Potential inner strength remains dormant until encounters with suffering jar it loose. Quality Christians experience enormous suffering and healing in the household of God. The Bible attests those who trust the Lord for help will discover their strength renewed.

As my Wallowa meditation came to a close, I felt a strong urge to get up, walk and run. I heard cosmic music, as if strains of Verdi's sublime *Requiem* were filling the evening skies. I found new strength to accept my anguish about the family below. Following my meditation, God's everlasting hills vibrated with new life born from above.

Alert once again to my physical environment, I moved down the mountain to rejoin the others. As I walked, I swayed among the wind-bent scenery as if I was riding on eagle wings.

W E mortals cannot comprehend God's mysterious Grace — it comprehends us. Vexing questions were on my mind when I returned from the Wallowas to my stately farm home. The Oregon accident raised issues about the ethical principle of justice. How did this tragedy relate to my miracle with the experimental parachute?

"Lynn," I said, "God must have distinctive plans for me or I wouldn't be here today. Let's pack the kids in the wagon and have dinner on the beach at church camp. Hopefully we'll run into Bishop Foote. I have some questions for him."

She packed hot-dogs, buns, and potato chips in a wicker picnic basket, and we loaded our dinner, the kids and the St. Bernard into our battered station wagon. Church camp was on the other side of Payette Lake, and it didn't take long to get there.

When Bishop Foote was in residence, our family felt church camp earned its name, Paradise Point, When we arrived, the Bishop and Ronny, his pet raven, were alone on the white sand beach. Our St. Bernard had learned the hard way not to bark at the Bishop's favorite bird, a 17-year old raven who pecked noses with great accuracy.

The distinguished Bishop looked as if someone had thrown a bucket of cold water over him when he saw our noisy gang pull up, shattering his lake shore peace. Nonetheless, he was gracious and asked us to share the small fire he had kindled from pine boughs earlier. Lynn poured him a glass of iced tea.

"Did you hear about my narrow escape last month?" I asked.

"How could I not hear about it? Some said you went to sleep and forgot to open your chute. Others said you just forgot to hook up."

He winked at Lynn with a twinkle in his eye, but he sensed I was disturbed about my deliverance.

"Well let's hear about it."

I began hesitantly. "I feel God has something important for me to accomplish, or I wouldn't be alive tonight. Dad says that eventually we are going to develop the choice — and last — ten acres of the farm into apartments and a small shopping center. He says I can manage the center and have a comfortable future.

"I wonder why God would spare me for that?"

The Bishop smiled. "What about your ministry?"

"I would become a self-supporting priest, earning my living by managing the center. Dad says we'll begin by developing the family farm into residences surrounding this choice site. When we've increased the value of the land, we'll develop the choicest parcel, and he says we'll realize a handsome profit on our early investments."

"What will you do with your profits?"

"Remodel the red barn into a counseling center, for persons who've lost their homes. We'll use the meditation chapel in the back yard for various services. The money from the last development will finance new ministries for people who need family and a place to call home."

Lynn roasted the hot dogs over the hot coals until they were almost charred black. She served the best one to the Bishop, who realized she was not excited about the idea.

"Lynn you look less than enthused about this family project," he said.

"I am. In the Van Geekherdt family, the 'Primogenitarian Kingdom,' everything benefits the oldest males. All decisions are made by the oldest men, who have a pattern of changing the rules in their favor. When they ask the rest of us to invest now and get our money back in one final project, I'm nervous. Mark happens to be the youngest child.

The Bishop scratched his head and swatted an enormous mosquito. "That's an old tradition for first-borns. The younger kids ... well, too bad for them,"

"If we invest our time and money," I said, "we'll realize a substantial profit in the last, and most valuable, project — the apartments and center."

"Do you think God spared your life to manage apartments?" The Bishop asked. "You are totally unequipped to play business games. One thing God and the wilderness have in common, is the fact they play no games. Trusting your relatives to play fair with you r money is like jumping a forest fire without a helmet."

"God spared you for more than that," Lynn said.

Biting into a juicy hot dog, I watched four people step out of a bright red Jeep. Skip, Bonnie, Hawk and Mary Kay joined us at the campfire with a picnic basket heaped with fried chicken and potato salad.

To the delight of everyone, a romance between Hawk and Mary Kay was gaining momentum. Theirs was a different friendship. She had been a widow for several years and was hesitant to remarry. She enjoyed a kind of platonic but very intense love for Hawk, but he loved just about everyone and there were times Mary Kay didn't think she was number one. Yet she certainly was, in Hawk's eyes, and he was not possessive in his love for her. She really didn't know how to love him, but longed to be with him every minute.

Their immediate concern was coping with the tragedy of the plane crash. It was Mary Kay who voiced the question that was on all our minds:

"Why did God allow the Oregon family to die in the Wallowas," she asked the Bishop, "yet allow Skip and Mark to avoid harm?"

"If we say God deliberately spared our lives, are we saying God turned his back on the Oregon family? Doesn't God will the best for all living creatures?" Skip asked.

"Considering that family reminds me life is transitory. Even love is temporary and imperfect," Hawk added, "The only permanent part of life is love blessed by and for God."

"I want to understand the meaning of suffering better," Lynn said. "From my own experience, when something comes along so we can't finish things, that's suffering."

"Suffering is related to freedom," Bishop Foote said. "Consider most forms of pain and suffering, and you will find freedom has been blocked or taken away. Suffering occurs when something happens to us which we can't control."

"This is certainly true of the Williams brothers," I said "People took their freedom away to feather their own political nests. Most people in their shoes would be bitter and vengeful, but they say prison has been their college. Suffering is the homework that gave them real character.

"Bland told me 'God gave me this opportunity to turn my life into something good,' and Eugene told me 'I asked Christ to come into my life in jail. If I hadn't been put there, I'd probably be an alcoholic.' He compared himself to Joseph in Egypt."

"How?" Skip asked.

"He explained it this way: He was put in prison because a guy named Waters gave false testimony. The wife of Pharaoh also gave false testimony against Joseph.

"Eugene was so innocent when he was arrested he didn't understand the word 'homicide.' Several years later, when he was only four weeks from dying in the electric chair, he was still more concerned about someone lying than his own welfare. He strongly believed God would vindicate him, as Joseph believed God would support him through the false accusation.

"He said, 'I was unfortunately black and convicted of someone else's crime by a white jury. But it's not complexion that causes wrong. It's misguided authority and the abuse of power.' "

"Or lack of power," the Bishop said. "Power tends to corrupt. It's unbalanced power in most anything that creates suffering."

"Eugene said he had no power to prevent him from dying in the electric chair; no power except prayer," I said.

"He must have turned his life over to the Ultimate Power," Skip suggested.

"Yes, and, from that point on, he was fearless. He experienced freedom in a situation where there was no sign of freedom. If the human heart, upheld by God, is free, concrete walls cannot restrain it. That's why Bland said he would rather die there than make a false plea for a reduced sentence," I said.

"That's not so different from Socrates choosing to drink the hemlock," the Bishop said. "Socrates said if there is nothing after death, he wouldn't have to endure the political uproar, and if there was life after death, he'd go right on teaching philosophy,"

"Consider some of our jumpers," Hawk said. "Nick enjoys little freedom. He is compulsively driven in self-destructive behavior. If Bland Williams could speak to Nick, what do you think he might say? "

"Another minister who called on Bland in the death house told him, 'Don't serve time. Make time serve you,' " I said. "Bland might say to Nick; 'Don't serve your emotional needs. Wake up and get well allowing them to serve you — a healthy you.'

"John Macquarrie says suffering occurs when people lose control of events to contingencies … cancer, for example … caused by things you can't control.

"When persons have incurable illnesses, they lose freedom to continue whatever they were trying to accomplish. When lovers lose their beloved, they are incomplete and their lives must continue in an unfinished manner. All forms of suffering involve a loss of something. There are no exceptions I know of," I said.

"Does God control contingencies? That is, does God decide who gets to complete things and who doesn't?" Skip asked. "This doesn't seem fair to me."

"Understand this," the Bishop said, "God doesn't direct decisions which promote suffering. He allows real freedom to happen, without strings attached. God intentionally causes good but never causes evil. I personally believe He uses angels to materialize the good.

108

"The Oregon families' agenda on earth has ended but will be completed in the next life. God had plans for them, but allowed a contingency to intervene and destroy the original plan. By God's Grace, the vocation for Mark and Skip goes on. Perhaps they will accomplish something that is vital to the well-being of others."

"Is that the end of the Oregon tragedy?" Lynn asked.

"No. Although God allowed that family to die," the Bishop said, "His ultimate plan has not been thwarted. When contingencies block a plan from completion, God ultimately surpasses it with a Divine plan. That little girl, born from above, is experiencing a higher form of life in Paradise. God always has the last word, and it's a good word."

"Dr. Macquarrie says God is not overwhelmed by suffering," I said, "but accepts and transforms it. When Jesus was crucified, ... the supreme suffering ... He said, 'It is finished ... it is accomplished.' I think He was completing fragments of our intentions,"

"What do you mean?" Lynn asked.

I almost launched a beach sermon.

"Jesus says 'It is accomplished', and offers us the broken bread of immortality. He gathers up all the crumbs of our endeavors; all the pieces of dreams or plans we've left unfinished. Christ restores meaning to the meaninglessness of our fragmented good efforts. Our completeness may be discernible only after this life. What a tremendous celebration there will be when our lives are joined together with the irreducible mystery of life,"

"Macquarrie also said, 'Action is the opposite of suffering,' " the Bishop said. "Self determination is one of my highest values. Suffering like the Williams' comes from outside our influence. What is vital, then, is how we choose to act. When we act, we help determine what will happen.

"The most inspiring person I know suffers from an incurable illness. Though she has begun many good things, only God can complete them in His time and place. We can't comprehend the 'why' of suffering, but only accept its reality courageously.

"I grieve for the Oregon family. In my opinion, Skip and Mark have been given more time to accomplish something only they can do."

The Bishop stood up and said goodnight and headed toward his cabin. His pet raven was not far behind, mumbling, "goodnight, good day, and goodby."

The evening star reflected in the still waters of Payette Lake as we began packing up picnic supplies and new understanding, perhaps going home, perhaps leaving home.

Hawk suggested we not focus on the loss of the Oregon family, but work on opportunities which we might somehow fritter away.

"We ought to love one another is such a way that our fragmented friendships can be completed someday by our Creator.

"We experienced the miracle of the loaves and fishes at the Whitehawk fire

109

with the women Hotshots. Afterwards, there were many fragments of food left over. Jesus said, 'Gather up the fragments left over, so that nothing will be lost.' Think of those abundant pieces of broken bread as bits of love which grow and grow when shared.

"Mark you and Skip have things to accomplish before you die. Get with it and God will bless your effort. I have one important goal and I'm working on it.

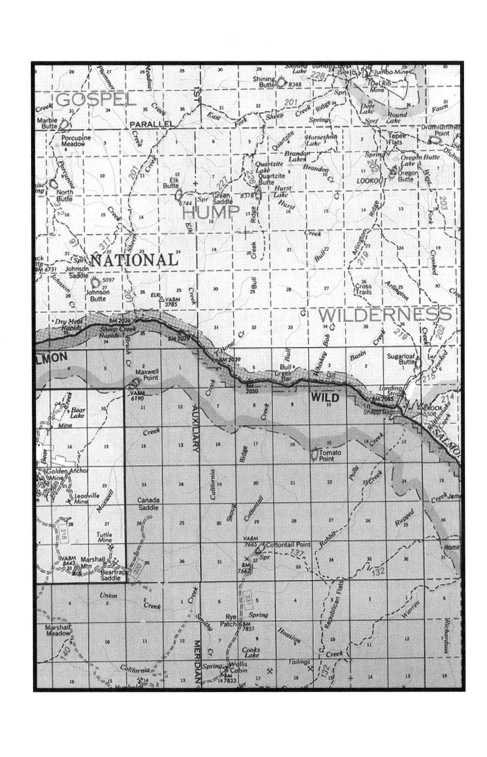

THE GOSPEL HUMP WILDERNESS

AN ABANDONED LOOKOUT

I DIDN'T SMOKEJUMP THE SUMMER FOLLOWING MY MALFUNCTION MIRACLE. I was wearing too many hats and collars. As Vicar of St. Andrews, I was shepherding a flock of mostly smokejumper families. I worked conscientiously on the board of directors of the Van Geekherdt Development Company.

I was also trying my best to make justice work in rural Idaho. I had been elected overwhelmingly to the office of County Probate Judge, Idaho's juvenile justice court, for crafting a program of senior citizens as voluntary probation counselors. Administering a chalice on Sundays, I wielded a gavel the rest of the week. On weekends I wore a striped shirt to referee football and basketball games.

My interest in juvenile justice had its roots in the New Jersey prison where I was a chaplain while doing graduate work at Princeton. I was sent to the dingy death house because the head chaplain didn't relish visiting death row.

I couldn't blame him. It's a gruesome little square gray building standing by itself in the middle of the prison yard. I had to duck my head to enter the steel doorway. The windows were small and high, like basement windows. Eighteen cells were on the right side of the gray corridor inside the entry. At the end of the passageway was a little room with the electric chair on a platform under a dim light. I couldn't look at it long. A shiver coursed down my spine as I imagined the leather straps in place and a final surge of deathly power. Inmates claimed the lights flickered throughout the prison when someone died in the chair.

Upon gaining admission to the Williams' concrete home, I was pleasantly surprised by the warm reception from Eugene's steel cage. Bland was polite, quiet and withdrawn, keeping his thoughts private. For some reason, known then only to Almighty God, I felt a special affinity with these brothers.

The Williams had been convicted of the brutal murder of a white night watchman near Perth Amboy, New Jersey. The man was beaten to death at a manufacturing plant. The apparent motive was robbing money from a heavy safe. The safe had been moved out of the room it was in, so more than one person was involved.

Three other husky black men were arrested along with the Williams. One was judged incompetent and sent to a mental institution. Another, in many opinions should have been declared incompetent since he had been in and out of mental institutions all his disturbed life. For his questionable testimony, he received a very light sentence.

With flimsy evidence and doubtful testimony, the brothers were convicted, perhaps to ease the public's cry for vengeance for the savage murder in a racially tense community.

Eugene told me a professional criminal named Alex, in the same prison, had lied on the witness stand. He begged me to call on him and persuade him to change his testimony. During the next two months I often called on him, but he argued he didn't want to serve another six months behind bars for perjury and frankly didn't care it the Williams brothers went to the chair.

After months of pastoral calls, though, we became good friends. A lawyer gave me legal papers for him to sign stating he had perjured himself and I convinced him to sign.

The next week I was barred from visiting him, by order of the warden.

I wrote a story for the New York Mirror containing this information, and Alex was furious. Later, at one of the Williams' trials, I was called to witness his change of heart. I witnessed his affidavit and the prosecutor asked questions about our conversations. There is no confidentiality in a prison cell. Neighboring cells had ears and the warden had a way of knowing exactly what was going on.

Under my oath as a minister, I absolutely refused to answer one of the questions, even under threat of going to the New Brunswick county jail. I explained that the reason I violated my clerical oath for the Williams at all was that it was a life-or-death matter. When I stepped down from the witness stand and through the bar, Alex, the tough perjurer, walked over and shook my hand and said, "You're all right kid."

Alex was not the only problem. As I learned more by studying court transcripts in New Jersey, I became convinced beyond any doubt of the Williams' innocence. There were many serious discrepancies in their prosecution.

For example, I learned that on the night of the murder, a police officer in Perth Amboy stopped a yellow car speeding away from the murder scene. The officer asked four youths to get out of the car and noticed a bloody baseball bat lying on the blood stained floor mats. The speeders told him there had been a fight at their school and the officer let them go without even recording their license plate number. Despite many events like this, the Williams brothers were arrested, charged and eventually convicted of the murder.

Their real infraction was keeping bad company with people they didn't know in a community they were visiting fresh out of military duty.

The Williams had been friendly with a man of questionable character who was linked to the murder. It was a terrible injustice by association. Every time I'd visit them in the concrete death house I became more disturbed by the lack of justice for black people.

After a few months of visiting the death house, the warden told me I'd been standing too close to the steel bars of their cell. I deliberately ignored him, shaking hands with men who needed a human hand to touch. They had strong hand grips and could have thumped me against the bars, but caring always involves risks.

When I left New Jersey for my first parish in Montana, we corresponded regularly and Eugene's "letters from prison" had a spiritual depth that must have been inspired by the carpenter's Son who bid us visit prisoners, and later became a victim of false accusations, Himself.

After seven years behind bars, Eugene plead nolo contendere or "non-vult," which meant he would not contest the charges. I wondered if he thought he was pleading "non volts." Bland would not plead anything but absolute innocence.

Eugene was out on parole, but Bland demanded a new trial to prove his innocence and consequently received a life sentence. His shining integrity cost him 17 years behind bars.

Sometimes, Bland sat on the electric chair after showering to tie his shoes just to defy the charges. He had been in the death house so long he built a tolerance for that ugly gray chair.

Shortly after we met, I gave Eugene a Bible. He enrolled in a correspondence course and later said he read the Bible, "until I knew it from Genesis to Revelations." One afternoon I was leaning on the one-inch bars while he gazed at the electric chair. I asked him if he thought he would someday sit there absorbing murderous volts of injustice.

"When I get my time out of the cell for a shower, I often look at the chair, but I know I'll never sit in it when it's hot, because God told me so."

"You didn't tell me God spoke to you," I said. "How did you know it was God?"

"I just woke up early one night. It all made sense to admit there is a much greater and more loving power in the world that would take charge of my life or my death. I said to Jesus, 'You must be the greatest Person in the universe. Please accept my life and do with me what you will.' My life has never been the same. Prison became my college and this cell my chapel. The early saints called their rooms cells. I have everything I need here."

"But how did God speak to you?"

"Later, I had a vision, but it wasn't in a dream or at night. It was like Paul's vision at noon. It happened at 11 o'clock, about the time they serve lunch, and the darkness was so thick in here you could cut it with a knife.

"All of a sudden, I felt something moving toward me through the prison shadows. I heard somebody walking in the dark ... talking. I couldn't understand what they were saying, but they were coming closer and closer. The light became brighter and brighter. When they got beside me, they put their hands on me like this." He gently touched my arm, which was against the bars.

"They were angels from God. There was a bluish light like I've never seen before. One angel spoke to me. 'Eugene you'll be all right. You are going to preach the Gospel.' The angel touched me again, and I never felt nobody touch me like that in my life. That message from God completely changed my outlook.

"I woke up spiritually at that moment, and I've been awake ever since. From then on I wasn't the same no more. That touch — I knew it was from God, — that's when I got stronger and stronger in my belief.

"Now when I read the Bible, God's Spirit guides me and talks to me. In order to get Scriptural messages, you've got to have the Spirit within you, and make room for the good news."

I was transported beyond prison's dismal surroundings into a glorious verdant wilderness for a few blessed moments as Eugene retold his angelic visit, envisioning Christ rescuing a lost sheep from a rustic well. During my summers in the Idaho forests, I came to understand why Jesus loved the wilderness to elevate His vision. Now the same Man from Galilee sent messengers to a prisoners housed in a wilderness of injustice. There are no bunkers too strong or wells too deep for them to penetrate.

I know Eugene's story of the seraphic visit to be true because some preeminent event transformed his life. He never doubted the good news, and even built a makeshift pulpit in his cell to practice preaching the Word. One guard expressed interest in Eugene's new faith, knowing intuitively that something mysterious happened in that cell.

"I told the guards I'm not dying here," Eugene said, " 'cause I've got a job to do and I know nothing could kill me here. Sometimes bad experiences has to happen to get you where God wants you at. So I pray for the people who put me in prison. They hurt themselves, not me."

"One of our hardest tasks is discerning God's Presence in unpleasant events," I said. "We prayed a collect last Sunday that sounds like your experience. 'Purify our conscience, Almighty God, by your daily visitation, that your Son, Jesus Christ, at His Coming, may find in us a mansion prepared for Himself.' "

"God knew without this happening I wouldn't have become awake. At times it seems like this is happening for the worse, but God will turn it into something good. That's the good news."

Eugene's radiance lit up his cell-chapel as he continued, "The Bible says don't do evil for evil, but do good for evil. It's harder to do good for evil than it is to get even. Anybody can fight somebody ... that's easy. But in order for somebody to fight you when you are not going to fight back, that's the hard part."

I got tired standing in front of his steel cage, but I wanted to hear him out. I was hearing the Gospel firsthand. The guard, who was also listening intently to what was being said, generously pulled up a chair for me. Then Eugene changed the subject. He wanted to know what news I could share from his family.

"Have you seen my mother lately?" he asked.

I had visited his mother and his sister the week before.

"Your mom's about the closest image of Jesus' mother I've ever met," I told him. "She's filled with God's love. She believes you're in good hands and you'll be released when the time comes. Every time I see her, she says, 'Leave it to God — He'll work it out.' "

"She's real happy I found my Lord and read the Bible. When I get out, I'll take her to church every Sunday to hear my sermons."

I hoped a time would come when Eugene and I could serve a church together. Each time I left the gray prison fortress, I renewed my determination to seek justice for the Williams brothers. Several opportunities came, including in the Court of Last Resort with the warm support of no less than Earle Stanley Gardner. But the strangest break came years later and was directly related to my job as County Probate Judge.

To improve my legal skills, I studied juvenile law at the University of Nevada in connection with juvenile court judges' programs. During one conference, we were invited to visit the Nugget Casino, whose owner was an alumnus of the University of Idaho and had worked in McCall.

The judges assumed we were old friends, and late one evening I was called to appear at a star-chamber hearing before four other judges in the lounge of our residence. I slowly descended the stairs to see what was expected of me.

I was directed to sit in a chair separate from the others. Judge Bellweather, a high court judge from New Jersey, was first to speak.

Judiciously, and grinning, the judge said, "This high council has met and ruled unanimously that you are to procure six tickets for this weekend's show at the Nugget. Petula Clark is singing, and we want to see her performance. Get us tickets from your friend, or we'll send you to solitary for Saturday night."

When I heard he was a high court judge from New Jersey, I said, "All right, but it will cost you a favor. I have two friends who have spent years in a New Jersey prison. I strongly believe they are innocent and they need help. So far the Court of Last Resort and the Governor of New Jersey have helped. When you go back to New Jersey, will you look into their dilemma for me?"

"You get those tickets, Mark, and I'll review the matter when I get home," Judge Bellweather said. He was serious.

I rounded up tickets for the Petula Clark show.

I took Judge Bellweather seriously, too, reminding him of his good will before I returned to my Judge's office. I pleaded with him to help Bland and Eugene.

Two months later, the judge wrote that he had researched the case and was disturbed by the transcript. I could rest assured, he told me, that he was actively involved. It was more than coincidence that Eugene was released shortly after Judge Bellweather's investigation. A month later, Bland was moved to minimum security.

When the Williams brothers were released from death row, I rejoiced, realizing God was operating in Trenton, New Jersey, via Reno, Nevada.

Some Christians avoid the Petula Clarks and casinos. Some are afraid to live life to the fullest, closing their eyes to God's love in show business. I know God lives in good people in Reno, Nevada, as well as in the rapture of wild creatures in the wilderness. We can't box God up and say He operates only in stained glass arenas or magnificent mountain ranges.

DURING THE NEXT FIRE SEASON THERE WAS MORE GOOD NEWS. In fact, it happened in the Gospel Hump Wilderness Area.

I was late that summer, reporting for duty in August rather than June. A week later I was patrolling for fires along the Salmon river, leaving the McCall airstrip before the sun rose. There had been a series of lightning strikes the night before. Our orders were to fly over the River of No Return area searching for flare ups.

It was no problem spotting small blue smokes aising their dangerous signals. The decision whether to jump or not was based on which smolders might blow up into major fires. If we simply let smaller ones burn themselves out, wildfires might clean up cluttered acres of deadfall, recreating a healthier forest.

We had been airborne three hours, dropping men and equipment along the breaks of the river, when Hawk began to question the wisdom of the extra cup of coffee he had earlier. The old Trimotor was great, but it didn't have a rest room.

"Would anyone near the door like to trade jumps with me?" Hawk joked.

118

His thick glasses, which had a sportsman elastic cord securing them for opening shocks, were beginning to fog up.

"What makes you think you're the only one who had coffee earlier?" Tex yelled back. Tex was now in the door and hoping to find a fire soon for his own relief.

Patrolling the backcountry was sometimes enjoyable, and sometimes boring, but always uncomfortable. The nylon jump suits fit like tight saddle cinches, so we were willing to jump about anywhere. I tried not to focus on my discomfort and instead thought of a recent discussion I'd had with Don Stephens, who was delving more and more deeply into self-understanding.

Don told me, "I attended a workshop where Dr. Jim Bugental quoted Marcel Proust: 'The real voyage of discovery is not in seeking new landscapes, but in having new eyes.' Bugental said we never know what's ahead, but life forces us to leap into the unknown, making the best choices we can, never knowing if they're the best ones. It's like jumping into the unknown, rocky places down there."

As we flew over the ridges of the Salmon River of No Return, searching for lightning strikes, I spotted a family of three white mountain goats running almost vertically up a cliff in the river breaks. It seemed impossible that they could get enough traction to bolt full speed up rocky cliffs, but that's exactly what they were doing.

I wondered whether anyone besides us ever got paid for touring Idaho's grandeur. And when the touring's over, there's something therapeutic about parachuting downwards in a tighter and tighter circle, hitting the spot.

Each time the spotter selected a fire for the next pair, I heaved a big sigh of relief. No matter where we jumped, I felt our jump spot couldn't be as dangerous as the last one.

Where the first team jumped, the turf resembled a giant pile of "pick up sticks" scattered on nature's living room floor. There were dead logs scattered like match sticks on the ground. They "treed up" in medium-height ponderosas so they wouldn't crash into the downed lodgepoles.

The second pair floated over a deep snow field near the top of Gospel Hump and landed precisely near a green bushy area beside an alpine lake in the midst of a summer snow bank. That green and white clearing on the upper side was the only safe jump spot, because bordering the water was a deadly rock slide. They waved their orange streamers as if they had scored a winning touchdown and immediately engaged in a snowball fight.

Don and Larry had an easier place to land, but confronted a more dangerous fire. The fierce flames were burning into a steep grassy area with small gnarled trees exploding. It could detonate into a major project fire like Mann Gulch if they let it spread over the ridge.

We had dropped their cargo when Hawk discovered a small pillar of blue

119

smoke three miles north. We flew over it, found an easy jump zone close by, smiled and relaxed.

"That fire's not going anywhere. It'll be into those rocks in a few hours and probably die by itself," the spotter said. "We'll keep flying north. If we don't discover a really hot fire, we'll come back here for a gravy jump for our philosophers."

In minutes, the pilot located smoke spiraling out of heavy timber on Quartzite Butte, one of the highest peaks in the Gospel Hump Wilderness north of the Salmon River.

We accepted the fact we had no choice, but as much as Hawk could have used some relief, he suddenly had a strong desire to stay airborne. Riding the Trimotor a couple of hundred feet over the rock-studded point didn't help. It was the sort of jump area that you have one chance to hit and that's it.

Sometimes it's a relief when choices don't exist. Hawk cemented faith and courage in the doorway of the Trimotor, ready for duty. Circling high above river rafters spinning around in the white water of the River of No Return, I asked myself why we weren't down there drifting over the rapids. Down there, if we fell off the boat, we'd get wet and that's all. Up here, a miss would be disastrous.

It was such a precarious jump, we decided to exit one at a time rather than going together. Caldwell, the spotter, told us where he expected us to land. Since it was such a dangerous jump, he dropped two sets of streamers to check the wind drift. He pointed out a safety zone if we ran into trouble, welcome news.

We decided the wind was moving away from the river canyon by watching the direction of the drifting smoke. Both streamers verified a drift away from the center of the river. The approach was directly south over the river. We were going to exit directly over the white water.

What a show we'll give the rafters watching us, I thought. It was a great picture for the people on the raft with cameras; a scary picture for two jumpers.

Hawk tightened his leg straps and put his right foot on the door step. Caldwell was completed absorbed in getting the plane in exactly the right place. If the wind let up, Hawk might end up with the happy rafters.

There was a manmade tower looming up on the highest peak. We wanted to avoid hitting it on our way to the jump spot. A long span of rock slides and cliffs stretched between the river and the jump spot. If we soared over the spot, our parachutes would hook up in some ponderosas. That could be highly dangerous, since the ropes in our jump pockets were only 100 feet long. The span between the branches and the bare ground could be more.

The Tin Goose was flying at right angles to the river when Bob cut the engines. In absolute silence, we glided a little farther, soaring like a Canada goose with its wings fully spread. You could hear a pin drop, if it had a place to land.

The silence was broken by Caldwell shouting "Go!" and Hawk plunged into the beautiful abyss.

Hawk had a habit of lunging headfirst into football games with little concern for himself. He also preferred diving toward the ground, while the canopy methodically separated itself from the rubber bands holding it to his backboard.

Once his chute blossomed open, Hawk immediately turned toward the spot. His forward speed carried him toward the old lookout tower. In the still air, he pirouetted once to test his forward speed and then moved parallel with the river until he was about two hundred feet above the spot, safely around the tower. Then he turned left and floated gently in between large rocks and trees. It was a perfect job of chute handling. It looked so easy, I figured even I could do it.

As I tightened up my leg straps and placed my right foot on the step, I thought for a moment, *What if this chute doesn't open, like that experimental one?* The River of No Return might be an appropriate place for my last jump.

When Bob cut the engines for me, there was a refreshing but terrifying pause. Then Caldwell slapped my leg.

Instantly I was the second solo act for the river runners, enjoying the breathtaking view of the Gospel Wilderness Area. Gospel Hump Mountain is an enormous stone mound north of the Salmon River with a mysterious aura encompassing the massive dome.

My chute opened gracefully. I felt like an exuberant eagle, alone in the morning sky, as if I was the eye on the pyramid on the American one-dollar bill, seeing in all directions. I had the whole world in my hands.

Moving toward the small jump location, I saw Hawk folding up his chute, ignoring my flying skills. I tried to hit his L-shaped orange streamer, but a gusty wind came up, and I had to fight with all I had so I wouldn't land in the pines. Grabbing my front lines, I pulled them down as far as I could. This decreased the lift of the chute and allowed me to drop very rapidly. It worked, but I landed like a ton of bricks.

Aﬞ FTER EVERY LANDING, I PAUSE AND THANK GOD FOR TWO THINGS; for being alive and being a smokejumper. There is a euphoric feeling following the completion of a dangerous parachute ride. You feel unified with every living being and that everything is right with the world. I felt I could accomplish anything.

The fire was up in a rocky area where plants grew out of the duff and rocks and no dirt. When we stirred it up, the duff and old pine needles ignited like a rolled newspaper sparking a fire in a fireplace. We worked and worked. We shoveled and carried burning embers to the rocks to burn out. We stomped on small smokes until our boots felt like Pele, the Hawaiian god of fire, had attached flames to our feet. We cut trees with our axes and removed the fuel.

When there were no hints of smoke, we lay down in the shade and enjoyed pineapple juice. After a sip or two, more light blue smokes surfaced. We tried everything, but nothing was suppressing the fire. This relentless game continued until the evening temperature cooled down affording us some relief.

We ate a cold dinner and watched crisp bright stars appear against a black sky. Imagine being paid for enjoying a view on top of the world in the most beautiful area in America! The starlit silhouettes of six mountain ridges suggested the leading edges of holy backdrops on a huge reredos behind a living altar.

"Why is this called Gospel Hump?" I asked.

"Gospel Hump rises over the other naves in our natural cathedral, emanating peace and goodness. Perhaps it is named Gospel Hump because it symbolized a peaceful window above a violent world for the early explorers and that was good news ... like the Gospel. In order to grasp this good news, we need to crank open windows of gratitude. Unless people express gratitude in all their journeys in life, they'll miss the good news of the Master Sculptor."

I took the tin pot sitting on a smoldering hot spot and poured us each a cup of coffee as I reflected on some clear windows of gratitude in my life.

"No matter how many summers we hike around, you can't avoid feeling thankful when you're out here," I said.

"Remember my namesake at Whitehawk?" Hawk asked. "Hawks in flight, riding air currents, are motionless, yet in motion. Isn't that a good description of relaxing here on Gospel Hump? In perfect stillness, we're moving spiritually. Spiritually, the stillness of God frees us to act on good choices. Healthy freedom precedes good character."

"Do you remember watching our pet bobcat make choices when you were at our home last week?" I asked.

"What's that got to do with this?"

"Benjamin's actions are directly related to his freedom. When we try to confine him, his potential to make good decisions is injured. When he is absolutely free and acting instinctively, there is no limit to his ability to act wisely. I think faith is like that. When we freely relinquish our need to confine choices to earlier prejudices, we're ready to move ahead."

"Prayer is movement," Hawk said. "A person afraid to move into uncertainty is bogged. A person may seek absolute certainty, but he's not going very far for the Lord."

"The only purely certain person I ever knew was six feet underground and quite motionless. Being alive requires movement, which involves plenty of risks," I said.

"One of my goals," Hawk said, "is to be in harmony with spiritual movement. Feel that breeze coming up from the river? There's movement everywhere in the wilderness. Here, our personal stream of consciousness can blend with a larger spirit if we allow it.

"We didn't merely observe rafts running the river when we jumped. There were people on those rafts. People are living rafts moving through the ups and downs of life's rapids. We don't know where spiritual currents are leading, but ultimately, faith will guide our movement to something good."

It was a good time to retire. I meandered down to check the fire lines for flare-ups, grateful for the limitless goodness encircling our camp on Gospel Hump.

I spread my sleeping bag on a soft mattress of thick layers of duff I had built earlier in the day. After reliving the exciting jump over the Salmon, I slept soundly, harmonized with the whole planet.

Early the next morning, the pine tree that lightning had shattered began emitting flames near its mangled top. We didn't have a 'Swede Fiddle,' (a cross-cut saw) so we had to chop it down with a pulaski. We flipped a coin to see which woodsman would chop through the thick butt. I lost, and it resulted in much more work than discussing the philosophy of goodness.

In the heat of afternoon, we rested to be refreshed in order to labor into the night. A solitary rain cloud appeared miles away, maybe as far away as Central Oregon. It was the only cloud on the horizon.

"Hawk, you believe. Pray that cloud over here with a little helpful moisture. That's the only way the fire will go out."

I laughed and stretched out on the warm duff to doze.

Hawk was a virtuoso of humor and this struck him funny. If humor is essential to human spirituality, wouldn't the Creator enjoy comedy? God answers all sorts of prayers. Who determines what's acceptable? Hawk began praying the little bundle of rain our way.

Before I went to sleep, I told Hawk about the Idaho preacher who was asked to pray for rain, The crops were parched, but when Sunday came, he forgot to pray for a cloudburst. As the parishioners were leaving church, an old farmer asked why he didn't pray for rain. Thinking quickly, he replied, "Because you didn't bring your umbrella."

"Humor is part of God's great design," Hawk said. "Out here it's impossible to take yourself too seriously."

Hawk's delightful prayer began with gratitude for the Gospel Hump Mountains. Then he joked a bit about getting that gray rain cloud exactly over the fire, mirroring Jesus' marvelous sense of humor. High upon the pristine pinnacle we basked in the Idaho sun, enveloped by the music of the spheres. Maybe natural rhapsodies inspired melodies from Bach, Beethoven and Mozart.

A radial engine suddenly intruded on our natural solitude, blaring a disharmonic crescendo, interrupting our siesta with its distinctive drone. A Travelaire, black and orange like a Princeton Tiger, was prowling around the Idaho sky. We didn't have a radio, but we hoped to receive a message; or better, two steaming T-bone steaks, baked Idaho potatoes, fresh bread and cherry pie. That would be highly unusual for a two-man fire, but this was an exceptional fire, in one of the highest chapels in Idaho's bioscathedral.

We raced to the top of the ridge near the lookout to see who was approaching. The answer was no one. Mary Kay was pulling away. After climbing the makeshift old tower, built during World War I, we watched her deposit two jumpers five miles downriver. She headed back toward McCall … no messages and no piping hot dinner.

A stiff breeze blew across the creaky platform. I noticed Hawk's rain cloud was fast approaching us from Oregon.

"Look! Your prayers are working, Hawk. Your cloud is moving this way like you had remote control. I better find my umbrella."

THERE IS MORE TO PRAYER THAN HUMANS IMAGINE. People forget to pray when they're in a delightful mood. God must receive a lot of dull prayers and no doubt enjoys jovial ones occasionally.

I watched the little, gray, puffy mass move our way with clear sky in every other direction, hoping it would not avoid us like the Travelaire.

"Hawk, if we get rain from that Oregon cloud today, you can preach during our highfalutin liturgy next Sunday."

Gripping the rusty cable handrail 24 feet above the ground, we might have been safer flying high over the canyon than standing on top of the makeshift tower. Yet, the timbers which held the observation tower together for many years were still strong and firm. There were eight poles, two stories high, cabled together with wooden crossbeams. The stairway was still serviceable, although a few steps were missing and others dangled on rusty nails.

We stood silently, awed by the grandeur of the Salmon River breaks far below us. We sensed our mortal lives, like the old fire turret, were temporary in comparison with the panorama of granite mileposts outlined by the river. Untamed ambiance urged nature's hymns to surge through natural organ pipes of hollow yellow pines with branches for reeds. The old Gospel lookout reverberated like an organ in a drafty choir loft.

I thoroughly enjoyed heavenly moments like this with my companion, Hawk. I enjoyed sharing my wild rapture because he never put down philosophical thoughts. He surprised me more than once by responding with an understanding of life much deeper and richer than any wisdom I had ever tuned into.

Carefully we worked our way down the wobbly steps. Hawk found the outlets for a hand crank phone near the bottom step. We looked for the phone, but couldn't find one.

We did find a small, windowless cabin hidden behind some trees not far from the base of the tower. It had not weathered the years as well as the tower. The roof still held together because it was built with hand-split shingles three inches thick. The walls had tumbled down on two sides. Ironically the moss-covered door was still in place, swinging noisily back and forth on rusty hinges.

Hawk stood at the entrance like a steel-helmeted doorman at the Portland Hilton, inviting me to enter. I saluted, but didn't tip him, and proudly stepped onto the broken floor boards. There were piles of old magazines dating from 1918. Several had been protected by old boards and were readable. We scanned *Country Farmers* and *Saturday Evening Posts*. I noticed others dated in the early '40s. This lookout had been active during World War II. I found a large green book under the magazines entitled, *A Saga of the Sawtooths*, by Hank Senger, and we headed out the door,.

A S I STEPPED OUT THE DOOR, a small rattlesnake raced out from under a broken board in the porch in my direction. Without hesitation, I stepped on the confused serpent right behind its dangerous little head. Smokejumper loggers are made with steel shanks in the soles. I felt safe as long as I kept him pinned down. Then, I glimpsed what I thought was another rattler moving near my feet. It turned out to be the tail of the same 16-inch snake, so I placed my other boot on his tail section.

It was a very young rattler, but I knew he was poisonous. The little serpent's "neck" was between my heel and sole so he was pinned down, but not suffocating. The way he was jumping around gave me the impression he was not a happy camper.

Hawk looked around his feet to see if he was also into snakes. He was safe and began laughing. "I've never known anyone to get into such ridiculous predicaments as you, Davis. I'll get a stick to hold his head down so you can move away safely.

"Don't move … don't run off. I'll be right back. Let me know if his big brother comes along while I'm gone."

I always liked snakes, but this was a little too cozy for comfort.

"Hurry up Hawk! What if I get a cramp or his family shows up?"

I waited a long time — at least it seemed like a long time — balancing my weight on one foot and then the other, heads or tails. It was a humorous situation, but if I took a hit there was no way to signal for help other than intentionally stirring up the fire so the patrol planes would notice a blow up.

Hawk took forever getting a stick. My legs started trembling. I was afraid to run, knowing the snake could move his head faster than I could push off. Throwing a rock, I might miss the rattler and smash my foot.

This cabin was the snake's home. I didn't wish him harm, but I nervously reconsidered my ethic of never deliberately causing harm to any living creature.

I didn't want to kill the agitated little serpent, so I conceived of a brilliant plan. I would crouch down and, with all my strength, jump as high as I could and land on the two-foot rock ledge in front of the cabin. Upon landing, I would run as fast as Mercury. No snake could go that fast even if he was very mad. Besides, he probably wanted out of the uncomfortable situation more than anyone.

I counted "one … two … three," and with all the nervous strength the adrenaline flooding my system provided, I lifted off that snake like a space shot toward the moon. I must have leaped four feet into the air, landing on the ledge and never looking back.

As I rounded the corner near the lookout tower, I saw Hawk had found a forked stick, all right. It was about six feet long and he was down near the fire holding it high above him, like Moses raising a staff in the Exodus, pointed toward the cloud. He had forgotten about my reptilian ordeal.

"Look," he said, "that little cloud's going to pass right over us and dowse the fire, even though the sun is shining all around us. God responds to all kinds of prayers,"

Hawk was rather pleased.

"We ought to pray more to preserve the goodness of the wilderness."

Neither of us mentioned the snake.

THE SERENDIPITY OF GRACE is the fact that God would care about our situation when there's appalling violence in the world. With so much suffering in the world, Almighty God still respond to prayers for rain. This is more than coincidence. If all God cared about was tragedy, he would be incomplete. God is empathic to all phases of life, sorrowful or joyful.

I studied the graceful movement of the cloud. God enjoys His wilderness much like He loves the people He created. The cloud appeared more businesslike as it got closer. A faint rainbow accompanied it, melting colors into the astonishing scenery.

We ran back to our camp and spread a reserve chute between several small trees, forming a splendid tent. In a minute or two, without a whisper of wind, we were in the midst of a warm summer downpour. The whole dynamic was too powerful for words, so we sat quietly pondering the power of prayer.

The solid soaking put the fire out for good. We poked our heads out into the purified air and walked through the thoroughly soaked duff. We were a bit stunned.

"There's not much to do now till the packer gets up here," Hawk said. "I want to be alone for awhile."

It was a good time to separate and soak up the vital spiritual friendship between good humor and good happenings.

After a couple hours of pure relaxation, we were invigorated enough to begin preparing dinner. We were down to our last rations and thankful this pesky fire was finished. We carefully found some dry boards under the lookout and sparked a fire.

As our dinner warmed up, we began to talk for the first time since the wonderful shower.

"Hey Hawk, let me read to you from *A Saga of the Sawtooths*, the book I found in the rattlesnake cabin. Hank Senger, an Idaho author, had a great sense of humor. He described wildlife out here that I never knew existed."

"Like what?"

"Here's a picture of a Mug-wump. He appears to be a moose with a bushy tail sitting right on the top of a sharp peak. Senger says, 'For weeks at a time he sits upon the high mountain ridges, with his mug on one side and his wump on the other, meditating on the cosmos.' "

We skimmed through the pictures together.

"How about this friendly cuss, who never makes a fuss, named the Whangdoodle:

> *Half human, half brute, he's a dandy,*
> *With skill that's plum cute he's most handy*
> *At carving great mountains,*
> *Turning rivers to fountains,*
> *Building lakes with big beaches so sandy."*

We laughed at such wilderness characters as the Whizzer Snifter who sawed trees for the smell of fresh sawdust. One enormous animal, called the Ithykasookus, resembled a dinosaur. He featured telescoping legs that enabled him to walk evenly over mountains and valleys.

> *Of all the strange palookas, the Ithykasookus*
> *Intrigues me the most I confess;*
> *He drinks from the showers; his food is fair flowers;*
> *He's loved for his true friendliness.*

Then there was the Idaho Side-Hill Gouger, whose left legs were twice as long as the others, enabling him to run around hillsides ... but, like people who can't change their minds, it can only travel in one direction.

The Wampus Cat, with its telescoping arm, concluded our exploration of Hank Senger's wilderness mythology. Sometimes it would be handy to have his extendible and retractable arm while reaching for fried chicken at church potlucks.

Hawk lit up like a meteor. "I've got a great idea. Let's tell the new smokejumpers these critters actually live near the Salmon River and are seen only by the most perceptive campers. We'll give them directions on how to avoid Side-Hill Gougers and speak to the Whangdoodles. I can hardly wait to get back.

"But, I didn't hear anything about young rattlesnakes."

"I've got a Hindu story for you about a converted serpent," he said.

"There was a ferocious snake biting everyone who came his way. A gentle man passed by and the snake discerned he was a holy man and declined to bite him. The holy man convinced the serpent to live peaceably and never bite anyone. The snake was so impressed, he made a decision to be a peacemaker.

127

"The snake began a pacific life, never harming anyone. Soon people didn't fear him any longer and began harassing him. They even tied tin cans to his tail. His life became miserable.

"A month later, when the sage appeared, he was deeply moved by the bruised condition of the snake. The snake told him what happened. The holy man replied that while we are not to harm others, it's all right to hiss now and then.

"Balance in everything is the key to a quality life."

AFTER FINISHING DINNER, as the sun brushed crimson shadows on nature's stately steeples, I walked up to the ridge to simply "be."

Silence is a refreshing gift of the wilderness. A gentle gust of wind whisked a few pine needles over a downed log I stepped over. A green branch rubbed against a trunk of another tree, and a red-breasted nuthatch fluttered somewhere.

The evening star appeared clear and bright, as if electrified by an enormous universal power station. I could envision the star over Bethlehem, complementing the conjunction of Jupiter, Mars and Saturn generating the holy light of nativity.

I sat on an old log about three feet thick. There was a chipmunk feverishly moving near the stump end. Chipmunks have two speeds … motionless or approaching the speed of light. Occasionally he would stop, perk up his little ears and listen. It was so peacefully quiet that I could hear his tiny feet racing across the old bark.

The sun descended and the stars ascended and I heard my favorite sound of the wild country; a great horned owl beginning a concert. Mozart can not improve the timing of the owl's extended hoots. There are almost always three, long, effortless hoots followed by a long pause.

On this enchanted evening near Gospel Hump, the owl soloed in a forest evensong. It was too dark to see him, but I felt he was sitting on the rail of the lookout. His charming voice carried for miles, with no imitations from jumpers, who often hoot to communicate. The owl, chipmunk and I were all one in a natural pew . I felt saturated by the universal good news like the generosity of the rain cloud. Enfolded by the rhythm of owl's arias, I prepared to meditate on the Gospel, the good news.

There was much good news in my past friendships with owls. I learned to imitate the great horned owl who lived in the poplar trees above our farm home. My children loved going into the yard at night to hoot with him. His solos above our house, like the carillon on the University of Idaho campus, chimed, "all is well."

Often, at our white house with the black shutters, I went outside and meditated on a stone wall constructed from table rock sandstone. On special occasions, the owl would descend to a lower branch and join my contemplation.

One night I was meditating on that rock wall, and a whole group of puffy round hoot owls roosted beside me.

After two years of friendship with the great horned owl, an irritable person living on the farm shot that magnificent winged friend. Mordred, the man in charge, said the owl killed one of his dairy cats. When we complained, the relatives agreed with Mordred.

I discovered higher values permeated God's wilderness than did our relative's farm. Out here, the beautiful wild owl was safe on the old lookout from Mordred mentality. I hoped he would sing forever.

As I thought about our friend owl, there was a long quiet pause. I tried hooting to the owl on the rail and he politely responded, in his own time. Then to my surprise, another owl joined the choral meditation. It sounded like the baritone and tenor duet in Bizet's opera, *Pearlfishers*. In that opera, two men find out they are in love with the same woman, which creates problems. Were these two owls courting the same female?

With two feathered friends singing in the background, I decided it was a good time to meditate on the good news. The only passage about owls in Scripture I remembered was in Zephaniah. He was upset with the direction his nation was headed when he said, "The owl shall hoot in the window, the raven croak at the threshold."

That didn't exactly fit my situation.

The music of the owls produced a mysterious mantra. I was humming *Shaéem, Elo'héem,* and *Christéem* and the ancient meaning of *Elohim* surfaced. It referred to God's Majesty as "the divine plurality in unity," reflecting God's love for all living creatures. *El Shaddai*, a name for God from early Old Testament times, means "God of the mountains." The lofty concept was highly appropriate but not a good mantra for meditation.

Perhaps thinking like Zephaniah, I brooded about the future of America, aware that God wanted me to work to nurture justice. I was elected probate judge while I continued serving as a priest. I blended these ethical vocations into one ministry.

After the elevated concert by the owls, the last verse of Zephaniah slipped into my awareness. "At that time I will bring you home."

My goal was to work for justice and dwell in the house of the Lord forever. As it says in Proverbs "By wisdom a house is built, and by understanding it is established … "

In hallowed darkness I found my way back to camp for repose in my wilderness home, where justice penetrates every aspect of life.

THE NEXT AFTERNOON, I CLIMBED THE CREAKY STAIRS TO THE LOOKOUT DECK to see if there was any sign of the packer coming. Soon the tower began shaking and Hawk appeared on the observation deck with me.

"Mark, are you hungry?"

"Yeah, why do you ask?"

"You'll have to stand here with your mouth open for a long time before a duck flies in. Let's go fix lunch."

A large bird with long, pointed tail flew by at great speed. We watched it become a speck over the river.

"I think that was a pheasant," Hawk said

"We had of a ring-necked pheasant in our yard at the white house. He had a crimson face above a dark green neck with a white clerical collar. The kids called him 'Reverend Ring-neck.'

"Reverend Ring-neck came to our yard every morning for a handout of cracked corn. He would crow, or actually, cackle, and pound his wings every time before it rained. When the bobcat was gone, he'd come right up on the front porch."

"I hope you were in a game preserve," Hawk said.

"We were, but it didn't protect 'Reverend Ring-neck'. My relatives believe they are above the law. They blasted Reverend Ring-neck with a 12-gauge near our front yard, spraying shot all over the place. Bill Pogue from Idaho Fish and Game, answered my call for help. He wanted to get a search warrant and arrest the shooters. When we talked it over, we decided to let it go, and try improving family relations. Besides, I didn't want relatives appearing in my court.

"I came home for lunch shortly after that to learn one of them shot our great horned owl. Driving down Van Geekherdt Lane, I noticed a big lump along the road. I stopped and picked up our magnificent opera singer with a bullet hole through his chest."

"It's hard for me to comprehend why some people are bent on destroying nature," Hawk said.

"It's hard to talk about," I said. "The worst happened last spring when they killed Scott's bobcat, Benjamin. I tried to get a search warrant to locate his pelt, but going against the status quo was futile. Since Dad died last year our incredible paradise has become paradise lost. The development company board of directors made important business decisions without informing me, and at my expense. When I objected, they voted me off the board."

"Don't you own the development land?" he asked.

"I thought so, but when Dad died, I found out we were trusting them too much. I cooperated 100 percent in developing a fine residential community. Long- term profits were to come at the end of the project in the choice 10 acres in the center of the project. Our plan was to build apartments, owned by all the family, around the Van Geekherdt homestead."

"My brother and his kids schemed together and snatched the 10 acres for themselves, cutting my family out. It was apparent they planned this grab throughout the development ,while we invested our effort and money in front-end costs in good faith."

"Maybe your beautiful house is not your real home," Hawk said as he searched the magnificent horizon for the packer. "This may be your real home, and all living things inhabiting this wilderness, your family. The Gospel says whoever willingly leaves a house will get back much more. Relinquish the idea that possessions are permanent, and accept the truth that we all abide in one universal home." Hawk said.

Hawk's vision was usually a light year ahead of mine.

"It's just a lot harder to relinquish houses, businesses, and even feelings, than it is to acquire them," I said, but the injustice of my relatives seemed to pale as I considered the invaluable living things in the wilderness.

What are you going to do?" Hawk asked.

"I've decided to put the house up for sale. I'll grieve the loss of my home, and pray that God will unveil a new dream. It's the land I loved since childhood, but my real home transcends Idaho and goes beyond this world. It's unclear now, but someday I'll know."

"Life isn't fair," Hawk said. "It's never easy to accept injustice. It's easier to accept hurts and pain than injustice you can't change. You must learn the Williams brothers' art of unconditional forgiveness and move toward whatever God has planned for you."

What are your plans?" I asked.

"Mary Kay and I agree Idaho may only be our temporary home, too. I may begin coaching high school football this fall, but I believe something far greater may be ahead. I love returning to Idaho in the summer to parachute and be with my dear backcountry pilot and the smokejumpers, but I have compelling things to accomplish beyond Idaho. The wilderness is my favorite home, but my mission goes far beyond it. I want the world to know God dwells in ordinary persons of good will, transforming the world through His image."

Below us, dust rose from the trail leading to the lookout.

"Here comes Packer John and his string of mules to escort us back to the ordinary."

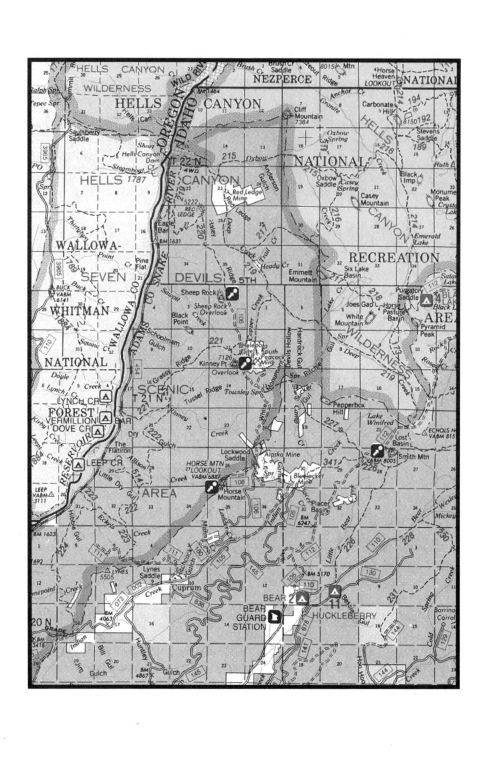

HELLS CANYON

THE SEVEN DEVILS MOUNTAINS

THE SEVEN SQUAD WAS PREPARING FOR WEEKEND STANDBY on a Friday so hot and dry that road dust was looking for shade. It was too hot to play volleyball, and the limited shade from three tall spruce trees had been staked out by Phil, Nick and Larry.

Friday afternoons were golden opportunities to earn overtime while relaxing around jump headquarters like city firemen waiting for a weekend call. If we were lucky we'd be dispatched to a fire, and earn even more money, but with no lightning strikes for three weeks, we had little hope to be in the woods for the weekend. Hunting season, which usually started a few fires, was still a month away.

Marvin Caldwell and Hawk muscled their way into the coolest spots on a shaded patch of lawn near the kitchen and were discussing philosophy. Caldwell was doing most of the discussing and a half-awake Hawk most of the listening, but soon the rest of the squad crowded in to hear the dialogue.

Earlier in the week, some of the men got into a heated argument about overtime pay. Nick said everyone ought to get extra pay, not just the men on the top of the jump list. He and a big kid from Oregon almost came to blows before Hawk stepped in between them and said, "Come on guys, we're all hot and short-tempered. Shake hands and let's be thankful we have jobs in the woods."

"Something doesn't balance out with your gentle faith and rugged lifestyle, Hawk," Caldwell was saying. "As a football player at Iowa you were trained to knock the opponent around the turf in very rough fashion."

When the subject of football came up, Tex became alert.

"He had a job to do and one means was to hit harder than his opponent," Tex said.

"Call it autonomy or whatever you like, but respect for others implies treating them as ends, not as means," Caldwell said. "True sportsmanship requires that all players be treated with dignity."

Hawk smiled with his eyes closed.

"Just let a tight end come across the line with the ball, and I'll treat him all right, as long as I can flatten him."

"Hawk's right, respect comes from strength," Tex added.

A wide grin stretched out under Hawk's heavy duty glass frames.

"Marvin, we ought to receive college credit for listening to your philosophy every summer. Give me an 'A' on Kant's categorical imperative ... 'Cherish others as ends, not as means for your own gains. Love people, and use things.' How am I doing?"

Caldwell sat up a little straighter. "You put your finger on a paradox I want to explore.

"The key to life lies within us, not in the environs, but natural surroundings enhances life's purpose. The forest evokes a reckless spirit of adventure, like the exhilaration generated in a football game. Nature's wildness strips away pretenses and reveals our gentler side. Urban society lacks this native gentleness, and as a result, people confuse wildness with violence.

"Hawk, here, exemplifies a gentle wildness, or is it a wild gentleness?

"Thoreau said, 'In wildness is the preservation of the world.' If our unhewn inner character — the animating force of who we are — could be drenched in the gentle wildness of nature, we would live in peace."

Marvin was talking to Hawk but reflecting on his own character. He was a gentle, even shy, intellectual who could press 325 pounds. Some old jumpers referred to him respectfully as "the Bear."

It was fitting because Marvin liked to wrestle bears.

Ivan Borsky often brought a medium-sized black bear named Igor to McCall in August, during huckleberry season. The bear wrestled local loggers and other crazies for money, which provided a living for Ivan, and fresh berries for Igor.

Ivan would set up a little boxing ring near the lake on a beach sand mat and everyone was offered a chance to pin the bear for five seconds.

The bear came out in bright red boxing shorts with a leather muzzle he managed to use like a hammer. Ivan took side bets on how long it would take Igor to win. It didn't take very long, averaging less than five minutes per surrender ... by pinning, not slugging. "Never slug the bear" was a ground rule meant to protect opponents' heads. Wise people wrestled bears with gentle respect.

A year earlier the professor had bet Ivan that he could pin Igor. Caldwell knew the bear was getting older. He thought this might be the year he could beat him. Handing Ivan a 20 dollar bill, he leaped into the ring while the bear was half asleep.

Any philosopher ought to know the maxim about letting a sleeping dog lie.

Marvin looked like a giant beside the little, cuddly bear. He began by giving Igor a bear hug, trying to throw him on his back. The sleepy bear pinched his arm so hard that Caldwell only had one good arm for the rest of the fight.

Caldwell, cheered on by the crowd as "Aristotle," was angry.

"That's unfair, Ivan. You have to forfeit the match. When I finish pinning your bear, I'm coming for you !"

The patient bear instinctively and methodically wore Caldwell down. He almost had the man pinned, but Caldwell blew in his ear. That startled the bear, he loosened his grip, and mankind came close to victory; but the bear began spiraling and spun Caldwell into the hot sand. With both front paws, Igor held the airborne philosopher down. Igor was declared the winner and given a cupful of huckleberries.

Hawk had also wrestled the bear over the years. As the bear got older, Hawk would say, "I'll get you next year." That didn't work because Ivan trained younger bears which made quicker moves.

Ivan had not come to McCall this summer, much to Caldwell's relief. Hawk's bear wrestling tournaments were over, too, because of his deepening friendship with Mary Kay. Hawk could stand up to a bear, but melted around his lovely friend.

"How's your left arm this year, Marvin? Igor squeezed it pretty hard," Tex teased.

"Hold up, Tex. You're not armed for the battle of wits. My arm hurts a little, but my pride hurts more. Animals never posture, never try being something they aren't. Humans pretend they are about everything under the sun, seeking endless approval. I should have respected that wild creature as an end — for being a bear — not a means to prove my strength. As strong as he was, he was still gentle with me."

"Remember the angel who spoke to Eugene Williams in prison?" I asked. "You'd expect a gentle messenger from God to appear in a lovely church building, not on death row. The very idea is rather powerful, isn't it?"

"Can anyone prove an angel spoke to him?" Caldwell asked.

"Are philosophers able to disprove the presence of God ?" Hawk asked.

Caldwell said, "The mystery about you, Hawk, is this: A tough guy like you could do about whatever you pleased, but you live by universal principles. I've never seen you engage another person with anything but gentle respect. 'Tough-But-O-So Gentle'. Many people do what's right because of fear. You just do it."

"Christians I've known who meditate regularly, are often quiet, unassuming people who are willing to risk tough sledding by doing what's right," I said. "Real power and gentleness go hand in hand."

Caldwell was gearing up for another discussion, but we were spared when the tower buzzer broke our quiet setting with two sharp blasts.

"A two-manner, Davis," Hawk shouted, "We've got it made in the shade. We'll have the fire out by midnight and enjoy a paid weekend in the mountains. I've packed extra fresh food for a wilderness stew. Let's go!"

He ran for the ready shack. "Marve, if Mary Kay isn't our pilot, tell her I'll be on a fire over the weekend."

"Marvin, tell Lynn I'm getting rich on a gravy jump and will be home in a few days." Running at full speed behind Hawk, I was elated. Friday jumps were best.

Wayne Weber was waiting for us, and I was not blissful very long.

"Where's the fire?" we both asked at the same time.

"First the good news," Weber said. "A team from Shell Oil is making a movie about parachuting. They want to film you parachuting into Hells Canyon. They have a Cessna and will fly along side the Travelaire for the pictures."

Hawk clipped his reserve chute to the front of his harness.

"I suppose the bad news is having to jump into Hells Canyon."

"Yeah, this could be a very dangerous jump. Be careful to stay away from the high cliffs near the canyon walls. We've dropped jumpers there before, so I know you can do it. Besides, you're going to be movie stars. Congratulations."

Mary Kay had the Travelaire warmed up by the time we got to the airport. The old airplane's black wings and orange body glistened in the sun. Mary Kay powered the Travelaire off the gravel runway and up about 3,000 feet. There, we easily distinguished the Seven Devils Mountain Peaks, with a grandeur like the Swiss Alps. In minutes we were flying below those peaks over an abyss deeper than Grand Canyon.

Flying among the Seven Devils, we searched for the fire. The view of the peaks was breathtaking. Twin Imps was the closest peak and beyond it were Mt. Belial, The Ogre, The Goblin, He Devil, She Devil and the Tower of Babel. These names did not give a jumper much confidence.

HAWK USUALLY LOOKED FOR ELK HERDS BELOW US or wondered whether this would be the fire where he would encounter a mountain lion, but today he was silent. Flying across the deepest ravine in America on your way to a fire is one thing. Finding a safe place to parachute into it, is another.

The fire was burning on Granite Creek above the barren, steep, rocky slopes that border the Snake River, and not spreading rapidly. Settlers who farmed the area in the 1800s called it Horse Heaven and abandoned it long ago.

I was scared, but I wouldn't admit it, and couldn't joke about it. I did manage to ask Weber how we would get out of the Seven Devils area after the fire was out.

"Don't worry about losing any overtime. A packer will come in for you in three days and we'll see you back at camp on Tuesday. Enjoy the scenery. This jump will be a piece of cake. One of my most pleasant jumps was below the Seven Devils, and I'm here to talk about it," he said.

Then he added, "They did have to carry Glen Beasley out on a stretcher from the base of He Devil."

Weber thoroughly ignored our apprehension.

"Look over to the south. There's a herd of elk in that dense group of Douglas fir. And down that ravine there's a herd of domestic sheep,"

"Look straight ahead!" I shouted, "That craggy gorge must be 7,500 feet deep."

Mary Kay flew beside She Devil and Twin Imps peaks, rising over 9,000 feet into the cloudless mountain air. We flew over old mining claims and deteriorating log cabins. The rimrock and alpine lakes below were breathtaking.

Mary Kay began a steep descent as we examined the small, blue smoke spiraling upward. We saw water birch and white alder directly below us, but we could barely distinguish a blaze. The movie makers, who wanted a dramatic fire roaring out of control, were disappointed. We liked the idea of being movie stars, but we were delighted with this small, innocent fire.

The Nez Perce wintered by the river for the relatively mild climate and abundance of game. Their horses grazed in the lush grass in Horse Heaven 150 years before Lewis and Clark's men crawled through the greasewood and mountain mahogany.

A Nez Perce legend describes a vision of seven dancing devils appearing to a lost Indian in this area. As we flew by, I renewed my commitment to Christ, sovereign over any spirits dancing below.

We made several sweeps to the Oregon side of the canyon where Douglas firs and ponderosa pines received more moisture and were larger. When the small Shell Oil plane pulled up beside us, the photographer looked more than a little air sick.

Mary Kay signaled Weber to come up to the cockpit and consider a jump spot below Twin Imps Peak, some distance away from the other peaks. Wayne preferred a meadow near the thin wisp of blue smoke arising from a family of alpine firs near a small lake.

"The fire's smoldering in the greasewood and creeping among the rocky cliffs below," he said. "We'll put you right in the meadow."

I had always worried about parachuting near Hells Canyon. Now, almost ready to jump, I was more relaxed than I expected We had flown so long, I was ready to jump anywhere, even between the Twin Imps Peaks.

The devilish names of the surrounding peaks seemed completely inappropriate. We were parachuting into a perfectly-landscaped, living cathedral.

The conditions were perfect for pictures but less than perfect for parachuting. A strong wind was blowing away from the canyon across the meadow up the hill, but since it was predictable, we knew we could make it. Mary Kay radioed the other plane and explained we would exit over the Snake River and a steady wind would draw us back to the colorful meadow below the gray peaks. People observing the movie could envision us jumping in the middle of the Swiss Alps, which pleased the camera crew from Shell Oil.

Once the jumping begins, the spotter, not the pilot, directs the flight. Weber told Mary Kay to fly directly into the wind over the selected jump spot. About a quarter of a mile later, he dropped two drift streamers. We watched them blow over the proposed jump spot, confirming the strength of the wind.

"Normally we wouldn't jump in this much wind," Wayne said, "we'd come back this evening. But, here's a chance to be movie stars. If you are short of the meadow, you might get smashed up, but it's up to you. What do you want to do?"

Hawk knew our nylon jump suits would float if we hit in the lake bordering the meadow. He voted to go ahead and asked for my opinion. I said I was going so I could tell my kids I was in the movies, though we both knew the film crew couldn't get close enough to reveal our nervous faces behind the steel meshed helmets.

I spoke to Weber one more time.

"What if the wind stops while we're in the air directly over Hell's Canyon? It's a long ways to the Snake River, and there's no safe area to land. If we pounded into the cliffs and rolled to the bottom, there'd be no reason to look for us."

"Look down there at the smoke. See how it moves almost parallel to the contour of the hill. I don't expect it to stop right away."

"Let's go for it," I said. "Weber, you can have my autograph when the movie comes out,."

I was trying to convince myself I wasn't terrified. Hells Canyon is narrower than the Grand Canyon, and from our airborne perch, it portended to be more formidable.

Hawk had faced danger many times. I hoped the cameras could capture the sheer determination behind his steel face mask. He carefully waited in the doorway with both feet on the wide step under the door of the Travelaire, winking at the pretty pilot. She flew directly over the Snake River thousands of feet below, and cut the engine. Hawk leaped out the door head first, like an Olympic diver going for the gold. I watched his feet as he entered Hells Canyon headfirst.

I was existentially involved in the success of his descent as his chute billowed open and he turned toward the meadow.

Weber looked at the terrified expression on my face.

"Relax. He'll get into the meadow all right."

We watched him spiral several times near the spot, knowing he had plenty of drift to clear the unforgiving cliffs on the eastern slopes of the canyon.

About 500 feet above the ground he turned directly toward the alpine lake. It appeared he actually wanted to splash down into the wavy blue water, proving the new nylon suits could float. He spiraled once more and landed right in the middle of the water. We watched in amazement.

It was a strange water landing. His shoulders surfaced immediately and he waved his orange streamer, half-submerged in the oscillating shallow water. We wondered if the Shell crew thought smokejumpers like landing in water or if they thought Hawk was giving them an extra gusto for their movie.

Weber checked my buckles and lines and said, "I'll let you off exactly in the same place, but avoid the water."

The water I wanted to miss at that moment was a roaring current in the Snake River 6,000 feet directly below.

I sat on the edge of the door with both feet firmly planted on the step. I was staring right at The Tower of Babel when the engine stopped. There was a two-second pause that lasted forever. Then Wayne slapped my leg.

"Go!"

I yelled "Geronimo" and leaped into an alpine chapel in Idaho's bioscathedral.

I wasn't cut out for movies. Something went wrong. I fell over backwards, staring at the Travelaire as my chute deployed. When the canopy caught air, my feet were directly above me, where my head should have been, and it jerked me around like a calf caught in the cowboy's rope.

Tremendous force swung me completely around like a trapeze star swinging back and forth, and for an instant, I was higher than the canopy. Fortunately, I slowed down the oscillation without getting any lines tangled up.

I had dropped several hundred feet and had to work hard to fly to the meadow. I "airplaned," pulling the front shroud lines down to my knees increasing my forward speed considerably. Straining every muscle, I sailed toward the meadow with 500 feet of elevation.

As I descended, I encountered a beautiful natural aroma, a fragrance like an expensive perfume store. Hawk was hollering, "Come over here. This isn't water. It's blue lupine."

I turned toward Hawk with the film makers off to my left taking pictures. The blue lupine "lake," waving in the breeze, was breathtaking, a celestial glimpse of the glory of heaven I've dreamed of since childhood. I was drifting in eternity, fully aware of being alive, erasing years of needless anxiety about Hells Canyon.

Sailing into the blue lupine, I came into reality; a floral garden surrounded by an enormous field of wildflowers including rocky mountain lilies, red columbines, and bright pink fireweeds as tall as my waist. Standing in the soft soil of a natural Garden of Eden, not more than 50 feet away, two white-tail deer accepted my arrival as if smokejumpers dropped in every day. They moved away when I waved my orange streamers .

Mary Kay understood why Hawk had chosen to land in the "water" when she flew by at treetop level depositing our fire packs into the "floral lake." Anointment with wildflower perfume in the meadow was preparation for the unfolding mystery of strenuous days ahead.

From the edge of the clearing, someone else had watched us drop in, a Basque sheepherder. We landed in the summer pasture of his herd of domestic sheep. He sauntered up the hill to welcome us. His skin was weathered and his beaming face revealed several missing teeth underneath a bushy mustache. He demonstrated an air of confidence as he approached us.

His name was Ignacio Onaderra and he had a surprise awaiting the two jumpers he had watched tour the deepest canyon in America on 20 pounds of orange and white nylon.

"I've already lined the fire, and it's not spreading."

He invoked some phrases in his native tongue, which we didn't comprehend. Then he said, "How about trading some food with you? If you share your fresh vegetables, fruit and butter, I'll provide fresh lamb chops, sourdough bread and red wine."

Ignacio had worked with jumpers before and knew what we would trade for the best sourdough bread in the West. Hawk had packed extra vegetables and fresh butter.

"It's a deal!" we shouted in unison, and the three of us wandered down the meadow toward his camp.

We laid our fire packs near his tent and outdoor table. Jams, sourdough bread and other essentials were on a table covered with a red and white checkered oil tablecloth. Everything was neat and tidy, including a small pile of books written in Spanish piled beside a tall thick beeswax candle. Two titles indicated he was a Christian. Those titles, translated into English, were: *The Spiritual Exercises* by St. Ignatius and *A Commentary on Saint Ignatius' Discernment of Spirits.*

Ignacio, carrying a shepherd's crook, led us quietly down the hill through the tall bunch grass. Carrying pulaskis and shovels, we avoided greasewood, difficult to pass through without getting scratched. We walked between alpine firs, brushing against their branches. From a small clearing, high above black basalt terraces, we beheld the heavily forested western side of Hells Canyon, aglow with nature's grandeur. The air was clean and inspiring to our lungs and hearts.

Jumpers approach larger fires from the windward side to avoid being overcome by thick and often deadly fumes, but there was little danger today. In a few minutes we encountered unmistakable forest fire fumes, but even the smoke was pleasant; like the smoke from the altar of an ancient Jewish sacrifice. When we climbed out of the alpine tree cover, Ignacio proudly showed us how little labor was left on this fire. He pointed to the top section of the two acre burn.

"What do you think of my work? Is it up to Forest Service standards?"

Upon close inspection, we found that he had carefully lined the lightweight fire with a cold trail. The soil was good, not rocky or full of thorns. Later in the summer lodgepole seeds would burst open and grow abundantly.

"Next year, fireweed or bright red Indian paintbrush will cover this spot like an English garden," Ignacio said.

There was something very good about this Basque sheepherder.

"I've been a jumper for seven years, and I've never seen a better fire line than yours," Hawk said.

"And I've never seen one completed before we got to the fire. This is incredible. Hawk, I'll take charge of the top of the fire, and you take the unexplored lower section,"

I knew full well that the first man out the door is always boss. Hawk just laughed.

We didn't locate any spot fires below us. We thanked Ignacio and walked around the entire fire to determine what we were dealing with.

In a slumbering fire like that, we strode right into the fire area, pulling logs apart. Two logs, close together, burn faster than single ones. Separating them offers more air, but without mutual support, they burn with less intensity, and usually burn out. Is this pattern similar to two persons in love? Two independent lovers maintaining a little space may fan their flames of passion. A respectful independence bolsters love's flame to burn brighter, but prolonged separation may diminish it.

We were careful walking inside the line not to step into holes left by burned-out stumps. After working for five hours, we decided it was safe to leave since the sun would soon drop over the horizon, allowing the area to cool.

When we trudged up the hill to camp, we watched the evening star appear and Ignacio disappear with his trusty dogs. We assumed he was leaving to count his sheep before nightfall. We cleaned up and spread Forest Service rations on his immaculate table. We hoped the sheepherder would join us for dinner.

Kindling a fire in the rock lined fireplace, Hawk said, " Maybe he'll broil the lamb chops tomorrow. Its almost dark. Let's eat our dinner and leave the fresh vegetables for him. It's been a long day for me. What's your pleasure Mark?"

I wholeheartedly agreed. I dug into tin cans of beef stew, snow peas, and cherry dessert, donating the fresh butter and oranges for Ignacio.

An hour after we had eaten and stretched out in our sleeping bags, the tired herder plodded slowly into camp. He knew these woods so intimately, he didn't need a flashlight. As he approached camp, it seemed a pale aura of bluish light accompanied him.

"There's some fresh food and canned things on your table," I said as he approached the fire.

"Thanks for sharing. One of my ewes got lost, and the dogs and I haven't found her. I wonder if a coyote got her. I counted the herd and she was the only one missing. We'll head out at the first break of dawn and look again. Tomorrow I'll cook a Basque dinner which you will never forget."

He was disturbed about losing one of his sheep. Two hours before sunrise Ignacio was up, brewing coffee, and left soon afterwards to search for the lost one. The coffee scent was more than I could resist, so I got up early and huddled up to a large tin cup of real coffee. Soon after, Ignacio disappeared over the horizon, guided by a brilliant morning star.

Imagine drinking coffee in heaven on the government payroll. As I nursed my hot coffee, I remembered the time I offered to jump on a hunter's fire after summer season, when most jumpers had gone home.

I had just come back to McCall from my judge's office at Probate Court. The sheriff had been talking about all the fires and not enough smokejumpers to cover them. I didn't have any pressing work in court for a few days, so I went to Sam Defler, Supervisor of the Payette National Forest, offering to jump the next morning.

"Thanks, Mark, but you're too out of shape. We'll bring some jumpers from Missoula, but you can help." He spiced up his rejection to my offer with a little humor. "Why don't you go to St. Andrews and pray for rain?" I immediately drove over to the church and prayed for cooler temperature and lots of rain.

By three the next afternoon, massive clouds covered the Idaho sky. Soon they were pouring moisture into the Payette National Forest. I couldn't resist. I sent Sam and the United States Forest Service a bill for one hour's "prayer" time. It came to $2.54.

A few days later I was busy in Probate Court when Fish & Game Officer Bill Pogue brought in a trophy hunter who had killed a mountain goat and left the carcass to rot. I was working with Pogue when the mail arrived with an official letter from Supervisor Defler of the USFS.

I read, "The government is prepared to pay Judge Davis $2.54. However, this particular lightning bust cost the USFS $250,000. Since the Lord caused the rain, He must have sent the lightning. Please remit to USFS, $249,996.46."

An option offered in lieu of payment was to get in shape and jump next summer.

What a delightful sense of humor Sam Defler has, I thought, as I poured a second cup of the sheepherder's coffee. Spirituality without humor, like faith without works, is deader than a doornail.

The next day was the Sabbath and a good day to rest. Hawk declared the fire officially contained, and we watched the shepherd moving up and down the mountain, looking for the lost sheep. Hawk was for exploring a nearby cabin, built years ago by homesteaders, but I knew him well enough to know he would search for the missing sheep while checking out the cabin.

The last time we had explored a cabin it was full of surprises, including that rattlesnake. The roof of this abandoned building sagged to the floor. Remembering the Gospel Hump incident, Hawk listened for the hissing of snakes. Instead, he heard a faint bleating. He discovered the missing member of Ignacio's woolly family in a five foot well near the cabin. She couldn't get out and had just about run out of strength to even bleat. Hawk jumped in, picked her up, and laid her on the grass. She was too weak to stand, so he threw the exhausted animal over his shoulders.

"I found the lost sheep," he shouted, racing around kind of like a Side-Hill Gouger with the good news, looking for Ignacio. He acted as if he had found a ton of gold rather than a very tired sheep.

I took a favorite paperback from my fire pack and went to the crest of the canyon in the midst of the Seven Devils. The cover and pages of Albert Schweitzer's *Out of My Life and Thought*, damaged from being carried to so many fires, were held together with a strong rubber band.

The Firestone Library featured Dr. Schweitzer's philosophy during my first year in Seminary, and the intellectual ambiance of Princeton inspired me to study his works. The Seminary also had its own spiritual vibrations. Albert Einstein lived on the campus, and just seeing him wander around was an inspiration.

Spending a day with Schweitzer high above the Snake River strengthened my devotion to all living things. Schweitzer was a musician, medical doctor, theologian and philosopher, but he pushed a life of fame aside and journeyed to Africa to serve a mission hospital. One day, returning from Europe, as he rounded a bend in the river, all his accomplishments came together in a fresh awareness of the meaning of life. He named it, "reverence for life." Out here we might call it "reverence for the wilderness."

I spread my lunch on a log overlooking Hell's Canyon, with the Seven Devils for my backdrop. I surveyed miles of wild beauty that didn't reveal a flicker of human activity, with one exception; unsightly sections of clearcutting on the next watershed.

Clearcuts are hacked out of the enchanting forest following a compass line rather than the graceful lines of the landscape. They were as grievous to me as if someone had indiscriminately gouged rectangular chunks out of the mysterious face of Mona Lisa, or scratched a checkerboard into a rosewood coffee table with a ten-penny nail. Thoughtless metes and bounds disfigure the flowing contour of nature.

Selective logging could have prevented this intrusion. It would provide a balanced resolution for both environmentalists and timbermen, avoiding the unreasonable demands of either extreme. Aristotle's philosophy of avoiding excess could negotiate harmony for extremists on both sides.

Everyone wants healthy forests, but viability of the wilderness demands balance. Selective cutting will maintain the old growth forests as ends, not temporary means. The *Via Media* — the Holy Balance — promotes complementarity for the timber industry and recreation. Both are essential for a good quality of life.

Not far from the log which served as my lunch table appeared a mountain quail who must have lost his family. His attire consisted of a beautiful combination of brown and gray topped off with a long black feather for a hat. Unafraid, with a delicate plume, he paused to consider me, with my shiny aluminum helmet. I enjoyed his company while reading Schweitzer and threw a few bread scraps his way.

To my left, high in a dead tree, was a beautiful, red-headed, pileated woodpecker. A bright, shiny, green hummingbird was also a companion while I devoured philosophy.

Teachers of prayer observe that meditators often hear the solos of wild birds while praying. Out here in the wilds of Idaho, I have yet to enjoy contemplating God without a bird singing or fluttering around me.

I love all God's "winged creatures." When smokejumpers hike down trails less traveled kicking rocks away, flickers and flycatchers often dart back and forth above them, looking for insects exposed by flying rocks.

Hummingbirds worried me on my last fire, when I prayed near a group of wartberry fairybell flowers. Darting around so quickly, I wondered if one might pierce my ear or eye by mistake while I was in deep contemplation. Once, I felt the vibrations of tiny wings. I was grateful she did not mistake my ear for a channel to the nectar in an evening primrose.

A Western bluebird could be mistaken for a robin. It sports a red breast with a blue head and wings. My favorite wild bird is the mountain bluebird, Idaho's state bird, with its soft, gray-blue body and bright blue wings.

Bathed in afternoon sun, I read several chapters of Schweitzer's philosophy, high in the choir loft of a chancel conceived by God's creative goodness. I read Chapter Four on the Last Supper and Jesus' attempt to build an ethical kingdom of God on earth. Then I slid down out of the "balcony" and sat on the warm ground with the log for my pillow. Contemplating the meaning of "reverence for life," I went soundly to sleep. The surrounding beauty ineffably pointed to the Source of all virtues, reverence for the living and to a holy rest.

This weekend jump was becoming the most important event in my seven years of absorbing wilderness spirituality. With the warm summer sun on my shoulders and the book in my lap, I dozed in perfect peace. When I woke up some time later, I wanted to express my inner joy in this vast expanse of Hell's

144

Canyon. Setting the tattered book aside and closing my eyes I repeated the mantra, "reverence for life," over and over.

I was not alone. Another little quail joined me, either from curiosity or from the attractive spiritual aura of prayer. I thanked God for her existence. Her presence permeated my love for creatures, great and small. I welcomed her and she stayed nearby for most of my meditation. Soon I was singing to her:

All things bright and beautiful, All creatures great and small,
All things wise and wonderful, The Lord God made them all.
Each little flower that opens, Each little bird that sings,
He made their glowing colors, He made their tiny wings.
The purple-headed mountain, The river running by,
The sun-set, and the morning That brightens up the sky.
He gave us eyes to see them, And lips that we might tell
How great is God Almighty, Who has made all things well.

A little later — I refuse to wear a watch into the forests — my stomach told me it was supper time. Ignacio might be serving fresh lamb. Piecing Schweitzer's book back together with the rubber band, I bid the quails goodbye and took the most direct route down to camp.

At noon the next day, as we were setting the table for lunch, the packer, Ray Yanke, led his three-mule pack train into camp. Ray rode a gray Appaloosa mare which was half the size of the sturdy mules. Ray was not much over five feet high himself. We wondered if he could throw our heavy packs on the mules. But that question could wait. Ray had other things on his mind: food. The packer joined us for lunch, at Ignacio's invitation.

After lunch, my question about Ray's ability to throw the jump gear on the mules was quickly settled. He had no problem tossing the heavy packs on Jenny, the smallest mule. He carefully balanced the two packs beforehand, taking my reserve chute and adding it to Hawk's pack. Perfectly balanced loads on pack mules are absolutely essential. This was especially true today as we would descend a steep narrow trail. One misstep and the mule and packs would roll all the way to the Snake River.

Our curiosity about why he put both packs on one mule and nothing on the other two came to a halt when he offered us an opportunity to ride bareback on the larger mules.

"I should tell you the big fire bust south of here took my regulars and so I had to use green ones today. Yesterday I was talking to my packer friends in Baker City and they asked me to bring a young mule along which has never been to a fire before. I don't know why I did it, but now we'll see if he can do the job. No one has ever ridden Triumph but you ought to be able to ride anything if you can manage parachutes into this canyon."

I didn't like that idea much. I have trouble staying on a good horse. He told me to get on old Thunder and Hawk to ride young Triumph, but as I approached Thunder, I got a dirty look from the wide left eye of an unfriendly worker for the U.S. Forest Service. He obviously didn't want a rider.

We bid goodbye to Ignacio, who expressed sincere appreciation for our friendship. We were disappointed that he hadn't shared his fresh lamb with us, but he hinted he would see us again. The formal recessional of our holy experience in the canyon cathedral began with Ray leading the way, Hawk next, then myself. The luggage followed.

Two others joined the recession. One was a big cedar waxwing who flew beside us for most of the day, sometimes so close we could see the little red tips in his wings and the mystical black mask streaking from his beak past his eyes to the back of his head. The rest of his flighty body was dazzling light brown. The other participant was Sheperboy, Ray's Australian sheep dog, and he was nursing a grudge with Thunder.

When Thunder relaxed, methodically plodding along the narrow rocky trail, the dog would slip in without warning and bite him on the hind leg. Thunder would jerk his large head around and try to bite the dog's tail or kick him into orbit.

This battle did not end until we got to the banks of the river, but it kept me alert, ready to leap uphill from old Thunder at any given moment. In spite of the continual dog-mule conflict, the mules sure-footed the rocky canyon, seldom even kicking any rocks over the edge. Rock-kicking jumpers clearing this spiny trail would have ruined their boots in the first mile.

Cliffs sloped several hundred feet from the rocky trail to the river. The bedrock may have been a vagrant group of islands years ago. The formation of the Seven Devils range and Hells Canyon had taken place 800 million years ago in the Preterozoic Era.

We trailed past an alpine lake where a family was camping. The entire group waved towels as we passed by, as if we were in a parade. Hawk waved back.

The government was paying us to tour one of the most beautiful landscapes in the United States. Constantly descending, we passed through scattered groupings of white alders with their smooth, light gray trunks, dark green leaves and delicate branches waving as we passed by. As the musical expressed it so well, "The hills are alive, with the sound of music."

Sloshing through a shallow stream under a group of water birch trees, Thunder abruptly stopped for a drink. The rest of the procession came to a brief halt. After gulping the clear mountain water, he decided it was dinner time. He tore away a mahogany branch, chewing leaves and stems. Hawk and I got down and drank upstream from the animals. After animals and riders were refreshed, the path opened into a clearing bright with orange Indian paintbrush among yellow daisies with a pileated woodpecker feasting in an old, tall snag.

Ray had been quiet most of the trip except for occasionally yelling unmentionable things at the mules, but as the caravan moved toward a clearing, he pointed to the cliffs high above us. He had spotted four white mountain goats racing up the cliffs as if they were on flat land.

An hour later, we passed two dilapidated homesteads. We expected thistle and thorn bushes near them, but to our surprise, beautiful flowers were abundant. There were forget-me-nots with sky-blue, round clusters of flowers dancing in the gentle breeze. They were contrasted by bunches of woolly yellow daisies growing out of rock piles. I felt everything along the way, even a cross-shaped stone, was praising God.

In late afternoon we approached a long sand bar bordering the Snake River , where we would camp for the night. We had been listening to the river's deafening roar for several miles but along the sand bar the dark, deep water was unusually calm.

About 75 feet from the end of the trail on the white sand, Sheperboy decided to risk it all and take a solid bite out of Thunder's belly. When he connected, I knew I was in Hells Canyon. I was instantly dispatched into orbit with a sharp re-entry into white sand and scratchy underbrush. My reserve chute might have been useful if I'd had it on. Thunder broke his tether and almost bit the tail off the mischievous dog. I wanted to get up and kick them both across the river, but it wasn't my battle.

An eye for an eye, and the game was over. Thunder and Sheperboy stopped their warfare, and peace flowed along the river. Hawk slid off Triumph, and the packer tossed our packs off Jenny near a clump of blue Jacob's ladder. He said a USFS pickup truck from McCall would arrive the next morning.

Ray collected his mules and headed down the road with only a "So long. Have a good summer."

The sand bar was approximately 40 feet long and 20 feet wide. At the upper end were several large flat rocks which provided a perfect, natural room for supper. We lay down on the warm white sand and enjoyed resting in the sun. Soon we collected our food and headed for the high flat rocks, sitting 15 feet above the white sand.

To our amazement, we were greeted by Ignacio. He had all the Basque ingredients for a last dinner together; garbanzo beans, chorizos, ensalad and goat cheese heavily flavored with garlic. Finally he unwrapped three fresh lamp chops.

Ignacio set the exquisite supper on the rock as I kindled a fire.

When the chops were cooking, Hawk said, "I've never smelled anything so good in my whole life. This is a feast we'll never forget."

He spread the red and white oil cloth on a smaller stone table.

"Ignacio says he had considered sacrificing his finest lamb for a special occasion. He wasn't sure just why. He decided against it, and yesterday, the lamb's mother fell over a cliff, and it was too young to make it alone."

The sheepherder didn't mind talking about it.

"You jumpers probably don't understand much about our history," he said, becoming very serious. "We consider that if the lamb could speak, he would be highly honored to give his pure, innocent life for others. We honor him, and he honors us. Is not that the essence of fairness found in the wilderness?"

We shared a royal banquet of lamb chops, potatoes, vegetables, sourdough bread, and fresh butter complete with Basque pastry. Even more, we shared royal friendship.

After dinner we sat around telling stories humorous and profound.

Ignacio talked about being a hunter. He said there is an unspoken bond between the hunter and the hunted, perhaps like our relationship to the lamb.

I repeated the experience of Eugene Williams at the Maximum Security Prison in Trenton.

"The angel said, 'You'll be all right.' Later, in his prayers, Eugene heard a voice say 'God wants you to preach the Gospel.' He knew after that he had work to do for the Lord. What impresses me is that God would send an angel into the death house to speak to him. Perhaps the same messengers speak to us in the wilderness. "

"What a contrast ... discerning God's call in majestic mountains or in prison. God is not limited by contingencies," Hawk said.

Our Basque host spoke of the mystery of life.

He began by reciting the Prologue to John in Greek, then translated for us,

" 'In the beginning was the Word and the Word was with God and the Word was God.'

"Life is all bits and pieces without much meaning unless glued together by the Ultimate Source.

"The world was created by a Word of Light, not a sentence of darkness," he continued, "but in order for this Light to make any difference it must shine within the hearts of God's people. The Evening or Morning Star — God's stars, so to speak — also sparkle within us. There are reflections everywhere of the true Light that enlightens every believer's heart, but I discern bright rays of that Light shining within you, Hawk."

"The Light is within believers everywhere," I said. "Remember Psalm 82. 'You are gods, sons of the Most High, all of you; nevertheless, you shall die like men, and fall like any prince.' "

Celestial music emerged above the table conversation in an aura of peace I had never experienced. I felt very close to Hawk, my jump partner of seven seasons, and a special bond with our mysterious host.

Up on the canyon wall, two owls sang evening prayer. They called back and forth, creating a natural Gregorian chant. Although it was summertime, I felt they were chanting, "Hark the herald angels sing, Glory to our newborn King ... " The mountains along Hells Canyon echoed their joyous refrain.

148

I told Ignacio for the first time I was a priest and asked where he had acquired such profound discernment of spirituality.

He remained silent for a long time, then said, "When I was a very young man, I went to a Jesuit Seminary, studying theology. I loved the Spiritual Exercises of St. Ignatius Loyola. Then, the Spanish Civil War devastated my life. The Nazis bombed our village. It was horrible beyond description. My family was killed, leaving me alone with just my faith in God. I never had a chance to finish seminary, but our Lord never did, either. When the war ended, I had to leave my beloved Basque country but not my St. Ignatius. I took his name and have enjoyed his gift of spiritual discernment.

"There are high mountains in the global cathedral where God reveals special spiritual truths, like Mt. Sinai, or the Mount of Beatitudes. I find Idaho mountains also blessed with God's mystical Spirit. Here in Hell's Canyon, I feel the Presence of the Logos — the Spirit of Creation — who is still creating wonderment.

"In order to penetrate the mystery, as you say, one must relinquish selfishness, create room for God's Spirit. Forgiveness opens the door for the Spirit to enter. Jesus said knock and this door will be opened for you.

"The Creator is not limited by His own Creation. When you become part of His Spirit, you are not affected by lesser spirits. Christ's Exalted Spirit within you enables you to communicate safely with other mysteries."

"How do we know our inner spirit is alive?" I asked.

"You know because the healthy spirit gives you a brand new way of seeing life," Hawk said. "You look through eyes of respect for all living creatures. Instead of just a bird out there tonight, you hear a little Northern pygmy owl, singing with the great horned owl. Rather than just an animal crashing through the woods, you see a mule deer. In the early morning you might see a Canadian lynx or bobcat quietly looking for a yellowbellied marmot. All living creatures have names and dignity,"

"What about wild trees? Are they alive too?" I asked.

"Yes indeed," Hawk continued. "No two are alike. All have their own beauty and purpose. One with broken branches may produce twice as much usable lumber as another which is more beautiful. Even a tree that survives a forest fire can become valuable lumber. A giant white pine may afford more shade than a Western larch, but each tree is unique and to be cherished.

"Those flowers are leafy-bract asters, not just white daisies. The point is this: When we wake up to appreciate creation, every piece of ecology has an important place and a proper name. Our task is first to enjoy them, and then to protect them for future generations."

"Are rocks sacred too?" I asked.

Ignacio said, "Not in themselves, I think, but the history of them is sacred. Do you know that most of the rocks near here came from coral reefs 100 million years old? Or that the Seven Devils are really squashed volcanoes? Or that during the Bonneville floods, this river was much higher than it is now?

"The mystery of the Idaho wilderness can be understood after we solve our own inner mystery through Christ. It is after our encounter with Him that we find out who we are and what we believe, what the world is saying to us," he said.

"My whole life was changed when I asked Christ to direct my life, but how do we recognize Him?" I asked.

"Look at ordinary folks with highly developed patterns of love. They have the key to the mystery of both inner and external wilderness," Ignacio said.

"Ordinary prayerfulness within ordinary people," I mused. "In the midst of my malfunction miracle, I asked my angel for help. Is prayer a means to meet our personal needs or a means to serve the Kingdom of God?"

Ignacio's eyes, glued upon the few glowing embers, said, "That's a paradox. It is definitely both. A life of all utility or of all prayer is not healthy spirituality. We need time in the mountains to develop spiritual vision. But leaving the mountains to labor in valleys of despair is equally important. I believe St. John of the Cross said, 'God weighs one good act of charity as more than many ecstatic Divine revelations.' "

Ignacio provided a resolution to the paradox of my own spiritual journey. We couldn't do community work without the inspiration from God's biospirituality. Hawk would begin teaching high school kids the art of wrestling in the fall, but he would teach spiritual growth as well. I dreamed of building a Merton Meditation Chapel near a university with a system where students could project slides of Idaho's sacred mountains upon a screen behind a natural altar, and visualize meditating in the natural sanctuary.

I spent summers in the wilderness of Idaho where I felt the presence of God very strongly. I left the mountain tops each fall to help improve the quality of life for others.

Marveling at the concerto of the wild owls, we sat at God's table, partially lit by embers of two fires ... interior and external. Hawk stirred the sparks of the glowing fire with a long thin stick just as Ignacio had stirred the divine within us.

Then Ignacio spoke. "I've got a little loaf of sourdough bread. Hawk, would you break the loaf into three parts and share with us?"

Hawk agreed. He took the bread and split it, saying, "Take this, knowing we share this bread in life, and we'll eat imperishable bread together in heaven."

Then, he filled our empty cups with the remaining red wine.

"May this wine become the Morning Star in us," he said. "May we live by the ethic of the wilderness and the covenant of love. Although this shining moment may pass away, the Lord of the Universe will be with us forever."

Ignacio asked me to offer an appropriate prayer. I opened my battered *Prayerbook* and prayed:

Lord Jesus, stay with us, for evening is at hand and the day is past; be our companion in the way, kindle our hearts, and awaken hope, that we may know you as you are revealed in the Scripture and the breaking of bread. Grant this for sake of your love. Amen.

Then Ignacio prayed in his native tongue. Lit by a mysterious glow, we cleared the rock table before leaving the chapel near the river. We didn't need flashlights to find our way. The fire had gone out but a pale glow remained around Ignacio and Hawk. The glow faded slowly away until I saw it no more, but heard it expressed in the collect:

O God, who before the passion of your only begotten Son revealed his glory upon the holy mountain: Grant to us that we, beholding by faith the light of his countenance, may be strengthened to bear our cross, and be changed into his likeness from glory to glory. Amen.

I wanted to share this with Ignacio, but I found he had vanished.

THE NEXT MORNING WHILE WAITING FOR THE TRUCK, I contemplated the words of the Eucharist about an island home.

"Hawk?"

"Yeah. What's on your mind?"

"There is something highly spiritual about last night. The words in Holy Communion keep coming back to me:

God of all power, Ruler of the Universe ... at your command all things came to be: The vast expanse of interstellar space, galaxies, suns, the planets in their courses, and this fragile earth, our island home ...

"This sandbar is almost an island. Are all homes fragile?"

Hawk listened intently and slowly responded, "You know the Scripture ... 'Everyone who leaves homes, lands and relatives will exchange them for something more important.' "

"It's going to be hard to leave my home, but I recall Psalm 104 which states birds have their homes by streams of water and sing in the branches. And Jesus said 'Foxes have their holes, the birds of the air have their nests, but the Son of Man has nowhere to lay his head.' Durable homes must involve movement."

"That's right. Spiritual movement gives life. Leaping out of planes into the unknown gives me new life, but even the Williams brothers soar far away from their cells by their absorption into the movement of the Spirit.

151

"Ignatio calls the Seven Devils area his home, but the truth is he allowed Christ to build him into a living house — a home for the Spirit.

"Healthy persons can't just stand in one place; in fact, they can't go backwards, but need to advance into the future, choosing to live in the house of the Lord all their days."

"I really have no choice," I said, "so I'm going to pray God will lead me wherever I'm needed. I'll love God first and leave the rest to Him. I recall Jesus saying He would make his home with anyone who loved God."

"Mark, the entire world is our island home in the ocean of God's universal love. He's got this whole world in His Hands."

"Thanks, Hawk."

Resting in the sun by the still waters, I wondered about Ignacio, the sheepherder who exuded spirituality. Was he a messenger like the angel that spoke to Eugene Williams in prison? Does Christ take residency in ordinary sheepherders?

D URING THE TIME WE HAD SPENT IN THE SEVEN DEVILS MOUNTAINS, a huge lightning bust was devastating tinder-dry Montana forests. The smokejumper unit in Missoula requested two Doug loads of McCall jumpers.

With 36 men gone to Montana, when we trucked back to McCall the next morning, Hawk and I were back near the top of the jump list. We may have been the most rested men in camp after our Hells Canyon experience.

We would have acted like movie stars if we had any idea how to act, but no one was impressed with our "movie star status," so we let it go.

Central Idaho was also absorbing extensive lightning strikes in the Salmon and Challis forests. Trucks carrying men and equipment whirled up the dusty road between jumper camp and the airport often. The tarmac was packed with fire-retardant planes loading reddish borate slurry. B-17s, B-24s and TBMs were flying east over Jughandle Peak at regular intervals, dropping retardant with pinpoint precision.

One of the former crack World War II pilots was Gene Phillips, who flew 11 South Pacific missions in a TBM, the Avenger Torpedo Bomber. The day before, he had been so exhausted returning from his sixth fire drop, he forgot to put down the landing gear. In the rush to refuel planes, no one on the ground even looked up as he approached the strip, wheels up, but they jumped straight in the air when they heard the "chunk-chunk-chunk" of a TBM propeller cracking into the pavement.

The Avenger was so stout that the only real damage was to the enormous four-blade prop and Phillip's pride. TBM pilots changed the course of the war at the Battle of Midway in these sturdy planes. A busted prop was a minor problem. The bright yellow warplane would fly five missions two days later with a brand new prop and an alert pilot.

After the wheels-up incident, we were unloading supplies from a ten-wheel truck into the Johnson Airlines DC-3 when Wayne barked orders over the outdoor speakers for the last nine jumpers in camp to report immediately.

"We have a radio call from Tex Lewis near Indian Creek," Wayne told us. "Nick is seriously injured. A snag fell on him, and they're having trouble stopping the bleeding from his broken leg. There are no helicopters available. We need to drop emergency medical supplies and a stretcher as soon as possible."

Wayne's voice changed as he deliberately chose his words.

"The afternoon air is extremely thin, with unpredictable winds. We're at the point of saying no more flights till flying conditions improve. Gene, who just dropped retardant on this fire, says the air may be safe but to be extremely wary of down drafts. Skip has volunteered to fly the AT-11. We're asking for a volunteer to drop medical supplies."

The AT-11, the twin-engine trainer, was a military aircraft from World War II. Many pilots remember it as their first multi-engine trainer. A rebuilt model called the C-45 was being flown effectively in Southern Oregon for medical "mercy" flights. Oregonians referred to their all-white, twin Beech with red crosses on the wings, as "Iron Annie." She had a reputation for saving lives and bringing hope to rural folks.

As we were mulling the danger in our minds, someone said, "Give me the stuff."

Hawk had voiced reservations about the backcountry flying ability of this airplane, which did not have turbo-chargers. He had also been a little nervous about Skip's lack of back country flying time, although Skip had been a top military pilot. Several others were willing to go and argued with Hawk, but he insisted that his experience favored him dropping the supplies right on target.

When it was settled, the rest of us heaved a sigh of relief and Weber told us to go back to work.

THREE O'CLOCK IN THE AFTERNOON IS A DANGEROUS TIME TO FLY in the Idaho backcountry. Not only is the air thin, but updrafts are unpredictable. Turbulence makes it hard to maintain altitude, so high speed is essential for lift and maneuvering.

Despite his lack of experience, Skip courageously faced the task ahead. Experienced pilots like Bob Fogg and Ray Arnold fly intuitively in air currents like birds of prey, but Skip was nervous about the tricky air currents. The twin-engine trainer could reach the fire in half the time as the old Trimotor, which soared serenely like blue heron without much speed. The AT-11 had good speed, but its gliding range was almost nonexistent.

Hawk loaded the first-aid gear in a cushioned box with fresh food for the crew. He hooked the box to a 24-foot cargo chute. The stretcher was tied on another cargo chute. When he stepped inside, Skip had the engines roaring.

A bright orange and gray B-17 retardant bomber landed, and Skip and Hawk were cleared for takeoff. Hot, thin air makes it essential to use as much of the runway as possible to clear the treetops at the far end. Skip revved up the twin engines as if he were taking off the deck of a carrier, as he had done so many times. The plane lurched forward and Hawk waved goodbye to jumpers working near the runway. Ray Hale, a World War II airborne veteran, threw them a salute.

Flying high at a safe altitude, Skip and Hawk had trouble locating the fire. The normally clear air around McCall was smoky from the Montana fires. The air was rough and turbulent when they found the intended drop area about three-fourths of a mile up the drainage of Norton Creek. It would difficult dropping the medical supplies close to the injured man, but so far, there was nothing unusual..

From the ground below, Tex watched Hawk toss a streamer out the door. A robust ground wind carried it horizontally.

Since the wind was coming from the west and the creek contour ran east and west, Skip decided to fly up the canyon against the wind for extra lift. This added risk. Mahoney Peak rose sharply in their path. There was only one way to exit, toward Little Soldier Mountain after a sharp turn away from Norton Creek. Flying beside Norton Ridge, 8,425 feet in elevation made the maneuver highly dangerous.Skip had the trainer screaming at full throttle, racing away from Shell Rock Peak, parallel to the familiar Marble Creek drainage. Tex and the crew were to the right as Skip turned upwind.

The AT-11 was being jerked around like a Ping Pong ball in a windstorm. Skip built up his airspeed and came in low. Hawk was in position in the door, holding the railing tightly with his left hand. He released the cargo at the right moment, pushing the stretcher out a second or two later. The cargo chutes opened, oscillated and landed near the crew, hitting the target exactly as planned. The crew waved their appreciation and Hawk waved back, pleased with a job well done.

Skip was satisfied but frightened. The twin-engine plane was not lifting fast enough. He fought furiously to bank it to the open side of the Norton Creek drainage near Little Soldier and into the open space near the Middle Fork of the Salmon River, but the trainer wasn't responding fast enough.

There were no turbo-chargers to provide extra power, the very concern Hawk had voiced so often. Skip gave the engines total power, risking blowing the pistons, but thin air was not giving the lift needed. Norton Ridge loomed closer and closer. He banked sharply to the left. A gust of wind hit the upper wing tip and flipped the struggling plane over, and the mercy flight plowed headlong into the ridge, upside-down.

Two courageous men who loved the wilderness were now part of it.

TEX AND ALL THE CREW SAW THE EXPLOSION ON THE MOUNTAINSIDE ABOVE THEM. No one said a word. In silence, 10 men joined arms and unashamedly wept.

IN MCCALL, WEBER WAS WORRIED. He knew that when pilots are busy, they report later, but the radio from the trainer had been silent too long. Then the McCall receiver barked the appalling news of the crash from Tex. Wayne was shattered when dispatcher Bruce Campbell relayed the details of the tragedy.

"It can't be true. I should've gone myself. Sound the buzzer. There's a chance Hawk jumped out the door and may still be alive. I'm going out there myself."

"Weber, I want to go find Hawk. Maybe he landed in a tree and is still alive," Larry pleaded.

"All of us want to go," I said.

Weber told the dispatcher to fire up the Trimotor. It would be safer in the bad air and unpredictable currents. The dispatcher agreed to send six jumpers to the site. Neal Yergenson, considered one of the best, would be spotter. Bob Fogg talked with a B-17 pilot after a recent retardant drop who said the winds near the Norton Creek drainage were calming down.

As we suited up for a rescue jump, a stunned Larry told us he was going to be the first man to jump for Hawk. Larry, a system opportunist, always came out a winner while Hawk stood by his principles, but none of that mattered now. He and Hawk had been honorable adversaries.

We loaded our rescue equipment and were airborne in less than 10 minutes. In hope, we threw a stretcher in.

On the way to Indian Creek we tried to convince ourselves that, though Skip was undoubtedly dead, Hawk would be alive.

"We'll find him, and he'll be all right."

The pilot took his time getting to the Little Soldier Mountain area in the corrugated Tin Goose. Weber decided the best and closest landing area was right below Whitehawk lookout, exactly where Hawk and I had jumped together three years earlier.

As we flew over the hillside that had been devastated in the Whitehawk Fire, I saw new, Kelly-green growth surrounding tall trunks burned black. When Hawk and I had worked there three years earlier, the area was covered with gray dust and charred ruins.

I could hardly believe the phoenix-like transformation that had replaced the ashes of the enormous fire. The heliport we constructed was now covered with young saplings. Lupine and fireweed flowered on the hillside. The bunch grass was green again and very much alive. Small evergreen trees were growing everywhere. In just three years, a mountain of ashes had been transformed into a cloister garden.

Yergenson said we would jump two-man sticks. The winds had calmed and smoke from the Indian Creek fire was now circling almost straight up.

A fierce fire had been ignited by the crash, pinpointing its location. I landed

100 feet downhill from the lookout. Wayne set a fast pace toward the crash and we literally ran down the hill after him.

Solemnly, we approached the melted pieces of aluminum which had been a rescue aircraft earlier in the day. Skip's badly burned body was still in the cockpit. The metal wings were almost totally burned, and the fuselage lay in a hole two feet deep and 12 feet long.

In what remained of the rear section, we failed to uncover any sign of Hawk.

"Let the fire burn, fan out in the flight path and look everywhere for Hawk, " Weber shouted, but the crew had already begun searching.

Words seemed inappropriate, but we thought he may have jumped to safety. "Hawk, can you hear us?" we shouted, hoping for any sign of life. We heard nothing.

From the Ford Trimotor circling overhead, Yergenson dropped two body bags and the stretcher. Weber began to walk on a line toward the rescue drop spot, isolating himself from the rest of us. We knew he wanted to be alone, but I knew that he was not alone on Norton Ridge. God's Spirit permeates every nook and cranny of His bioscathedral.

We searched in every direction, hoping Hawk was alive. We knew if he was, he would be somewhere between the cargo drop for Nick and the crash sight. We looked high up into the ponderosa pines convinced he may be hanging on to a branch. We searched beneath smaller trees in the hope that one of them could have softened his fall. We couldn't go fast enough; all the time hooting for Hawk, hoping for any response.

After six hours, we returned to the shattered aircraft; dejected, knowing our hope for finding him alive had been dashed. We searched for any clue ... a burned boot, his heavy belt buckle, anything to indicate Hawk went in with the plane, but our search there was in vain. There was absolutely no evidence of Hawk's body.

Surrounded by the dark emotions of grief, my heart was warmed by an unknown appearance of aural Light ... as if the Morning Star was shining in broad daylight. I knew that Hawk and Skip were part of that Eternal Light. Then, the most beautiful Swainson's Hawk I have ever seen spiraled skyward into the hot air currents and rose out of sight. Moments later I heard the sad haunting melody of a Mourning dove in the forest below. The passage from John's Gospel where Jesus said, 'You will search for me and you will not find me,' reverberated in my mind.

After the crash blaze was contained, we devised a plan to transport Skip's body to a site below us, near the Indian Creek Ranger Station. We carried his body to the heliport Hawk and I built three years earlier. We cleared away some bushes and rolled away a large stone and cleared the landing area. I considered it a mountain monument.

God is graceful in the fact He does not reveal what suffering may be ahead.

Life had been carefree when we built the heliport, flying to Salmon City in the evenings, living it up in Salmon.

A FTER A SERIES OF RADIO CONVERSATIONS WITH HIS FAMILY, it was decided to bury Skip's body near the airstrip at Indian Creek, not far from the Middle Fork of the Salmon River. A search team was coming for a more thorough investigation and to search for Hawk's body. We placed Skip's body safely in the sacristy of the lookout for the night, high above the mountain.

Nick had been flown by helicopter off the fire and was recovering in the Salmon hospital. The accident was devastating to him. He felt responsible. Nick considered Hawk the finest man he'd ever known and himself the worst. Guilt, ignored for his entire life, came home to roost. Hawk sacrificed his life for Nick. My strong intuition told me that Hawk's agape love would be a turning point for Nick's rebirth.

Early the next day, we flew Skip's body to Indian Creek.

There was a unity achieved in laying his body to rest in a courtyard of nature's cathedral. Tex's crew joined us in digging his grave, taking turns shoveling. We used nylon jump ropes to lower his courageous body tenderly into a crypt in the evergreens. Tex reverently threw the first shovel full of dirt to fill Skip's grave. Phil fashioned a cross out of white pine boughs and placed it devoutly at the head of the grave. Then Wayne asked me to share a passage from Scripture.

I chose a verse from I John.

" 'If we love one another, God lives in us, and his love is perfected in us.' A person would have to be spiritually blind not to have witnessed God's love in Skip and Ken."

Then I read a short passage from Colossians on the mystery of love with all its joy and agony.

"God will reveal to the saints the 'riches of the glory of this mystery, which is Christ in you.' The Lord who loved lakes and rivers enables each person to unlock the mystery of his life. The key to understanding life's mystery is within ourselves, and the wilderness helps us uncover this inner nature. The same Lord who loved the wilderness near the Jordan River is the Dean of nature's cathedral here at Idaho's Indian Creek."

I told them what Ignacio had told us a few days earlier.

"He said Christ lives in ordinary people. Saints are ordinary persons like Skip and Ken who never consider themselves very holy. They are what genuine spirituality is all about."

"Christ is the Light of the World ... the 'Morning Star' in the Bible. From now on when we gaze at the Morning Star, we'll also think of our friends who were always the first to say, 'I'll go when called.' "

Our thoughts ended with "the hope of glory," not the gloom of despair.

"Both men tasted eternity in the Idaho wilderness. Now they're seated at a banquet in heaven, dwelling in an unbounded garden which blooms eternally."

We closed with prayers from the *Book of Common Prayer*:

> *Almighty God, who hast knit together thine elect in one communion and fellowship, in the mystical body of thy Son Christ our Lord: Grant, we beseech thee, to thy whole church in paradise and on earth, thy light and thy peace. Amen.*
>
> *Into thy hands, O merciful Savior, we commend thy servant Skip. Acknowledge, we humbly beseech thee, him as sheep of thine own fold, a lamb of thine own flock, a sinner of thine own redeeming. Receive him into the arms of thy mercy, into the blessed rest of everlasting peace, and into the glorious company of the saints in light. Amen.*

AFTER THREE DAYS OF INTENSIVE SEARCHING, no trace of Ken Shuler's body was found. A bloodhound was brought in, but was unable to detect a trace of him. I had an intuition where he was, but hesitated to share it with anyone.

Ignacio had prepared us for this event.

Later, separate memorial services were held for them near the Indian Creek landing strip, and we learned something about Skip that had been a secret since his family moved to McCall.

When they first arrived in McCall, Skip and Bonnie didn't have any furniture. The congregation at St. Andrews quietly went around the community locating used sofas, chairs, beds and rugs, filling their rented home. They never complained about making ends meet, and politely thanked everyone. They were just like the rest of us, struggling to make ends meet. You can imagine our surprise when Skip's parents flew their twin-engine, six-passenger Beechcraft to Idaho for the service?

Skip's family allowed his body to remain in the Idaho wilderness. They felt it was the proper final resting place for a courageous father, husband and son who loved Idaho. At the memorial service, I told his family, "Skip often attended the 7a.m. Eucharist. Recently, he flew all the way from Missoula in order to arrive at St. Andrews for early Holy Communion. He has now transcended time and is seated at Christ's Holy Table. In my opinion he arrived too early, but he'll be there when we come together."

The family had requested a brief service, and I ended with this commendation from the Book of Common Prayer:

> *In sure and certain hope of the resurrection to eternal life through our Lord Jesus Christ, we commend to Almighty God our brother Skip; and we commit his body to the ground; earth to earth,*

ashes to ashes, dust to dust. The Lord bless him, the Lord make his face to shine upon him and be gracious unto him, the Lord lift up his countenance upon him and give him peace. Amen.

The Trimotor and smaller airplanes ferried people in and out of Indian Creek landing strip throughout the day. Over strong objections, Mary Kay Clark piloted a Cessna in, preferring to fly alone.

At 3 p.m., we gathered for the Hawk's memorial service. More than 50 persons assembled on the southern end of the airstrip. They circled around a large picture of Ken on a natural altar of wild flowers. Although most smokejumpers were miles away on fire lines, we felt their presence.

"L ET US BEGIN WITH A COLLECT EXEMPLIFIED IN KEN SHULER. " 'Purify our conscience, Almighty God, by your daily visitation, that your Son, Jesus Christ, at His Coming, may find in us a mansion prepared for Himself.' Amen."

The absence of my best friend overwhelmed me so we next had a period of silence. Then I cleared my throat, and said, "The magnificent bioscathedral of Idaho has many natural rooms prepared for people's enjoyment. Individually we ought to prepare special rooms or homes within our selves for Him. Ken created a spiritual mansion, as the collect directs, and Christ definitely lived there. We saw this with our own eyes.

"Consider this short passage from 1st John:

> *We declare to you what was from the beginning, what we have heard, what we have seen with our eyes, what we have looked at and touched with our hands, concerning the word of life — this life was revealed, and we have seen it and testify to it, and declare to you the eternal life that was with the Father and was revealed to us.*

"Hawk's magnanimous life spoke louder than any words I might offer, so my homily will be brief. Later I will ask for your comments."

I cleared my throat and tried to continue, but his loss was too painful. My voice cracked, but Ken's friends listened to living voices singing in the verdant breezes, and soon I was able to speak.

"In this Scripture, John refers to the Lord of the holy hills. Over the last seven years, I've become aware of a comparable mysterious light shining through Ken. He made so much room for the Great Fisherman inwardly, he acted and thought like Him most of the time. It's no wonder we loved him so much.

"Was it St. John or Hawk who said, 'Let us love not in word or speech, but in action.'? Ken, who walked in the light, never hated anyone, loved everyone, and always kept his word.

159

"Ken Shuler personified unconditional love, seldom placing his own interests above the rest of us, ignoring opportunities for promotion.

"Sending the fire retardant to protect the Hotshot crew on the Whitehawk fire three years ago, he set their welfare above his own. When everyone was safe from that inferno, we celebrated by sharing fish and breaking bread. Ken carefully picked up the leftover fragments of that meal.

"I believe God will pick up the pieces of fragmented friendships and unfinished love in His merciful arms. He will bless them and piece them together with eternal love. No human effort to love — however small — is ever lost in God's boundless love.

"God cares about the forests. Not far from the terrible accident, three years ago Ken and I built a heliport. The hills were dusty and void of any signs of life. Last week I ran down the same mountainside and it teemed with new life flowering the slopes If God resuscitates forests back to life, will He not restore his people to eternal life? Are humans not of more value than trees?

"Three years ago on the Whitehawk fire ... "

A Swainson's hawk spiralled down over us, catching my attention. I left my notes, when I could continue.

"Last week I sat near the site of the accident and saw a hawk ascend — spiral — into the clear sky. Now one like it appears overhead. What does this mean?

"Everyone take a moment and examine this little hawk circling overhead. Notice of the markings on his underside, a white cross surrounded by brown feathers ... light in the midst of darkness, joy in the midst of sorrow. We can only see this, like Ken and I did three years ago, when the hawk is airborne. The flying cross prompts us to keep moving. I pray the winds of God will lift our wings to forge ahead through our sorrow, as a tribute to Ken."

After completing three full circles, the little brown hawk landed near the top of a young pine tree not far from the altar.

"Swainson's hawks are special because they are social, migrating all the way to Argentina in huge flocks. Swainson's, different from other hawks, are known to be gentle. Rising high on warm thermals, they soar for miles as families.

"Hawks have the keenest vision of any living creatures, binocular vision. Our beloved Ken had extraordinary spiritual vision. Spiralling above us spiritually, he perceived our highest hopes and deepest dreams. Yet he could dive, like a hawk, into areas of our personal suffering, sharing his unique courage."

Suddenly the little Swainson's rose from the pine bough and began spiralling skyward. I waited until he was out of sight before I returned to my homily.

"Ken was a man for others. When the call came to rush medical supplies to others, Ken ... that is, Hawk, ... was first to volunteer. Is there greater love than laying down one's life for others?

"Out of respect, we ought to emulate his values: Living without illusions while graciously accepting reality. Strengthening happiness in others, and rewarding virtue. Keeping our word even when it is not to our advantage. And above all, respecting all living things.

"Ken, we'll miss you. We saw Christ's Light shining in you as in no other."

It was time to conclude.

With my voice wavering, I asked."Would anyone like to share any thoughts?"

Several friends spoke up.

Gene Crosby said Ken's favorite song was *Go Tell It on the Mountain*, and he hoped we could sing it together. Max Blanton, who loved classical music said Ken's life was the missing movement of Schubert's *Unfinished Symphony*.

Marvin, the philosopher, standing in the back, spoke up.

"This man blended the good for individuality with the goodness of community. The ethical life is properly balancing them. Ken lived the maxims of Immanuel Kant. He cherished other persons as ends in themselves, never using them as means for his own success. He avoided all excesses in life except one — he was excessive in his respect for life. I've never met a such a man."

Phil walked to the altar. He spoke so softly Marvin asked him to talk louder.

"I'd like to retell, in my own words, the story of the Stranger on the road to Emmaus.

"After the first Easter, two disciples were walking along the road to Emmaus when Jesus drew near and walked beside them. God prevented them from recognizing who He was. As they walked, they spoke about the resurrection, angels, and the empty tomb. The Stranger told them that Christ had to suffer before his glory.

"It was getting late and they still did not recognize the Stranger, so they asked Him to stay for supper. He did and as He broke bread, their eyes were opened. When they recognized Him, Jesus vanished.

"Later, they remembered their hearts burned within them as they walked together."

Phil then cleared his throat a few times and continued. "I walked down many trails with Hawk, and frankly, my heart burned within me when we were together.

"Was our friend Ken Shuler," Phil asked quietly, "or did we walk with Jesus, the Stranger?"

When Phil returned to a place in the outer circle, Wayne Weber, who stood off the the right side, faced the group. "We can summarize Ken's good life in one sentence. He always kept his promises."

I closed the service with a passage from St. Mark echoing the same theme expressed by Phil.

"Jesus appeared in another form to two of them, as they were walking into the wilderness."

"On a stone table in Hells Canyon last week, a stranger shared bread and wine with us before Ken's sacrifice. What does this mean? Like Phil, I wonder if we have met the same Stranger, in the life of a smokejumper, here in the wilderness.

"I believe we have. And if so, we will continue to walk with Him throughout our lives wherever we go. If we have been raised with Christ, let us seek the things that are above.

> *Depart, O Christian soul, ...*
> *In the name of God the Father Almighty who created you;*
> *In the name of Jesus Christ who redeemed you;*
> *In the name of the Holy Spirit who sanctifies you.*
> *May your rest be this day in peace,*
> *and your dwelling place in the Paradise of God. Amen.*

People were silent for a few moments, listening to the alleluia choruses of wild birds in God's natural atrium, echoing praises for our beloved friend.

The service ended when Tex Lewis, stationed 50 feet up the hill, played his bagpipes ... flawlessly ... inspired by Hawk. The familiar tune of *Amazing Grace*, echoed throughout the forest. The memorial for Ken Shuler closed with prayer:

> *Almighty God, we give you thanks for surrounding us, as daylight fades, with the brightness of the vespers light; and we implore You of Your great mercy that, as You enfold us with the radiance of this light, so You would shine into our hearts the brightness of your Holy Spirit; through Jesus Christ our Lord. Amen.*

Don set up a Native American tradition to share for Skip and Hawk's friends after the service. It was called "Otu'han," a Lakota word translated as "giveaway."

In their memory, he thawed 20 pounds of elk steaks from his freezer. The coals were white-hot under a makeshift grill he had rigged. Don barbecued elk for the entire group who gathered to honor the sacrifices made by our brothers. The McCall kitchen staff sent food, including Ken's favorite, apple pie. Friends lingered, sharing good memories from Skip's 40 years and from Hawk's 32.

Phil and I ate supper together away from the crowd on a log at the end of the runway high above the river's roar.

"I spoke with Nick. He's experiencing dreadful shame for their deaths," Phil said. "On the other hand, he absolutely maintains his life is changed forever. With a completely new outlook, he's going to make everyday a good one. No force can be as powerful for change as someone dying for you.

"The Seven Squad has come to an end, but it's a new beginning for Nick, and me too. I'm going back to Central America as a social worker. What are your plans, Mark?"

"As you know, a prophet has no honor in his own country. It's hard leaving our family home, but I've decided to move and craft a Center for Biospirituality.

"I hope to build a natural chapel resembling the wilderness with evergreens, wild flowers and native rocks throughout. Behind the chapel's stone altar, I envision a large screen where worshipers can project slides of the countless chapels in the bioscathedral. When they meditate, it will be as if they were in the wilderness, surrounded by natural sounds recorded out here. I want it to be a center for Christian meditation blended with a deep appreciation for nature.

"I feel my heritage is ministering to others — hopefully to students. Jesus never owned a house, yet the whole world was His home. I'll always have a home in the Idaho forests. I hope Christ will make His home in me, and I will dwell in the house of the Lord.

"My Ordination vows mean more to me after living in the Idaho woods, 'You are to love and serve the people among whom you work, caring alike for young and old, strong and weak, rich and poor.'"

> *"One thing I asked of the Lord,*
> *That will I seek after:*
> *to live in the house of the Lord*
> *all the days of my life,*
> *and to behold the beauty of the Lord,*
> *and to inquire in his temple."*

When Phil and I finished dinner, people had begun flying home. Mary Kay asked me to accompany her to McCall in her Cessna. Without hesitation, I accepted, and soon we lifted off the little landing strip and were soaring high above Shell Rock Peak.

"I need time in the sky to rebuild a future without my best friend," she said. "Pilots understand this. It's how we cope with difficult times."

She banked the plane away from Indian Creek toward the White Clouds mountains. Mt Borah loomed before us.

"Before you joined us as a pilot we had a fabulous fire down there near Stanley," I told Mary Kay. "We had a smokejumper party at the Ranger's station and got in a little trouble. Hawk assumed the blame, but said it was well worth it."

She turned north toward Salmon City.

"What was he like before I met him three years ago?"

"One of the first things he said puzzled me. He said we can't pick apricots off ponderosa pines, but every tree is known by its fruit. Hawk always lived in harmony with God's fascinating order of creation. He lived on equal terms with others, without the need to control everybody."

We plunged down between the mountains barely above tree tops, and soon were flying low over Salmon City.

163

"Here's a good reminder of the sort of guy he was. We flew into Salmon City in the chopper in the evenings from Whitehawk Lookout. I remember flying right over the Big Dipper Motel, 500 feet above Main Street, looking for a vacancy.

"Ken took care of Nick here when he was in serious trouble. When the rest of us thought Nick had a good thumping coming, Hawk bound up his wounds and paid his motel bill."

I wished we could rewind time back to those happy days.

Mary Kay turned the high-winged aircraft west. She wanted to fly down the canyon of the River of No Return, where they met on the river.

"Look way over there to your right toward the Selway-Bitterroot mountains," I said. "I know what Hawk meant about knowing each animal by name. In my first summer, I meditated over there with a moose near a hot springs. Every wild thing, whether a Rocky Mountain bighorn sheep or a black-masked raccoon has its unique place in God's scheme of things.

"He treated every individual as unique."

We soared without words, enjoying the breathtaking view of the river, relishing our good times with Ken, wondering what life would be like without him. In some way he was there between us, as if we were headed to Emmaus.

"Mary, see those clear-cut sections hacked out below us? Ken was concerned that some people clear-cut groups of others using square, unforgiving judgments. He said churches ought to operate more like selective logging, going into the forests of needy people, individually nurturing the healthy and the weak."

"Gain altitude and buzz over Gospel Hump off to your right, about three miles ahead," I said.

Mary Kay increased our elevation. In a few minutes we were directly over the old World War I lookout where Hawk and I encountered the baby rattlesnake.

"See that little clearing between the cliffs that goes all the way to the Salmon River? That's where we landed. Did he ever tell about the time he prayed a rain cloud all the way from Oregon? Afterwards he sang, 'He's got the whole world in His hands ... He's got the wind and the rain in His hands.' "

"Yes," she said. "He believed God had a sense of humor and cared about little things. I am going to miss Ken's humor in ordinary things,"

"You can't be a saint of God if you don't know how to laugh." I said. "If you will circle the top of the Little Five Mile Creek Drainage, I can tell you more about the Christ living in Hawk's short life."

She neatly circled the airplane over the spot where we had encountered the herd of bighorn sheep and I spotted the congregation of wild sheep again.

"Did he ever tell you how he got that nasty scar on his right arm?"

Mary didn't say anything, perhaps miles away in her own thoughts.

"This is where he literally saved my life. True goodness has a way of coming back to the giver. I expect all of us who really loved Hawk will continue benefiting from his goodness."

"Ken enjoyed singing," she said.

"On this little fire, as strange as it may sound, we were singing, *I Want To Pass It On*. Now I want to shout from the highest mountain tops to share Hawk's life with the whole world.

"Everything and everyone in the wilderness sings. It's always possible to enjoy a sonata in the stillness of these hills."

"We've got about a half-hour before dusk," Mary Kay said. "Let's fly over to the Wallowas. The rescue jump you made over there had an enormous impact on me."

When we reached the site of the Oregon family's fatal crash high above Wallowa Lake, Mary Kay made one pass and then began to cry unashamedly. I awkwardly took the controls and made a long bumpy turn back toward Hells Canyon.

"I'm sorry," she said with tears streaming down her lovely face. "Ken and I talked about the meaning of suffering after that accident. Now, I'm the sufferer — not an observer. It's different. I loved him so much. He's gone."

My only response was to mourn with her in silence. I had kept most of my composure through the burial and all the rest. But now I couldn't hold back my own emotions. I'd lost my friend. It's all right for men to cry. What she said was true. Ken for her, and Hawk for me was absent.

Mary Kay used a hankie and regained her composure.

"I'd better take over again or we'll never get home," she said. "Your Bishop said suffering meant 'unfinishedness.' What did he mean?"

"I can't express it as well as he did, but it is something like this: Throughout our lives we attempt this and that but never quite finish. Unfinished friendships remain fragmented and never see completion. We develop lovely companionships, but contingencies come along and without warning some of our best friends are gone forever. The longer we live, the more bits and pieces of friendships and scattered projects fade away in our lives. Unfinished business causes pain and suffering. Are you with me?"

"More or less. Go on."

"Jesus said on the cross, 'It is finished.' I think He meant, 'It is completed.' What was completed? His perfect sacrifice and the gift of eternal life. This love attracts, then collects our bits and pieces of good efforts and unfinished intentions, recasting them into sacred meanings. Each piece of human love and effort, however small, has a place. There is a room of honor for every person's sincere contribution to God's eternal plan in our heavenly home."

"So God will complete my love for Ken someday," Mary Kay said.

"Yes, our every effort to love others will fit into a master plan someday."

We approached Hells Canyon, where Ken and I made a last jump together before his courageous sacrifice. Of all our jumps, this one was elevated above all others and included the most mysterious man we ever met in the woods.

Mary Kay smiled for the first time.

"I never told you, but I flew over here last week to drop Ken a loving message. I couldn't find you guys, so I hightailed it back to McCall before my boss found out I was trying to see Ken."

I pointed out the right window. "We were down by those alders and lupine. Let's drop a note for Ignacio, telling him about Ken."

I hooked a brief message to a streamer. We saw dust coming up from a band of sheep moving in the clearing but we couldn't see Ignacio. On the third pass Mary Kay shouted, "Look over there above the meadow. It looks like he left a message."

We flew over the message several times before I realized what it was. Lined out in white stones were the Greek symbols, γινοσκω.

"That's a Greek word from the New Testament."

"What does it mean?"

"It means, 'I know.' "

AFTER GAINING ENOUGH ELEVATION TO CLEAR GRANITE PEAK, Mary Kay asked, "What does that word have to do with Scripture?"

"When the Bible talks about 'knowing,' it is more than mere information. It means experiencing the truth, referring to action rather than theory. At the final supper with Ignacio, Ken referred to a verse in Philippians: 'I want to know Christ and the power of his resurrection and share in his sufferings by becoming like him in his death.' Ignacio knew Christ was in Ken and he would sacrifice his life for someone.

" 'I know my Redeemer Lives.' That is the statement of faith put to music in Handel's *Messiah*. Several passages from Scripture also come to mind. I'm sure you know John 3:16. But consider I John, 3:16; ' We know love by this, that he laid down his life for us; and we ought to lay down our lives for one another.'

"In I Corinthians, St. Paul said we look into a mirror dimly in this life but someday we'll see Christ face to face. After that he said; 'Then I will know fully, even as I have been known.' "

We drifted home by the light of the evening star, engulfed in an orange sunset as bright as if it were ablaze with Indian paintbrush. The evening star grew brighter and brighter following the silver and gold of the sunset blaze.

We circled Payette Lake, lighted houses outlining its shoreline, like a constellation in the heavens above. Mary Kay turned on her landing lights as we approached McCall runway. She broke our silence, "Thanks Mark, for flying with me. Ken was truly a man, laying down his life for his friends."

O Lord, support us all the day long, until the shadows lengthen, and the evening comes, and the busy world is hushed, and the fever of life is over, and our work is done. Then in thy mercy, grant us a safe lodging, and a holy rest, and peace at the last.
Amen.

THE END

NOTES

(These pages for notes precede an index of Scripture and references and are provided to be of assistance to readers who wish to pursue the ideas and ideals portrayed and discussed by the characters of *Jumping Skyward*.)

NOTES

NOTES

NOTES

$\mathcal{S}$ CRIPTURES

INDEX OF

THE AUTHOR RESPECTFULLY REQUESTS THAT A PERSON READ THE BOOK FIRST, AND THEN CONSIDER THESE REFERENCES.

CHAPTER I

> *A false balance is an abomination to the Lord, but an accurate weight is his delight.* — Proverbs 11.1

> *Say to this mountain, 'Be taken up and thrown into the sea.'*
> — Mark 11.23

CHAPTER 2

CHAPTER III

CHAPTER IV

CHAPTER V

CHAPTER VI

CHAPTER VII

178

R EFERENCES AND NOTES

CHAPTER I

Collects: *The Book of Common Prayer,* New York: Oxford University Press, 1979. Episcopal collects are short forms of prayer used throughout Jumping Skyward. (Quoted throughout text of book)

Scripture: *The New Revised Version of the Holy Bible,* Nashville: Thomas Nelson Publishers, 1989. Used with permission of National Council of Churches of Christ, USA.. (Quoted throughout text of book)

Dr. Bruce Metzger, Editor, and my seminary advisor, states in the NRSV preface, " ... the Bible has been more than a historical document to be preserved or a classic of literature to be cherished and admired; it is recognized as the unique record of God's dealings with people over the ages."

Wilderness: "An area untrammeled by man, where man himself is a visitor ..." 1964 Wilderness Act.

Peace: "Go placidly amid the noise and haste and remember what peace there may be in silence." Desiderata, 1692.

Angels: St. Francis, visited by a Seraphim angel with burning love, embarked on a new existence with Christ dwelling within.

Wilderness in a New Jersey Prison: Following the trail of false accusations, and unjust imprisonment of Eugene and Bland Williams, an angel encountered Eugene in his cell.

Dr. Tate, as prison Chaplain, worked closely with these African-American brothers for many years. Bland spent 17 years in prison, much of it in the deathhouse. Eugene, currently a Gospel minister in Tampa Florida, leads a special Bible ministry to people in prison called the 'Grassroots Gospel.'

A cabinet in the Christian Centering Place, Moscow, Idaho, contains details concerning their journey toward justice, including years of correspondence. Neither brother harbors animosity toward the system.

Seven: "The number seven is one of the more mysterious marvels of our universe. Virtually all religious ... systems include the number somewhere close to their holiest of holy sanctums." — Godwin, Malcom. *Angels, an Endangered Species,* New York: Simon & Schuster, 1990.

Cathedrals: Edwards, David L. *The Cathedrals of Britain.* Wilton, CN: Morehouse Publishing, 1989.

CHAPTER II

It Don't Cost Very Much. (The Good That You Do.), Tom Dorsey, played by Turk Murphy's Jazz Band. "You may not be an angel; You may not go to church; but the good that you do will come right back to you ... "— Merry Makers Record Company, Mill Valley, CA 94941.

Spirituality: "If we believe that all things are saturated by the Spirit of God, that we are surrounded and buoyed continually by God's presence, we will, in fact, begin to notice the signs that this is so." — Liebert, Elizabeth, SNJM, *Changing Life Patterns,* The Paulist Press, New York, 1992.

CHAPTER III

Wildfires: Fuller, Margaret. *Forest Fires, An Introduction to Wildland Fire Behavior, Management, Firefighting and Prevention.* New York: John Wiley & Sons, Inc. 1991.

Wildfires: Maclean, Norman. *Young Men and Fire, A True Story of the Mann Gulch Fire.* Chicago: The University of Chicago Press, 1992.

Walt Rumsey raced to safety in the Mann Gulch Fire. We became close friends. While watching our sons in a sporting event, I asked him if his faith saved him. He pondered awhile and said, "Yes, but my good strong legs really helped."

CHAPTER IV

Native Americans: Brown, Joseph E. *The Spiritual Legacy of the American Indian,* N.Y., Crossroad Publishing Co., 1982.

Smokejumpers: Cohen, Stan. *A Pictorial History of Smokejumping, Missoula. Montana.* Pictorial Histories Publishing Company., 1983.

Smokejumpers: Cooley, Earl. *Trimotor and Trail.* Mountain Press Publishing, Missoula, Montana, 1984.

Smokejumpers: Schmaljohn, Dale. *Smokejumper.* Hyde Park Press, Boise, Idaho, 1982.

Ford Trimotors: Smith, Steve. *Fly The Biggest Piece Back.* Pictorial Histories Publishing Company, Missoula, Montana. 1988.

CHAPTER V

Suffering: Macquarrie, John. *In Search of Humanity: A Theological and Philosophical Approach.* New York: Crossroads, 1983.

Spirituality: Macquarrie, John. *Paths of Spirituality* . New York: Harper and Row, 1972.

Theology: Macquarrie, John. *Theology, Church & Ministry.* New York: The Crossroad Publishing Co. 1986.

Biomedical Ethics: Tate, Stanton D. *Pastoral Bioethics: Pastoral Care and Biomedical Ethics.* 1989. (unpublished).

CHAPTER VI

Psychology: Bugental, J.F. T. *The Search for Authenticity.* New York: Holt, Rinehard and Winston and Irvington Publishers, 1981.

Courage: Olsen, Jack. *Give a Boy a Gun.* New York: Dell Publishing Company, 1986.
This is the true story of the senseless murder of my close friend and outstanding Fish and Game Officer, Bill Pogue.

Wilderness Humor: Senger, Hank. *A Saga of the Sawtooths.* Caldwell, Idaho: Caxton Printers, Ltd, 1938.

The sacred earth: "Those who would take over the earth and shape it to their own will never, I notice, succeed. The earth is like a vessel so sacred that at the mere approach of the profane it is marred and when they reach out their fingers it is gone." Tao De Jing, 1958.

CHAPTER VII

Respect: "Until he extends his circle of compassion to all living things, man will not himself find peace." Albert Schweitzer.

Heros: "A hero is someone who has given his or her life to something bigger than oneself." Joseph Campbell.

EPILOGUE.

SMOKEJUMPER KEN SALYER AND PILOT BRYON 'SKIP' KNAPP crashed on Norton Ridge, in the Boise National Forest on July 9, 1965. The Rev. Stan Tate officiated at 'Skip's burial near the Indian Creek Ranger Station, near the Middle Fork of the Salmon River, on July 11, 1965.

Dr. Stanton Davis Tate

ABOUT THE AUTHOR

D R. TATE GREW UP ON A LARGE DAIRY FARM IN BOISE, IDAHO. Ordained in Presbyterian and Episcopal churches, he has spent the majority of his ministry outside traditional parishes, counseling and teaching.

He has been chaplain for a prison, hospital, the 124th Fighter Interceptor Group, McCall smokejumpers, the Canterbury House at Oregon State University, and the Idaho Chapter of Sons of the American Revolution.

Currently he is Bioethicist for Gritman Medical Center, and Latah Health Services, in Moscow, Idaho, and ethicist for the Idaho Juvenile Justice Commission. He taught courses in religion at Boise State University, and is now a part-time instructor in ethics for professional counselors at the University of Idaho. An avid outdoorsman, Dr. Tate is currently researching subjects related to wilderness spirituality throughout the Northwest. He would like to be considered chaplain to the Idaho Bioscathedral.

Dr. Tate in his smokejumping days at McCall, Idaho

His rich experiences as pastor, counselor, teacher, probate judge, meditation instructor, and smokejumper/priest, are interwoven throughout *Jumping Skyward.*

185

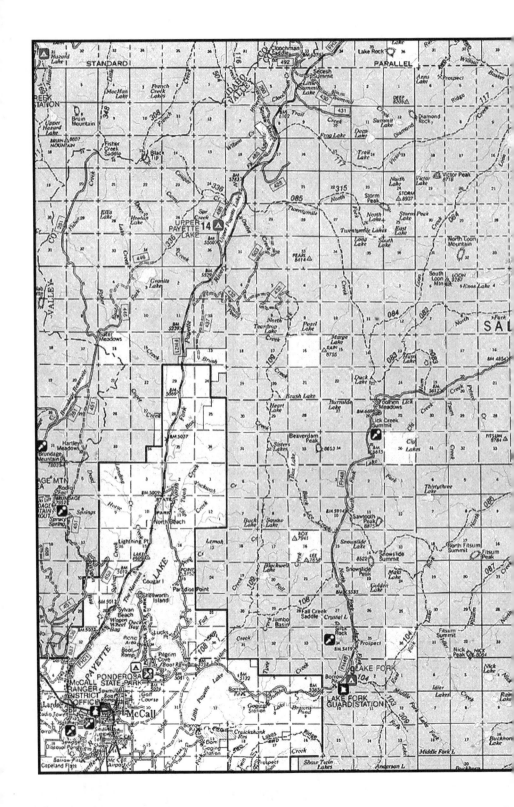

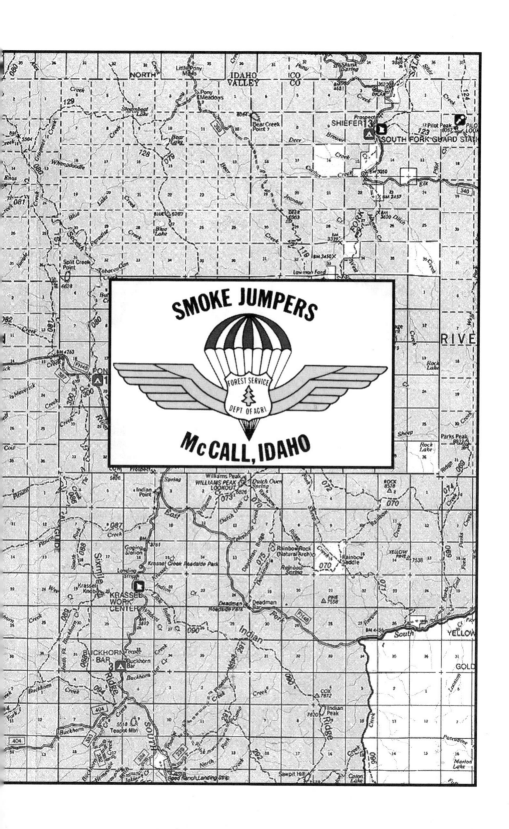